A NOT SO DOLCE VITA

A

WARTIME STORY

OF

TWO BRITISH CHILDREN

IN AMERICA AND BEYOND

A NOT SO DOLCE VITA

REFLECTIONS IN A RED CONVERTIBLE

JULIA FALKNER-TOMPKINS

authorHOUSE®

AuthorHouse™
1663 Liberty Drive
Bloomington, IN 47403
www.authorhouse.com
Phone: 1-800-839-8640

Published by AuthorHouse   05/12/2012

ISBN: 978-1-4685-5744-2 (sc)
ISBN: 978-1-4685-5743-5 (hc)
ISBN: 978-1-4685-5742-8 (e)

Library of Congress Control Number: 2012903636

Cover Photo Courtesy of Bay City Motor Company,
Bay City, Michigan

CONTENTS

Part IV

Part V

Part VI

Part VII

Part VIII

Amen,
Well, not quite yet!

Dedicated to:

Our Second Parents

Aunt Dodie and Uncle Larry

Dr. & Mrs. Lawrence M. Stanton

Who cared, beyond caring.

And

RHJ

who believed in me!

PREFACE AND ACKNOWLEDGEMENTS

The New York Times, published the following at the time:

It is twelve o'clock in London. Hitler has spoken and [Foreign Secretary] Lord Halifax(then Britain's foreign secretary), has replied. There is no more to be said. Or is there? Is the tongue of Chaucer, of Shakespeare, of Milton, of the King James translations of the Scriptures, of Keats, of Shelley, to be here after, in the British Isles, the dialect of an enslaved race? Words falter. There are no phrases for the obscene ambition that attacks, for the magnificent mobilization of a people that defends, unshaken and unafraid. We can only pray that soon the time will come when the vultures no longer defile the British skies and the cry goes out from John O'Groats to Land's End: Twelve o clock and all's well!

And so the fight would go on: Churchill:

We shall go on and we shall fight it out, here or elsewhere, and if at last the long history story is to end, it were better it should end, not through surrender, but only when we are rolling senseless on the ground.

And on June 4, 1940:

> We shall fight on the beaches, we shall fight on the landing
> grounds, we shall fight in the fields and in the street, we
> shall fight in the hills: we shal never surrender.

Given this rhetoric, this incentive, the British would fight on until
death following Churchill's latest remark:

> Hitler knows that he will have to break us in this island
> or lose the war. If we can stand up to him, all Europe
> may be free, and the life of the world may move forward
> into broad sunlit uplands: let us therefore brace ourselves
> to our duty and so bear ourselves that if the British
> Commonwealth and Empire lasts a thousand years, men
> will still say, 'This was their finest hour.'

One can but wonder at the perversity of Fate, to change the course
of history, ways of life, careers, different influences and environments
to bear on malleable minds. Where, today for instance, would the two
babes uprooted in World War II be, if life had continued more or less on
a smoother course? One can but guess. Our uprooting, while giving us
a wealth of experience, also changed our lives irrevocably. Too, as most
children, we became resigned to the curious events happening around us
all part of some scheme over which we had no control.

Many have been the truly tragic, destructive and obscene details of
war, even some farcical, born out of the horror of that war, with the
loss of millions, the destruction, the suffering, uprooting of further more
millions. Yet, I would add a happier note, for this is a story of love, devotion,
patriotic duty amid emotional upheaval and above all, survival and pride
of spirit. This tale is from childhood memory, of which I had many due
to the extraordinary events occurring around me, all interspersed with
letters of the time, written by our parents as they lived through the days

between 1940 and1944, their background so influenced by the Victorian and Edwardian age, when all had been "Rule, Brittania!"

So, why have I written this book? Because there was no way not to! It was partly because many, who have already heard it, have found my story to be unique. Also, having latterly taken a memoir writing course, I felt compelled to write my story. Too, while temporarily living in England in the 1990's, friends and I attended private readings given by a psychometrist, a "reader" who picks up vibrations from objects belonging to the owner. I took my Royal Air Force brooch given me years earlier by my RAF Air Commodore uncle. The reading by the psychometrist surprised me by its accuracy; that is, until he came to the future. I'd be writing a book, he pronounced, further flabbergasting me when he said I'd go on to write a second. No way! Impossible! What did I know of writing? Yet, the first book was written and published,* and now, amazingly, here the second!

Several years ago I chanced upon Alistair Horne's book *A Bundle from Britain*** the story of his move to America after Herr Hitler threatened to invade Britain in 1940. Thorne was one of many children bundled off, as we were, to safer shores. His book further inspired me to write my own, and after taking a memoir writing course with the eminent Dr. Winifred Bryan Horner, teacher and author of books on writing, I began.

Part of my story tells of the separation from our parents at a very young age, and of our voyage to safety in America, away from Germany's threat of invasion upon the British Isles. Perhaps we were the lucky ones, for the majority of children displaced from the slums and inner cities of the south to north England and Scotland, were more or less dumped upon families in small towns and villages, who often found these refugees crude, rude and illiterate, many lacking in discipline, and with head

---

* Keith Falkner *Ich habe Genug*, A Biography. Thames Publishing, London, 1998. ISBN: 0 905210 87 5. All unsold copies remain in my possession, @$22.00 plus postage.
** *A Bundle From Britain*, Alistair Horne, 1993, St. Martin's Press, New York. ISBN: 0-312-11136-3.

lice. Often assigned to households so dissimilar from their own, these youngsters found it hard to readjust, to cause trouble and resentments on both sides.

While Alistair Horne, some eight years older than me in 1940, may have protested his displacement to the States, my two-year-old sister and I, had no understanding of the cause for such desperate urgency to save us from invasion. We were in fact, some of the lucky ones, despite the terrible wrenching of tearing families apart, for we experienced adventures on the high seas and the protection from war with mostly caring families in America, becoming cosmopolitan in the process.

Thanks to American generosity, ours would be a mostly happy experience. Most children survived their separation from parents with aplomb; but had difficulty when parting from parental surrogates with whom they had formed strong ties, yet having to say goodbye yet again, before returning to their barely remembered parents. In the end, all the sad and tragic upheavals would be fore naught; for, following the RAF's Battle for Britain in the summer of 1940, Herr Hitler in mid September, postponed Operation Sea Lion indefinitely, never to try it again. But who was to know that in that June of 1940?

ACKNOWLEDGEMENTS

About six years ago Pippa Letsky, editor, teacher, musician, and a second cousin on mother's side, suggested I join a writing course taught by Dr. Winifred Bryan Horner. Her course was an eye-opener for me! Though timid at first, I found I could write and since, have found myself unable **not** to, hence this memoir of events which shaped our family's life, its togetherness, its future from 1944 onward. Some years have passed now, some of the participants of that class continue to meet once a week to share, discuss and critique our endeavors, having pared down to a "precious few." Thanks to them, my efforts have led me to write this second book, the one I never thought to write! These trusted generous persons are Libby Gill, author: *Live It to the Brim,* friend and confidant; the very caring brilliant-thinking Avis Kopcha; Jeanne Oldweiler author, *The Ant Hill Challenge*, about her Nebraska upbringing, and very much in great particular, Peter Hasselriis: educator, singer, writer of the Foreward and editor twice over of this effort. There is also the wonderfully funny and intuitive "spot-on" Lynn McIntosh who helped give title to this book; Whitney Hicks asked for definitive answers; the occasional funny and amusing writings of Jan Tompkins, (no relation), and George Washburn. My long-time friend Mary Larkin, and more recently Jo Manhart offer continued support; as has Betty Littleton, author, friend, and advisor. Also Neil Carr for his assistance in the book's final presentation, and to, of an evening, my son Jeffrey Keith Wheeler, so like his South African cousin John Keith, who has patiently listened to my scripts, offering suggestions as necessary. With thanks to all, this is my story. Also with kind permission, their photo of red Chevy convertible, from BayCity Motor Company, Michigan. Thanks to all.

FOREWORD

In the Preface to her book, Julia Falkner-Tompkins sets the stage for the adventure you have agreed to join, the adventure that is her life from the time she and her sister were sent away from Britain to the United States during World War II until she was 18 years old and newly married.

If someone other than Julia had written such a memoir it would of course have been decidedly different. But, most of the people who might have written it would have been born in the United States and would have had experiences more closely resembling mine than hers. Like Julia they would have been young children during World War II, and their experiences during that time would have been protected from any real knowledge of the war or from any of its dangers.

People who grew up quite close to New York and others of America's heavily populated cities, can remember air raid drills in which a siren would sound that caused everyone to stay either in their homes or on their own property outside until the "all clear" sounded. They can remember that the top half of car headlights had been taped so that only a minimal amount of light could shine, making them less visible to enemy airplanes. Air Raid Wardens, men who lived nearby who wore white helmets and patrolled during air raids and blackouts, made sure no lights could be seen from houses or apartments. I'm sure my mother wasn't the only resident who read in the bathtub or another room whose light couldn't be seen outside the house. Also, I wouldn't have been the only kid whose father was an Air Raid Warden, and our row house near New York City wasn't the only one that had a red, white, and blue bucket of sand and a shovel on its stair landing. Houses had such equipment to be used in case an incendiary bomb was dropped.

Talk to people in the U.S. who lived through the time of World War II, and they'll tell what they remember about ration books and ration stamps. When word came out that the butcher shop had meats that no one had been able to get, people would crowd in and would push and shove, ration books in hand, toward counters for meats and other staples like sugar, salt, and butter. Gasoline for cars was scarce and tightly rationed, but most people didn't have cars anyway. Auto factories were making tanks and airplanes, and there was virtually no rubber for domestic tires. People who held vital positions that depended on car travel were able to buy as much gasoline as they needed. Doctors, volunteer firemen, and farmers were members of that group.

Schools in the states held occasional air raid drills, and kids were sometimes surprised to be taken to strange parts of buildings like boiler rooms. Such places were judged to be the safest places to be should enemy planes be nearby, and, during the drills, boys and girls were crammed into a very limited space. There were, of course, no actual air raids on any American cities, and no public announcements were made of any attacks that were made. Children in particular were sheltered in ignorance of such news. They had no idea, for example, that German U-boats managed to get as close to New York City as Long Island Sound. They thought nothing of seeing the U.S. Navy blimps that regularly flew over people who were enjoying a day at one of the nearby ocean beaches. They knew the fliers were looking for submarines, but no one ever even hinted that any had been found.

Julia Falkner-Tompkins was alive at this same time, but she was born in England to her musically gifted mother and father. "The parents," as she refers to them, became fearful for the wartime safety of Julia and her younger sister, Philippa, and accepted friends' offers to take care of them in America during the war. She describes how it was for a four-year-old and a two-year-old to be taken from their parents, put on a ship with a nanny, and sent from England to America to live with strangers for four years; that is, from 1940 to 1944. That this did not turn the two girls into psychological wrecks is a testimonial both to their own fortitude and to the compassion and competence of their parents' friends. The experience of course affected their lives, and it did influence those lives in ways you will discover continuously as you see their world through Julia's eyes.

You will be delighted to become part of a family whose friends are as well known in the world of music as today's Neil Diamond and Yo Yo Ma. You will travel with Julia to Italy, where her school experiences were decidedly different from the ones she would have enjoyed in the states. Her experiences in Italy enriched her upbringing in ways you and I can't begin to imagine.

After her schooling in Italy her father returned her to the states, this time to Ithaca, New York, whose Cornell University had offered him a wonderfully prestigious position. Julia graduated from high school in Ithaca in 1954, and that is where the two of you will part company. Before leaving you, Julia will have shown you what it was like to grow up where she grew up, and she will have described those places so well you will feel you were there with her. You will know what it was like to have famous parents whose priorities were their professional lives rather than the lives of their children. When she has graduated from high school and has immediately married, she leaves you. By then the world has changed, and Julia will continue in it as a young mother, a college graduate, and a working professional. She will have a rich, fulfilling life, but we will have to await this book's sequel for its details. In the meantime, it's time for you to find out why she titled her book as she did. Enjoy!

REFLECTIONS IN A RED CONVERTIBLE

May 1956, had been the month my parents left Ithaca, New York, bound for New Zealand, leaving me, recently married and newly pregnant, to act responsibly in my new status of wife and mother-to-be finishing the first year of a business administration course at Ithaca College. How disappointed they must have been! For one thing, I had been unable to shake off that awful feeling that I had made the biggest mistake of my life so far, this on December 27th the previous year, when at age eighteen, I had exited St. John's Episcopal Church on the arm of a husband. While he beamed, I had felt remote, asking myself, over and over, "What have you just done? What, have you done?"

Realization had suddenly hit, and hit hard, for, dismayed, I found I had leapt from the proverbial frying pan into the fire, to give up an exciting and rich life in music, in exchange for a very ordinary one. I did remain an optimist, for sooner or later there had to be better experiences. Nonetheless, I couldn't help but wonder who I might have become, or what I might have done had I not tied myself at so young an age, to a man of Dutch Baptist puritanical background. Leading up to the marriage however, I'd had no qualms, and no one could tell me a thing, for I knew, or thought I did, where I was going, what I was doing. This poor benighted immature fool had been so very wrong!

In love with love as I was, I had been swept off my feet by William Hawley Wheeler, an Air Force communications officer recently returned from Darmstadt, Germany. At some point, he told me that, with only a glimpse or two of me in some college hallway, he had decided then and there, I would be his ideal wife and so, had set out to woo me, egotistically assuming I would also think him a perfect mate. As it was, I was flattered, charmed and wowed, standing in awe of this veteran whom, it appeared, I had "snowed." Perhaps, if life had been easier under what I considered to be at the time, mother's irrational yoke, I might not have been so hasty to wed. Yet, wed we had, and on graduating, Bill had eagerly accepted a position with radio Station WEEU in Reading, Pennsylvania, where he soon became a beloved radio host.

So it was, with Bill in Reading and my parents far away, I decided to enjoy a last month of freedom, and, with no one to stop me, wasted no time in doing so. If this had to be a last fling, I'd do it in style, the bigger the better before settling into my rashly chosen new life. Car! That was it! I'd rent the brightest, flashiest red convertible I could find; perfect, just as previous ones in my life had been. So, with some wedding monies and driver's license in hand, I set off for a car dealership, where with papers signed, no questions asked, I was off.

And, what a trip it was! Such fun driving around campus, showing off, always with the top down on those late May and early sunny days of June. I soon picked up a bunch of newfound friends: not odd at all, I suppose, how the seemingly endowed attract! So what! We had a blast: swimming, picnicking, smoking, drinking, dining and dancing, even to bed a faithful red-headed classmate or, just driving around. Did we ever go to class?

I suppose I had thought by having a last fling, I'd get immaturity out of my system but I wouldn't, couldn't, loving life as I did. After all, the Falkner motto is "Live in order to Live! I was just following instructions, enjoying my then last dregs of hedonistic freedom. That wonderful month had been such a blast, a wonderful whirl-wind of frolicking, but had to end. Time to behave sensibly, to return that flashy joy-toy to the dealer, before Bill, who had been too busy to travel to Ithaca these past few weeks, arrived to reclaim his errant bride and discover her transgressions, not the least of which was wasting money on such a frivolous pastime as leasing a shiny red convertible! So one might ask what business had I had, to marry so young? None. But, here I was and pregnant besides, so would have to pretend, at least for now, to be a sedate wife and loving mother. Oh, piteous me!

For me, the tires of that beautiful red automobile, mine for so brief a time, rotated far too swiftly back to the dealership. On the way, I thought to glance in the rear-view mirror, making sure juvenile Julia looked pretty enough, for she never knew who might be around to flirt with! But, instead of seeing my face, a jumbled stock of memories flashed in the mirror, some sharp, some vaguely glimpsed, then, just as suddenly to disappear, leaving my soul with the events which had composed it from the time Britain declared war on Germany, that third day of September, 1939. Reminded, I remembered, r e m e m b e r e d and, r e m e m b e r e d . . .

Julia Christabel flower girl

With Dear Daddy

THE BEGETTORS

It was not until the mid 1990's that I began to see that through no choice of my own, I had lived a rather unusual life. Children do not give thought to the lives of others, are only aware of their own, and assume all others must be pretty similar. Right? Wrong.

In the first place, it is miraculous we are here at all, derived as we are from primitive oceanic cells. Then, on to dry land to mutate again and again and yet again, to travel down eons of time, eventually to migrate out of Africa. Our particular clan settled in northern climes to become fierce Norsemen. My DNA tested so. Of course it is miraculous to have survived at all, what with endless wars, poisonings, illnesses, and antiquated medical practices often causing more harm than good. Then there were the plagues. In England in 1350, the Black Death killed half the population. It is sobering to realize that had any one of my forefathers succumbed to any of the above, causing them to miss their so-called appointment with destiny, I would not be here at all. Clarence Darrow, the famous lawyer, believed his very existence came about through one gigantic lottery, or as the wit Dick Cavett put it, "If your parents never had children, chances are you won't either."

So, my family is descended from murdering, marauding, plundering and philandering Norsemen or Vikings. That was their way of life. Adventuresome and artistic, they were said to be virile and handsome. It would have been interesting to meet some of this polyglot of ancestors, long ago settlers of England, Scotland and Ireland. On father's side, the Falkners (falcon trainers) belonged to the Keith Clan of the Scottish Sutherland and MacPherson tribes, and were connected to the earls of Kintore near Inverurie; some said from the wrong side of the blanket. The

1

Celtic Irish side, the Clarks, fled from Ireland to England and America between 1846 and 1857, during that great agrarian crisis, the potato famine. In England, the Clarks married Wrights, Ports and Falkners. Most Falkners were a charming lot and, because of their looks and temperament, often tempted into affairs. It's only human after all, and one grows more tolerant as one matures.

On Mother's side the Fullards (silk and wool merchants) were from Norway, and, with untold others, settled in France in the area known today as Normandie. After the Edict of Nantes in 1685 declared Protestantism to be illegal, some 200,000 Huguenot families fled to England and other countries to escape persecution. The Fullards settled in London and aligned themselves through marriage with Divers, Parnells and Stannards. Interestingly, the Falkner/Fullard alliance came full circle when my youngest daughter, Jocelyn, married the Frenchman Freddy Canesse from Bethune, in Normandie. Was it another coincidence that my mother's favorite cousin, John Arnold Stannard, killed in World War I, is buried in La Pugnoi Cemetery (Plot T, Row E, Plat 6) in Bethune? I wish I had known this when Mother and I traveled there in 1988.

This interesting blend of blood lines and genes throughout the ages produced some talented family members. While there were several generations of career soldiers stationed anywhere from Crete to New Zealand (where a number of relatives still live), others were artists. The famous painter Joseph Wright of Derby (1724-1797) was one. There were numerous educators including Sir Ivan Port, founder of Repton School in 1557. Also, my father's mother, Alice Hannah Wright, an educator herself, was a direct descendant of Ports and Wrights, while her husband, John Charles Falkner, father's sire, was administrator and teacher for thirty seven years in Sawston, Cambridge. On mother's side, Alfred Diver (1824-1876), famous cricketer, who until his death was also a professional tutor to the famous Rugby School, a school that his relatives, my mother and her brother, the World War I Ace pilot Philip Fletcher Fullard, attended some forty years later. Mother, Christabel Margaret Fullard, (1902-1990), was a brilliant pianist who could have had her own career but elected to be her husband's accompanist in all things. My father, Donald Keith Falkner, (1900-1994), was the eminent bass baritone of the 1930s, acclaimed by the conductor Sir David Wilcox as the best singer of Bach for his time. Keith was also a world-class cricket player and could just as well have made this his career. He was an educator at Cornell University in upstate New York from 1950 until 1960, and then was appointed Director of the Royal College of Music, London, where he served, from 1960-1974. Mother, bound by the culture of her education and class, had her own travails to deal with. As a much loved, and I suspect, somewhat spoiled second child of Maud and Thomas Fletcher, Christabel was devastated at age nine when her father died of pneumonia. Her brother*, five years older and a war hero, became her idol.

In the 1930s, it was my time to be born. I arrived under the sign of Capricorn, the Goat, on January, 10, 1936, with double Leo rising. No one gave a thought to this at 17:30 GMT, the afternoon of my birth. Father bustled in to hospital shortly thereafter to see his wife and baby daughter. In a hurry, on his way to sing at a concert that evening, he burst into the room with some flowers, kissed his wife, peeked at me and was away, never having much time for babies. So what had the fates ordained? What fairy-godmother gifts bestowed or evil bewitched brews to imbibe? Time would tell. Things were about to change; but on that day, I lay gently protected in my mother's arms.

---

* See: Testimony of War—1914-1918 by Peter Liddle. Michael Russell (Publishing) Ltd. 1979.

Before I heard the news

RUMBLINGS

Babyhood had been kind but now, ominous vitriolic rumblings of war had begun to fill the air, to echo around the world. After World War I, the 1918 Treaty of Versailles had severely punished Germany, which country now sought vengeance, with calls for reprisals given added impetus by the Nazi party and its leader, Adolf Hitler. Ripe for war by 1939, Germany annexed Austria and invaded Czechoslovakia.

I was oblivious of course, my small world consisting of a strict nursery regimen, an "early to bed, early to rise" routine. It took time before I became aware of other things and other people, so, in a sense, we are born twice: first, that of birthing, then, of consciousness. My memories are few of this time with one exception, that of my "Gambu," daddy's father. "Gambu" must have greatly impressed for me to remember him at such a young age: to this day, should he happen to materialize, I would recognize him instantly, perhaps the reason I have a penchant for men who resemble him. This grandfather of mine and I adored each other, or so I was told; he often pushing my pram, taking us for long walks with daddy's dog "Bee," a Jack Russell, so named for being as busy-as-a-bee, when rabbiting. I was about two when "Gambu" died, his death caused by injuries suffered in a car crash, of which, he had had premonitions. From a reliable clairvoyant years later, I learned "Gambu," has been my guardian angel throughout my life, and I believe to be true for any number of reasons. Bee, on the other hand, stayed near me, and would be more protective than ever upon my sister's arrival two years later, and consider her an intruder in the nursery. Philippa would eventually win him over by dumping most of her porridge on Bee's head, which she, if not he, thought great fun. As for the other grandparents, my memories of Gran, Maud Diver Fullard, mother's mother, would come later. It was a great pity I never knew my paternal grandmother Alice Hannah, a good writer herself, who died on a trip to South Africa in 1927; nor, my maternal grandfather, Thomas Fletcher Fullard, who died in 1907.

Stories of baby and tot-hood were oft told over the years. A vague memory lingers, that of lying on the sofa listening to my father practice, often singing my favorite at the time, "Sheep may safely graze" from Cantata 208. Give me Bach any time! I have no memory of my sister's birth in 1938, but, before her arrival I have a hazy memory of walking with mummy in a meadow when a ladybird landed on my arm. Mummy told me to blow the ladybug on her way as she recited: "Ladybird, ladybird, fly away home; your house is on fire, your children are gone." This made me cry as mummy tried to console me: was this a sign of things to come? Also hearing my parents talk about "Gambu's" untimely death, caused me to ask mummy, one evening as she gave me my bath: "Die with me Mum?" She about died then and there. Mummy always called me "Baa" (little lamb), and her emotions got the better of her again when I turned to her one day to exclaim: "Baa do love Mum! Baa do!" We shared this love, but it was never the same after our enforced separation.

Any time I balked, it was the parents' practice to tell me King George (VI) would want me to do whatever it was that I didn't want to do. As most children will, I soon picked this up. One evening, having been put to bed and not staying there, mummy, having come to the foot of the stairs to order me back to bed several times, gave up. Finally, daddy took charge: "Julia," said he, in his sternest voice gazing up from far below, "Get into bed at once or I shall come up and spank you!" "Oh!" said the pert little miss leaning over the banister, "And what would King George say to that!?" I can almost again see the grin on daddy's face as he beat a hasty retreat.

The rumblings in Europe were no longer rumbles: rather, no thanks to most Germans' belief in Hitler, the world plunged into its second world war in twenty-five years, this one to last six long years of atrocities and agony. On September 1, 1939, Germany invaded Poland, catapulting

France and England into war on September 3rd. Canada, Australia, New Zealand, and South Africa joined in a few days later, the war escalating, so that, when finally over, some sixty million people would have lost their lives, leaving much of Europe and Asia in ruin. It was between May and early June, 1940, that British forces fighting in France, became pinned down in France at Dunquerque (Dunkirk). By some miracle, 338,226 of those troops were transported safely back to England, by boats large and small, heavy equipment necessarily left behind. Uncle Phil, finding himself temporarily stationed in France, spent those last days and hours, helping to ditch military equipment and lorries into the English Channel, preventing use by the encroaching Germans. Returning to England, uncle declared it was only a matter of time before Britain was invaded by Germany, and he repeatedly urged our parents to accept offers for our safety which were then arriving from the United States and elsewhere, particularly Canada, Australia, New Zealand, America, even South Africa. Did our parents ever consider sending us to this last country? It was where Aunt Mercy, daddy's older sister, lived with husband Austin Sutton and son, John Keith. Alternatively did they consider Vancouver, to Aunt Kitty, with her two children, Alex and Ailsie, she the widow of Keith's older brother Ivan, dead from wounds suffered in World War I? In both cases, we would have been welcome; yet an imposition, for neither family could afford the extra expense. In later years, Ailsie told me she had been thrilled to think she might have two little sisters for the duration. As it was, the parents elected to accept the generous offers of great friends, the Jacobs in Cincinnati, and the Stantons, in New York City. So they set about to arrange our passage, to make sure we would be out of harm's way. They, on the other hand, chose to stay in England to do their bit for the war effort.

How the parents must have agonized that June, so fraught with anxiety over our future. According to Jessica Mann, author of *Out of Harm's Way** some parents "wondered why they had brought their

---

* Jessica Mann: *Out of Harm's Way,* Headline Books, London, ISBN: 075531139

children into the world only to be faced by this Germanic threat . . ." The idea of sending children to the United States was daunting for many British, as it was said to be populated by Indians, movie stars, skyscrapers and mobsters. However, the parents knew more, so were easy in their thoughts. Up and down we went, to and fro, to London, to and fro to the American Embassy in Grosvenor Square, where we sat for ages. Well trained, we sat quietly in our matching pinafores, Mary-Jane's and little white gloves, playing quietly on a small side staircase as Embassy staff marveled two such small children could sit so calmly for hours on end, waiting for bureaucracy to revolve. Every time I'm in that embassy, the sense of déjà vu overwhelms me.

For England it was time to again "batten down the hatches" as our stiff-upper-lipped nation calls it, and once again, King George was called upon in our family to help ease heartaches and troubles. This was small comfort to my few years though, for how could they make me feel better when I was about to be sent abroad, parted from my adored parents, for how long, perhaps forever? Winston Churchill, King George, and Queen Elizabeth would eventually do much not only to win the war, but also to back those at home and abroad where troubles were escalating in earnest.

Would Britain survive this threat of Germanic invasion? King George VI and Winston Churchill were trusted to bring the country safely through the war, the latter, newly in command since the resignation of the rather pitiful Neville Chamberlain privately referred to by Hitler as an "arschloch."* Certainly, our uncle Phil doubted Britain's ability to withstand the invasion, doubting Churchill's assertions to the contrary. In the meantime, the citizenry, separating from their children, did all that was necessary; inner-city children were evacuated to northern parts of the country, as night after night, German bombing raids caused heavy losses inflicted upon the country; as night after night, gallant young men of the

---

* The Defense of the Realm: The Authorized History of MI5, Christopher Andrew, October 5, 2009. ISBN: 978713998856.

RAF fought them off, their emotions and the country's fired by Churchill's "V" for victory sign,** and his rhetoric.

We were set to sail late June, 1940, part of the second wave of some three thousand children shipped overseas to welcoming hosts, this just before the increase of U-boat activity in the Atlantic. As it was, the crossing was perilous. Until that time, through June, submarine warfare had been somewhat sporadic, limited by the number of U-boats available to Nazi Admiral Karl Donitz. From July onwards, German Wolfpacks, consisting of multiple U-boats, began their prowls across the Atlantic in earnest. Formed of six or more, these packs would attack convoys at night, creating heavy losses to British lives and shipping.

At four, it was difficult for me, even with my good memory, to remember the trauma and disruption to our lives, perhaps blocking out the pain, as I continued begging not to be sent to America. The parents were often saying, along with King George, that we'd all be together again when the war was over. But, at my age, what did war mean? Such shocking upheavals at so young an age often sharpen the mind, fragments of images, fleeting moments, remembered by many of us who were evacuated during the war, hardening us to reality. Sad to realize, in hindsight, that all the turmoil, the upheavals of wrenching families apart for deportation, turned out to have been totally unnecessary, for the threat of an invasion of the British Isles was over by late June 1940. By then, we were already on the high seas, bound for America. I was four years old; my sister, Philippa, was two.

** While Churchill used the "V" sign initially with palm inward, an international insult; and later with palm forward to signify peace; the BBC with an audible code of three dots and a dash, used the opening bars of Beethoven's Fifth for the rest of the war as call signs for programs beamed to occupied Europe.

Daddy, Mummy, Philippa and me, soon to part

ASEA

As the day of departure had neared, poor Mummy had to put up with outbursts of, "But I don't want to go to America!" Almost unhinged, she patiently and lovingly reminded me King George wanted us to be safe. As soon as the war was over, she said, we would be together again, she having more faith than many at the time. War meant nothing to me, but I sensed urgency in the air.

In late June, before we departed, and, while we were still at home, Charles De Gaulle, the very symbol of French resistance, arrived in England following the dastardly occasion when Premier Marshal Petain, Chief of State for Vichy France 1940-1944, capitulated, choosing to align his country to armistice with the Germans. General De Gaulle then had broadcast, from Berkhamstead to France, the formation of the Free French Resistance Movement. A garden party had followed the occasion, and De Gaulle was introduced to my parents. As they talked, De Gaulle occasionally glanced down, smiling to pat me on the head, as I gazed upward. I thought him a giant as indeed he was at 6' 5", and not just to children.

With a few days left, the family made its way by train from London's Euston Station, a dark cavernous building at the time, for Liverpool. There, my Liverpudlian godmother, Aunt Nan, spent hours with us, as did Uncle Phil, to see us off, and, I suspect, to offer what support they could to our parents. As a parting gift, uncle had given me a doll nearly my size, whom I had named Miss Hamilton for some long forgotten reason. She was difficult to cart about, but she remained by me for some years, and was someone I could hang onto in my darkest moments.

Just before we sailed, I had again asked if I really had to go to America and, gently assured so, was introduced to a new person, barely remembered now, a temporary nanny to take us across the ocean to America, where she would join a British family already relocated. Many families did flee Britain for Canada or America, but most felt it their duty, even honor, to stay and fight off the Bloody Boche, Boche a disparaging term for Germans in both World Wars, which they could do safely, knowing their children to be safe. From the beginning, Nanny had her hands full. Trouble had started with my two-year old sister desperately crying; screaming, as she struggled in poor nanny's arms, stretching her chubby baby arms back towards mummy, as we walked up the gangway, more like a gang-plank, and disappeared behind a tarpaulin. The separation must have been agonizing for everyone, not knowing when, if ever, we might return. Was I crying? I think not, believing this event to have been my first instance of "shutting down."

From that time on, I have been able to drop what is called a portcullis, an iron or wooden grating lowered when enemies loom, a defense mechanism for castles preventing invasion or, in my case, the feelings of desperation and abandonment, thus, a shield from pain. A portcullis allowed outward sight, and as I am and remain an eternal optimist, I looked outward for rays of hope and sunshine. Years later, mother recalled:

> So, we went on with the ghastly morning in Liverpool. Given the same options again, I would never have parted from them: the war and separation changed our lives irrevocably. Yet we survived, when many did not.

I can hardly bear to think of the anguish mummy must have suffered as she caught that last glimpse of us going to an unknown future, provided, that is, we weren't blown to smithereens by the U-boats that were then actively patrolling the vast Atlantic, doing their best to dispatch vast tonnage to kingdom come and the deep. Aside from London, Liverpool would be the most heavily attacked city in England. Whole areas were bombed, and killed thousands, particularly near the docks, for the Germans knew Liverpool was an important port, and therefore a target. If, for whatever reason, we had not sailed that particular late June afternoon, it is likely I would not be here to tell this tale, for that evening the Luftwaffe bombed the docks almost to smithereens.

Into whatever future, we had sailed just hours earlier for safer shores either under the government's Children's Overseas Resettlement Board (CORB) or privately, the former would cease on September 13th, 1940, when the *City of Benares*, with ninety children aboard, was sunk by German U-boat #48, some 600 miles out into the Atlantic, with only thirteen children surviving.*

After our departure and to be met by at the Cunard docks in New York on arrival by Dr. & Mrs. Lawrence Stanton, mummy wrote to them, miserable as she must have been in the telling, trying, I suspect, to convince herself all was well:

> The children went off in grand style. Julia was magnificent, only once did she say she didn't want to go. I felt very proud of them. It is such a grand experience for them to be launching out as pioneers at their time of life that I cannot grudge their going. I am purposely not mentioning when the boat sailed or its name.

Nevertheless, every day and night we were on the high seas, "Pop," as we called him, was able to monitor our ship's progress across the ocean, via his Royal Air Force 'Ops' room. He had re-enlisted at age forty, his singing career, with few exceptions, put on hold. Though able to monitor

---

*   Though described as an atrocious act by U.S. Secretary of State Cordell Hull to be a most dastardly act, the commander of U-Boat #48, testified at trial that he had been totally unaware children were aboard.

our progress, for security reasons he was unable to inform the Stantons of name of ship or, arrival date, a suspenseful time for all. It was not until the sixth of August, sometime after our arrival, the Stantons received this note:

> "It has been a great wrench, extraordinary how precious our 'whippersnappers' became as soon as one had to say goodbye."

Aboard, it seems I was at liberty to roam the decks. I was never seasick, unlike nanny who mostly stayed in our cabin anyway, with her hands full with two-year-old Philippa. Somewhere in mid-Atlantic after a storm left roiling, rolling waves, I was on deck early one evening, leaning on a rail as the ship plowed through the swells, watching the white-crested undulations rove back from prow to stern to join the ship's wake in a boiling froth-like cauldron, every wave taking me further from home. More hopeful perhaps, I turned my face skyward, watching the evening turn from pale lavender to darker blue where a first star twinkled for me to wish upon: "Star light, Star bright, first star I see tonight. I wish I may, I wish I might have this wish I wish tonight,"* my wish, of course, was to return home. It was then that a gentle man, gentle in dealing with youngsters, stopped beside me. After a few questions mostly about why I was traveling, why going to America, he too looked at my star then back at me. "All is well," he said, "You will return and, fairly soon." It was his belief and trust that I held onto instinctively, trusting in his optimism that all would be well. In later life, I would wonder how he knew this to be true, and whether he ever wondered what happened to that four year-old whom he had so consoled? A quote from William Broderick's book *The Sixth Lamentation* (Viking 2003) somehow seems appropriate:

---

* "When you wish upon a Star," Disney's "Pinocchio," 1940, sung by Jiminy Cricket.

> You'll find as you get older, you start seeing yourself from
> the outside, particularly your childhood. You'll see a child
> enacting her part innocently, while you watch, knowing
> what is going to happen, unable to intervene.

At our age we knew so little: where were we going, to whom and for
how long, time being eternities at our age. As children we were adaptable
and malleable, the one constant in our lives once in America, were the
Stantons, who gave loving care with parameters, and forever after, were
interested in our well being. In hindsight, we owe much to the Stantons,
though I fear my sister and I took all for granted, too young to realize the
sacrifices made and the beneficences of the many substitute parents who
helped save British children. As New Englanders, the Stantons would have
been embarrassed by an effusive gushing of sentiment. They did what
they could out of respect for and the privilege of helping Keith, then
the pre-eminent Bach singer, and of his beautiful and courteous pianist
wife, these four who had shared, before the war, musical evenings in that
gorgeous salon at 867 Madison Avenue.

As expatriates, my sister and I also became international children, to
become influenced by a new life-style, vastly impressed with America, and
to fall in love with the country, we now barely aware of the war no longer
on our doorstep, as it was for those remaining in Britain. There had been
questions raised about the effects of parent/child separation in 1940, but
many parents, including the government felt, if it was possible, parents
should proceed with the wrenching separation. But what were or would
be these effects on children separated from everything they had known in
their short lives? Case studies conducted after the war by the Department
of Psychology, University of Helsinki, revealed,

> "Despite the significance of childhood trauma in later
> life, there is little evidence of long term consequences of
> parent-child separation: those evacuated in toddler hood
> (aged two to four years) or aged four to six, seem to [have

been] the least affected from later depression . . . those separated from parents for no more than four to six years, fared best."

Despite the agony of separation at this early stage, neither of us suffered depression in later years, though it left me with vulnerabilities. Of course there could not help but be changes in relationships between parent and child on return. In a poignant memoir, the British author and journalist Vera Brittain, also having decided to send her children to the States, parted from them on June 26, 1940, very likely on the same ship as ours. Watching her two disappear on board, she later wrote,

> The small gallant figures which disappeared have never grown up in my mind, for the children who returned were not the same; the break in continuity made them rather appear as an older brother and sister of the vanished pair.

For many, the lasting negative of separation would be, if we ever returned, the loss of closeness and devotion for and from parents, who, while doing what they thought best at the time, also lost the intimacy ordinarily shared in earlier untroubled years. On return, if there was to be a return, difficult readjustments would have to be made all around.

LAND HO!

While remembering much so early, it's strange I don't recall the rest of the voyage, but perhaps it was a blessing as I would have sorely been missing my mother; too, the monotony of convoy travel, zigzagging across the Atlantic, can be incredibly boring, daily life-boat drills aside. However, I do remember the day we arrived in America, a glorious mid-morning as our ship sailed into New York Harbor with Ellis Island on the left and the ever welcoming towering Statue of Liberty. Most passengers were on deck, my sister and I included, as tugboats tooted, whistles blew among all the other noises of a busy port, along with the occasional shuddering sound of a large ship's horn, as our ship was gently eased stern first into one of the Cunard docks located between West 46th and 54th Streets, at the time, primarily used to deploy troops overseas.

As we had entered the harbor, a man standing next to me at the rail leant down to ask: "Is this your first trip to America? "Yes," I replied rather proudly. "If this be so," said he, "for good luck, you must throw your right shoe overboard." "Really?" asked the gullible Julia, ready to believe anything told her by an adult, so ingrained at home to obey she tended to take others at face value, a sometimes unfortunate trait. "Oh yes!" he emphasized, "Only then can you settle happily in this country." Years later, I wonder where he was from, what tales he had been told, where going; certainly I did not see him throw his own right shoe overboard. Believing this strange ritual must now be performed Philippa, who always copied everything I did, and I bent down, removed our right shoes, and with glee watched the two splash into the water to slowly sink into the bay's murky waters far below. Moments later Nanny emerged from wherever she had been, took one look at our right unshod feet to scold, admonish, huff and puff in annoyance as our Mary-Jane sneakers, which had matched our floral-patterned summer pinafore dresses and sun bonnets, sank further toward their muddy end. Nanny of course would have wanted us to look our best when we met the Stantons dockside, yet here we were as in the nursery rhyme: "one shoe off, one shoe on, diddle diddle dumpling . . ." not my son John, but two little girls upsetting her plans.

Of meeting Dr. and Mrs. Stanton, I have no memory, nor of nanny's defection, or even of arriving at 867 Madison Avenue, known as the Rhinelander Mansion. Built in 1898 in the French Beaux Art style which heavily influenced American architects between 1880 and 1920, it was commissioned by the New York heiress Gertrude Rhinelander Waldo, though never occupied. The mansion has five stories, which remained empty until 1921when the first floor was converted into shops and two large apartments were carved out of the upper four floors. In the 1950s, the entire mansion was leased as the home and studio of the Mexican-born photographer Edgar de Evia (1910-2003) who, in turn, rented office space to the interior decorators Tate & Hall. In the 1960's the mansion was purchased by a nearby church, before the fashion designer Ralph Lauren obtained a lease in 1983 to start a massive overhaul of the building, making it his flagship store, which, at various times had also housed Olivetti, the auction house Christie's, and Zabar's, the gourmet food store. The mansion was added to the National Register of Historic Places in 1980, its purchase price continuing to soar from $6.4 million in 1984, $43 million five years later, and in a sale in 2005, brought a whopping $80 million. Sometime in the 1930's Lawrence M. Stanton, a well-known doctor of homeopathy and his second wife Dorothy had moved in to occupy the upper three floors facing Madison Avenue and 72nd Street.

To think we once lived in this handsome mansion, if ever so briefly! In my day, you entered from Madison and went past an Italian-owned florist on the first floor to take a rather elaborately brass-gated elevator to the second, where, exiting, you faced the offices of Uncle Larry and his secretary, Eleanor Francis. To the left, a wide blue carpeted hall led to a large parlor with fireplace, perhaps the dining room—hard to remember.

At any rate, the dining room was carpeted again in blue, this time royal. A butler's pantry and immense kitchen came next with floor-to-ceiling cupboards, staff accommodations leading off from there. A largish cook held sway yet was always very afraid of breaking her neck as she climbed a tall wheeled ladder to reach the uppermost cupboards for special pieces of china. As she climbed up and back down, she seemed to take delight in telling us gruesome tales of cooks she had known who had broken their necks or backs doing just what she had safely accomplished.

Turning right from the elevator, a hall stretched farther and farther westward, emptying into a vast salon, its ceiling twenty or more feet high, a room so vast it housed a small stage at its southern end. Five tall arched windows faced west over Madison in front of which stood Aunt Dodie's large desk, Central Park a block away. The two upper floors, reached by staircase, contained bedrooms and baths, grownups' on the third, ours on part of the fourth, the rest of it and the fifth floor the second apartment. The Stantons would continue to live here until Uncle Larry's death in the late 1940s.

Mrs. Stanton, or Aunt Dodie as we came to call her, somewhat younger than her husband, was tall, stately and a somewhat uptight New Englander, both music lovers and instrumentalists. The white haired doctor, Uncle Larry, with an aging malleable-looking face and bushy eyebrows, often played his cello for us, while Aunt Dodie, thick gray hair always worn in a French twist, was an accomplished pianist. Both had met daddy during the 1930's when he had consulted the good doctor for throat or nasal irritations while engaged for performances at New York's Carnegie Hall. A deep friendship developed, the Stantons without hesitation offering safe haven to the family as war in Europe loomed, or, acting as sponsors for Keith's children. And, lo and behold, here we were: our first day in America.

With no children of their own, the Stantons must have found our invasion tryingly tiring in spite of our genteel manners from two such small people. Not quite believing this, Uncle Larry put us to the test on our first day. It was at lunch, the grownups were seated at a long mahogany table where, at the end of theirs, Philippa and I sat at a smaller table several levels below theirs. What followed is vivid, partly because it seemed, at least to me, such an outrageous request for an adult to make. Glasses of fresh orange juice had been placed before us—something we had never tasted before, when Uncle Larry, possibly having had one glass too many before lunch, spouted "Right! If you're so damned obedient, I dare you to kick your table over!" So requested, we dutifully complied with flying colors and gleeful shrieks as orange splashed upwards then dropped to seep into royal blue carpet. Only momentarily shocked, Uncle promptly burst into roars of laughter as Aunt Dodie glared at him furiously while I decided, then and there, I liked this new and rather eccentric uncle very, very much. The rest of the meal was calm enough, though Aunt Dodie never forgot my reply when she asked if I'd like a second helping of dessert: "No thank you," said I, not having had the unknown tapioca pudding before, each word distinctly expressed: "I have had ample sufficiency," a reply hard to believe, but then it was a different age, a different up-bringing.

We were just beginning to settle comfortably with these two warmly affectionate people with whom, to this point, I had shed no tears, so was surprised several days later by the arrival of a Mrs. Andersen, a nanny hired by a Carl and Frieda Jacobs in Cincinnati, another musical family, friends of our parents who had insisted, generously, we join their household of four boys. Mrs. Anderson was to be our escort to Cincinnati there to stay and care for us: another upheaval, another venture. Not understanding the ins-and-outs of the matter, I suspect I was thrilled with the idea of my first plane ride, the first of many over the years.

Far away: aged four and six

CINCINNATI, HERE WE COME!

So, we were about to travel to our new host family in Cincinnati, flying out of the new airport known as LaGuardia located in nearby Flushing Meadows. Opened for business the previous year to commercial traffic, it soon became popular, its planes flying within the States and Canada. Proposed by Mayor LaGuardia, the project was originally thought a $40 million boondoggle; yet the public, now entranced with flight, flocked to the airport's observation deck to pay a dime a time, the sum soon amassing $285,000, everyone eager to watch the silver birds take off and land. We too had been treated to such a visit in preparation for our first flight, learning airplanes could take you to far-away places with speed. Could one, would one, get us back home someday soon? Please?

After about a week with the Stantons and more or less settled, I was reluctant to leave, though the excitement of our up-coming flight may have assuaged some sadness, as hand-in-hand, the Stantons led us out onto the hot tarmac and up the steps to the plane, Mrs. Andersen fussing with our small carry-on bags. In the doorway we said goodbye to our new aunt and uncle, briefly hugged and patted, and joined other excited passengers on first flights westward. The stewardess took us, dressed again in our flowered pinafores and sun-bonnets, to our seats and soon we were taxiing down the runway. Then came the upward thrust of lift-off into "Beyond the Blue Horizon,"* where indeed, I hoped a beautiful time awaited us as we roared upward. Our British accents caused fellow passengers to come by to say hello, ask where from, where going, while in the seat behind

---

* Words and music: Franke Harling, Leo Robin & Richard Whiting, recorded by Jeanette McDonald in 1944.

us a traveling salesman perhaps, opened his case, leant over our seats to hand each of us a glass pendant suspended from pale green velvet ribbons worn as a necklace. The pendant encased a genuine four-leaf clover, that from the white clover plant, the original shamrock universal symbol of good luck. "Charms," the man said, "to bring you luck while you're in America." We thanked him and thereafter in spring and summer, searched grasses for this rarity—surely the more we found, the sooner home?

As with the Stantons, I have no memory of meeting Carl, a prosperous lawyer, nor his society wife Frieda "hostess with the most-est," who in Cincinnati perhaps vied for a position similar to that of Perle Mesta in Washington D.C., best known for backing Harry Truman and her soirees, bringing senators, congressmen and other luminaries together. The Jacobs, long supporters of the Cincinnati May Festivals, had met Daddy during performances in the 1930's, when street banners had proclaimed this, or something similar: "FALKNER SINGS BRAHMS!" As the Jacobs were involved with the Festival, I suspect they also had something to do with housing artists in their ante bellum-styled mansion located on the outskirts of Cincinnati named "Red-Wing Farm," so named for the number of cardinals nesting in the area, and incidentally, where my sister had been conceived three years earlier.

The Jacobs' four boys ranged in age from thirty-two to fourteen: Carl Jr., Stewart, Robert and John. The eldest was already in the army; the next two would enlist following Pearl Harbor. John, a lanky schoolboy, kept his distance from us "babies;" just as well for we were not adjusting well. I had soon realized we were here to stay a long way from mummy and daddy for some time, perhaps forever. I cried, and because I did, so did Philippa, even harder when she broke out in boils caused by a diet far richer than that served in Britain and so, inconsolable, we clung together sobbing our hearts out. I can feel, though not as agonizingly, that anguish, the awful loneliness and massive re-adjustments to all things foreign. Our Mrs. Andersen despaired, as did Frieda, who soon began calling us her "wailing women," exclaiming in a letter to Aunt Dodie: "All they do is cry!" There had been no such scenes with the Stantons. Perhaps, if Frieda had given us more care and attention, it might have helped us to settle.

Aside from Mrs. Andersen, a black chauffeur-cum butler, a cook and a maid made up the staff, while outside two enormous Great Danes kept encroachers at bay bounding freely within the large acreage. Every time we stepped outdoors these large creatures at first frightened us until we became used to their bounding excited leaps when they placed their huge paws on our shoulders knocking us to the ground delivering slavered slurpy doggy kisses upon us. So friendly did we become with these two, they allowed us to munch on their over-sized dog biscuits. UGH! Actually they tasted better than some stuff we had for breakfast like the unappetizing Ralston, a high fiber cracked wheat cereal, black spots too, invented in 1898 and still available today. I wonder how many children in the 1940's sat at American tables pushing the stuff around and around until the mixture became congealed slop. Threatened with sitting there all day until finished, the only way I would eat it was with cream and brown sugar.

Unkindly perhaps, in retrospect I feel the Jacobs' interest was not necessarily altruistic; rather, their offer of safe haven an ostentatious display of civic-mindedness by extending a hand to English friends, very much the in thing to do at the time. In our case, I suspect we were nothing more to the Jacobs than two waifs to be shown off, given little affection or comfort in our misery while showering us with "things." When at last I did stop crying, Frieda was pleased to show me off to friends, relations and church members; parading me about in a new sailor outfit with smart navy cap worn half-cocked, nautical streamers hanging down the back. On many a Sunday morning I sat beside her in the family pew during Catholic services; all parishioners' eyes upon me, as, wearing white gloves, I diligently placed my quarter in the collection plate, all nodding approval. The novelty of "me," Flip too young to be paraded about, soon wore off, dismissed then to purgatory in the church basement for Sunday school, to color endless bible pictures.

Then, one day, Frieda in her chauffeured Cadillac, took us to the very concert hall where our father had sung and where, embarrassingly, word was out that the Falkner girls were in the audience. That's how well-known daddy was in those days. A queue formed, ostensibly to talk with Frieda, at the same time eyeing her two waifs as we sat quietly waiting for the music to start. Was it Beethoven's Fifth they played that afternoon with its four-note opening: 'V' for Victory? This being my first real concert, I was totally spellbound by the music and the players, absorbed by the sound of an orchestra in full flow, wanting the magic to go on and on. Next day the *Cincinnati Herald* displayed a photograph of us:

> "The girls, Julia and Philippa, are the daughters of Keith Falkner famous singer who performed often at our May Festivals before the war, here seen walking to their seats for the concert in their jaunty patriotic sailor outfits. They now live temporarily (no doubt thanks to the generosity of) the lawyer Carl and Mrs. Jacobs . . ."

From there on, things began to deteriorate as we had discovered there were no parameters. Only meals, naps and bedtimes were set. Everyone seemed to be trying to make us feel at home through 'things," about which we had no complaints, no expense being spared, though no pony supplied; tons of new clothes, a huge doll-house, farm and a crawl-in greenhouse with plants which soon withered away, and the run of the boys' old nursery with its train set wandering throughout the large rooms on the third floor. As if this were not enough, I clamored for a bicycle, so one was bought, my challenge from the Jacobs to learn to ride it that very day. With no one to help, I despaired as the long day went on—I was brought a sandwich and glass of milk at noon, then it was back to the struggle. Day began to turn to dusk, the evening loomed and I knowing I wasn't to be allowed inside until I had learnt, became frantic until, finally, I was allowed in to be put to bed without supper, for I had failed, and failed again. It was several days later before I got the hang of it when after a few wobbles, I took off. Despite all this spoiling generosity, our favorite games were simple: playing store with crates and empty cans from the kitchen or hiding underneath the large rhododendron bushes in the middle of the circular driveway, pretending to be Carl Sr. smoking his endless Havanas, ours the curled—up brown, unlit rhododendron leaves.

I began to put on weight from eating celery sticks with, no, not cream cheese—bad enough—but butter; even oranges, weird as it may seem, always a hefty pat on salted radishes, double helpings of dessert, ice cream, nobody paying a bit of notice. Unable to fulfill her duties properly, Mrs. Andersen had had enough, whether of us or her employers I can only guess, but enough she had had, as throwing up her hands for the last time, she decamped. From then on we were supervised by a maid lax in her duty and language which arising from the kitchen and up the back stairs to our nursery, was a wonderful concoction of profane language: all wonderfully new sounding words which, being children, we quickly picked up and bandied about, only to have our mouths washed out with soap.

Many days seemed endless especially when stormy. Ohio weather was variable so we were often marooned in the nursery, pining as we watched the rain teem down windows, sheet off roofs as the great oak outside my bedroom window, bowing in the wind, knocked, rapped or tapped its lofty branches against the panes: most scary at night. Yet, despite all, these two seemingly interminable years were not without pleasure. There were parties; Christmas, with a live Santa, where in 1942 we thought we were getting guns,—well it was war-time—the guns turned out to be matching umbrellas, a big disappointment; birthdays were richly celebrated and at Easter a supposed bunny left all sorts of baskets around the great gardens then full of flowering magnolia trees; New Years, and 4th of July were big occasions with grand firework displays on the grounds, which, after exploding, festooned the sky as small parachutes drifted downward to land a small army of dolls which we retrieved the next morning. Early one spring both of us came down with whooping cough (Pertussis), and were farmed out to live with the gardener's family for some six weeks. On return, each of us at different times were treated to a lunch party of favorite foods: mine sliced honeydew melon, creamed sweetbreads (thymus or pancreas glands of beef or veal) with peas and mashed potatoes, followed by homemade peach ice cream and wafers. The entire summer of 1942 we spent at Magnolia Beach in Massachusetts before returning for me to be enrolled in first grade at a nearby country day school. I was driven there at first by the black butler in the estate's wooden paneled Ford, patriotically repainted red, white and blue. Thereafter, I'd soon be riding back and forth in a bright yellow bus, feeling very grownup.

SUNDAYS IN CINCINNATI

Not too many months after the Sunday novelty of my being shown off in the nave of Frieda's church, then being demoted to purgatory in the basement, came the shocking and monumental blow to the United States, the bombing of Pearl Harbor. Not all, but some like us, if not exactly *personae not grata,* were less welcome Americans now at war themselves, needed to think of their own sons and daughters whether away fighting or at home. Despite all, the usual alternating Sunday dinners between "Red Wing Farm" and the home of Frieda's parents, the Heines, went on as normal. How we giggled when we heard their name, Frieda a Heine herself, referred to bottoms as such, bottoms for children . . . well, you know, something very funny.

The Heines lived in a gloomy old house in an older section of the city, not a house liked by small children for everything was dark and ponderous, everything from the sepia-toned photographs in dark leather frames to the drawn-down shades with ecru-colored lace curtains overhung by darkly drab velvet drapery; to the heavy old Germanic-style settees and chairs draped with antimacassars. Clocks, in or out of wooden or glass cases, proclaimed the passing of hours as each quarter chimed in an assortment of discordant notes, pendulums swinging unceasingly back and forth, back and forth. Then and there I decided never to own ticking, chiming, dinging, donging, gonging, pinging, pealing or cuckoo-ing clocks! As for Mrs. Heine, I do not remember her husband, I can still see her, a small plumpish woman grey hair piled atop her head, wearing old-fashioned purplish, (I've hated purple ever since, especially when later Mummy told me the color was for old ladies!) sateen dresses with lace collars, shawls draped about her shoulders, as she clicked her way in small French heels across the highly polished parquet flooring, trying not to take a trip upon the maroon and marooned Persian carpets.

It was not just the house and furnishings that were heavy and dull, so too the food, unremittingly the same every Sunday. However, the highly polished mahogany table with lace mats was always laid in proper order with glittering crystal and silver, complete to dainty glass finger bowls with tepid water and thin lemon slice for the purpose of the genteel rinsing of, heaven forefend, greasy finger-tips! The first course was always homemade beef consommé, brown of course which I admit was delicious served with slice of lemon, sprinkle of parsley. Our hostess, amid polite conversation, no slurping of soup allowed, would when all had finished, tap her foot on a bell hidden under the carpet, summoning the maid to remove the two-handled soup bowls which one never, ever picked up: the refrain for children being: "As little boats go out to sea, I push my spoon away from me: as little boats come in from sea, I push my spoon into me," swallow. Soup cleared, the ever-standing over-cooked rib-roast, no rarity here, followed surrounded by darkened toast points and over-grilled gills of mushrooms. Shriveled roast potatoes, green beans cooked to death and boats of cooling greasy gravy completed the course. Desserts were not much better; none I can remember. The bonus came later for, if we had been good, on our way home we visited an ice cream parlor for green mint ice cream with hot chocolate sauce, a real treat.

After this stodgy repast, it was back to the gloomy sitting room with coffee for adults, chocolates for all, as briar-scented tobacco, cigarettes, or Cuban cigars fugged the air amid the chatter of war, shortages, while bandages were rolled and knitting needles clicked. The mania for knitting had suddenly become a patriotic duty under the auspices of the American Red Cross, who gave basic instructions to women picking up needles for the first time. An issue of *Life* in November, 1941, featured a young woman on its cover busily knitting away, inside instructions for "how to." Eleanor Roosevelt was often photographed either carrying her large knitting bag, or with knitting needles in action, effectively launching the national knitting effort by hosting a "Knit for Defense" tea at the Waldorf

Astoria in New York City in September 1941. Not three months after Pearl Harbor, American women were taking up the craft making with the Army's regulation olive drab khaki-colored yarn, sweaters, socks, mufflers, fingerless mitts and other garments to keep their fighting men warm. Bandages were also knit using white cotton in straight knit (each row a knit, rather than alternating rows of knit and purl) allowing bandages to stretch. Before shipment to medical units they, the bandages not the knitters, were sterilized. All very admirable, but at age five or six, it was a relief to be dismissed for a nap, freed from chattering adults, the clicking of needles and smothering smoke.

On just such a Sunday I was excused to take my nap upstairs in Mr. Heine's study, to find his room surprisingly light with mid-afternoon sunshine streaming through tall windows bouncing off dark built-in floor to ceiling shelves crammed with leather-bound tomes. They, of little interest to me, my attention wandered to a tall brass stand where, perched in a gilded cage sat a bright yellow canary chirping happily away. The nearer I got, the more it sang, the more I wanted to see this tiny "cantatrice" close up, so pulling up a straight-backed chair I climbed aboard. The canary seemed to welcome my attention, fluffing up its little jonquil-colored feathers singing away loudly hopping to the floor of its cage and began scattering seed, splashing water as it took minute sips from a tiny dish. Hopping half-way back to its perch, it stopped, tiny claws clinging to one side of the cage as it looked at me. Should I, would I, could I open his little gate? Yes, for then I could stroke his tiny head as he fluffed up his plumage, maybe he'd even sit on my out-stretched finger. Thinking this I tried to lift the little latch but found it difficult to open. So leaning in further to get a better perch, a better angle, my balance shifted, the chair on the highly polished floor sliding slowly then gaining momentum as I grabbed at air and cage alike as seemingly in slow motion, we crashed to the floor stunned. Frightened, my little golden friend began to squawk hopping about while I, having banged my nose on the hard floor cried, my tears mixing with blood dripping from my nose. Running steps were then heard tearing up the stairs, along the corridor, people bursting through the door causing it to crash back against a book case. Then we were being picked up, canary first, me second, our very varied ruffled feathers soothed, I for awhile inconsolable, missing mummy wanting her comfort rather than hearing, as my nose was seen to, the chill remarks of "pull-yourself-together, you naughty, naughty child!" To my sorrow, I was never allowed to rest in that one bright room again. Needless to say, there was no green mint ice cream with hot chocolate sauce for me that day!

On alternate Sundays we dined at home at one p.m. sharp, where sometimes I was allowed to join the grownups. I happened to be among them Sunday, December 7, 1941, the elders eating, imbibing and chatting, while I, bored stiff, felt a nap coming on. Suddenly the butler rushed through the green baize door to place a portable radio next to Carl Senior: "Pard'n! S'cuse'm !" he stammered, "But y'all got to hear de news!" as almost sobbing he continued, "America bin attacked by de Japs! Dey bombed Pearl Harbor!" I remember the event well, this perfidious act on what FDR would call "a day of infamy." This invasion by the Japanese resulted in a rush of young men eager to volunteer for the armed forces; the end of isolationist sentiment in the United States united now in feverish fervor. At the time the significance of the event meant nothing to me but to eventually change our lives again as it would do for many others with their hosts' homeland threatened with invasion and war.

Cincinnati Sunday afternoon on best behavior

COUNTRY DAY SCHOOL

A bit of background. Of course I was too young to know what was happening in Europe during 1940, 1941 and 1942, where all Jews were in grave danger and Germany, having broken her pact with Russia, invaded that country on June 22, 1941, in operation Barbarossa. Things progressed from bad to worse when Germany invaded the Ukraine on July 19, to round up and slaughter 33,771 Jews on the twenty-ninth. Meanwhile, the Italian Fascist government of dictator Benvenuto (the welcome) Mussolini, which had taken over in 1922, had garnered an empire in Ethiopia and had annexed Albania to then join forces with German Chancellor Adolf Hitler. On November 13, the British aircraft carrier Ark Royal, based at the British colony of Gibraltar, engaged in escorting convoys to Malta, was torpedoed by U-boat 81 off Gibraltar, sinking some fourteen hours later. A month later, on December 7th, came the big blow to America when the Japanese attacked the American fleet at Pearl Harbor, Hawaii. The following day, the United States and Britain declared war on Japan; while three days later Germany declared war on the United States. By doing so, Hitler had hoped to entice Japan to invade Russia from the east while he invaded from the west, final push to attain Moscow. Shades of Napoleon. As it turned out, this megalomaniac ended up fighting a war on two fronts, a similar fiasco suffered by Germany in the First World War. Had Hitler not pursued this strategy but relied instead on Admiral Karl Donitz and his U-boats for control of the Atlantic, Germany conceivably could have won the war, even though at the beginning, Donitz had only fifty-seven U-boats in service rather than the three hundred he had requested. By the end of 1942 production of U-boats had increased so that the admiral was able to send out "wolfpacks," formed to intercept and attack convoys at night, which often included merchant shipping protected by naval escorts. As wolfpacks hunted and destroyed, they also created havoc among the escorts who were often thrown into disarray, with huge loss of men, materiel and shipping. The merchant fleets of both the United States and England were not permitted to stop for survivors of torpedoed vessels, as it was considered too dangerous to do so. If they did, it was very likely they too would become targets, and their cargos of war materiel considered of far more import, particularly fuel, for Britain. Admiral Donitz, who lost his two sons during the war, was disillusioned for he had hoped his wolfpacks would help tip the war in Germany's favor. Designated by Hitler as his successor, Donitz, as head of state and President, eventually expelled Goring and Himmler from the Nazi party before committing suicide. Meanwhile, in a surprise military attack, the Japanese had attacked Pearl Harbor, its purpose to keep the U.S. Pacific fleet from interfering with Japanese expansion of its empire.

After Pearl Harbor, Daddy wrote to the Stantons:

> On December 7, we listened with trepidation as the news of the Japanese bombing Pearl Harbour came through. Apart from the horror of the devastation, we wondered about our children's fate and could only feel that, at last, America was fighting with us. We had a lovely weekend together in July, a lovely interlude to this life of 'je ne sais quoi'! We ended with an air raid on the last night, but were too tired to do more than turn over in bed. So blase does one become.

For me, September, 1941, seems to have been a happier time, adjusted to first grade in a one-room school house, so different from the previous dull months, though apparently I learned little, for that fall Mummy wrote to Aunt Dodie:

(At last) "a long letter from the Jacobs with twelve photographs of the children. They look absolutely grand! . . . Julia now goes to school but has not learned much. I do not mind this as one could not expect her mind to work on too many details. Also her heart may have been a bit sore . . ."

How could it not have been?! Our separation was still taking its toll. Nonetheless, because of our young age, my sister and I were adapting more quickly to our surroundings than older children in our situation.

A Mrs. Hencock was in charge of the lower grades in the school, she was not a bad old bird fussing about like a mother hen; thus living up to, in part, her oxymoronic surname. The headmaster taught grades five through eight, where a number of rowdy boys were often in enough trouble so that, with impunity, indeed some enthusiasm, he punished them in the shuttered kitchen, all of us able to hear the thwack of wooden paddle on bottom, and the howl of some poor boy.

All the grades were housed in one large room. On either side of blackboard that covered the west wall stood two flags, that of the United States, the other the flag of Ohio. Above the blackboard, was a big rolled-up map of the world—as it was then—that could be lowered for geography lessons. On the south side, windows overlooked the playground. My desk stood halfway along the north wall, near the metal shuttered kitchen. Behind it, on most mornings, the odor of bland boiling beans and ham hocks seeped out into our room. At noon, lunch time, the metal divider would, with a tremendous clatter, be drawn up so that food could be slopped onto our tin plates as we diligently filed past. As we finished munching at our desks, plates returned, the shutter would, just as noisily, drop back into place. I found it best to bring my lunch from home in my own lunch pail.

A great deal of time was spent indoors that winter, the schoolroom reeking of damp coats, mittens and rubber boots competing with the smells of paste, crayons, chalk, not to mention that inevitable aroma of beans, unsalted, unpeppered and, without a sprinkling of clove or sage. The noise was non-stop: the banging of desk lids, scraping of chairs, voices, rustling of papers, snapping of note and text books, snipping of scissors, that awful screech of fingernails on blackboard, teachers' voices and the tomfoolery of the older boys who were always ready to dip pigtails into ink wells. We bobbed for apples on Halloween; Frieda brought cupcakes to school for my birthday. On Valentine's Day, an older boy named Dick came to my desk and gave me a heart-shaped card which I still have. Pitty-pat went my heart! It would not be my first such experience, nor the last!

One awful Friday afternoon in first grade, I had forgotten something in my desk and rushed back in the school before the bus arrived and staff locked up for the weekend. Inside, a small hallway led to the large classroom into which I ran just missing the headmaster as he emerged from his small office. He did not see me nor I him as I ran to my desk, gathered up what I had forgotten, and raced back to the front door. But, it was shut, and now locked. Through the glass panels on either side of the door, I could see Mrs. Hencock and my schoolmates waiting for our bright yellow bus, the headmaster waving to all as he left the grounds in his car. I shouted, banged on the door, and rapped ever harder on the glass panes for attention. Somebody, somebody had to hear me or at least notice I was missing. Nobody did, and I panicked.

In moments of stress small children tend to let irrationality take over, can not think straight, the worst imagined, and about to happen. I was convinced that not only had I been forgotten but would never be found again. What would happen if I had to spend the entire weekend in the school? I might die from cold and hunger! Imagining long, lonely dark nights wherein who knew what horrible creatures roamed about, was even scarier. It did not occur to me Mrs. Hencock would be counting heads, or, if I didn't get off the bus at the Jacobs driveway, people would start looking for me. There are no sensible thoughts in these very juvenile situations, at least not in mine, just the horror of being abandoned, something I already felt I knew something about.

I was now quite irrational, hoarse from shouting as I pummeled the door, banging window panes ever harder. Suddenly heads turned, children pointed towards the school. Mrs. Hencock turned and with what must have been a squawk of astonishment, flew towards me across the school yard. The big key grated in the lock, the handle turned, and the door opened. Tearfully, with a gasp of relief, I fell into my teacher's arms as she, clucking, ever the mother hen, fussily dried my tears and calmed me down. "I was about to count heads before the bus arrived," she said. "I would have noticed you were missing and come to get you." But, I was not so sure. As we walked back to the students, the bus pulled up and we all clambered aboard. I was soon safely on the way back to my temporary home, a place I had been positive I would never ever see again. I had had my own little battle to fight and had come through it. As it turned out, a few months later, I would be gone from "Red Wing Farm," not to see the Country Day School again.

A TRAIN TRIP

That June of 1942, Frieda took us by train to Boston, then by car to their summer home near Magnolia Beach in the township of Gloucester, Massachusetts. Everyone needed the break from war news coming from east and west alike. In January more than two-hundred and thirty American ships and fifty tons of war materiel had been lost; not counting innumerable sailors, merchant seamen and others who did not survive U-boat attacks. That April the Fall of Bataan had occurred with the surrender of American and Filipino troops, when 72,000 of them, diseased and starving, were forced through jungles on the seventy mile Bataan Death March, some18,000 to 20,000 dying on the week-long trek from dehydration, untreated wounds, shot execution-style or bayoneted. Of good news that same month the first air raids on major Japanese cities had been led by Colonel Jimmy Doolittle. In May Corregidor fell, followed by the Battle for the Coral Sea, both leading to the defeat of the Japanese Navy, yet fighting continued to rage. Frieda and Carl constantly worried about their boys fighting in various theaters, hoping a holiday might cheer everyone up.

The journey from Cincinnati to Boston was, if you'll pardon the expression, a real hoot of excitement: the noise of engines gathering steam to roar and roll ever faster, flashing passengers across the countryside amid the clickety-clack of steel on steel. Whistles, throaty hoots, and sonorous peals resounded while metal bells swung back and forth atop chugging engines, cow-catchers welded to their fronts. The train, swaying slightly from side to side, hurtled and thundered past crossings of stripped barriers, alternating flashing red lights, semaphores swinging back and forth with a 'dang, dong, dang, dong'. The train slowed when trundling over high trestles or bridges above sparkling blue rivers bubbling over boulders far below. Tunnels were approached with loud whistles, trains hurtling into gaping black maws thundering through with tremendous clatter as travelers, gazing out darkened windows found they were staring at themselves until trains, disgorging, blasted from blackness to sudden brilliance. Approaching trains roared past to startle with their strident screeches, high-pitched whistles and tremendous swoosh of air to disappear from whence we had just come, one supposed. So it was at night when the piercing glare of on-coming train's headlights flashed past illuminating carriages briefly to leave all in darkness again.

Too grand to stop at small stations, we watched as our train tore through them, extending a long metal arm with hook to retrieve canvas mail bags hanging from tall stanchions alongside the tracks, their contents sorted en route in the post office compartment; later delivered to a main office down the line. When the train did pull into a station, the conductor, a black (right word at the time) man in an impeccably smart uniform and cap in black with red trim, opened the outside door at the back of whatever carriage was best suited for descent to the approaching platform, the heavy iron plate covering steps leading to it, lifted. As the locomotive eased to a stop, the conductor jumped down to place an iron footstool for alighting passengers, who, having departed with heavy luggage, needed the assistance of redcaps and porters. Time then to resume the journey, timetables to be met as a flagman signaled from the rear all was clear so the engineer, having re-stoked the engine and taken on water, released brakes to get his heavy train moving again. Slowly the big locomotive; sometimes two for gradients, chugged and puffed, pushed or pulled, big wheels slipping at first then gaining momentum as the conductor, heavy footstool back on board, hopped back on as with deafening metallic clang he dropped the heavy iron plate flooring back into place and slammed shut the heavy door.

Though wonderfully exciting, the trip was not without its perils, for we found it frightening as we moved from carriage to carriage having to cross an expanse of grinding metal plates coupling carriage to carriage, which swayed alarmingly with the speed of the train, we, afraid our feet might slip between them, caught in this deadly device. Our time otherwise was fun in assigned seats gazing out at the unfolding scenery, or coloring when not tumbling about in the observation car. Always eager to eat, we had to wait our turn as passengers ate in shifts in dining cars with tables set before plate glass windows on both sides of the two carriages. Each table had a bud vase with fresh rose, menu card set in silver stand set on linen napery with heavy silverware polished to high sheen, goblets agleam. Food, which even at six I knew to be good, was served by black waiters in impossibly white jackets and gloves. Perhaps it was the contrast? If we had behaved during the meal, ice cream was allowed with slim crisp waffled wafer wedged on top. But then, horror of horrors, we had to make that awful trek back to our carriage, back across that great grinding divide of lurching metal plates under our unsteady feet. "Girls!" admonished Frieda, a woman of little patience giving no quarter, no encouragement, tried to hustle us across: "Keep moving!" Of course her boys would never have been so nerveless!

At night we shared a "drawing room," lucky me in the top bunk, my sister below, Frieda nearby. These night journeys for me were fraught with anxiety for when trains pulled into large terminals in the middle of the night, locomotives, carriages, Pullman cars, tankers, freight cars and cabooses were unlinked, shuttled, shunted, re-linked and re-routed in what sounded like total disarray. Our Pullman coach often seemed to be sidelined in darkest night, the quiet convincing me we had been stranded somewhere, lost in the wilds of unknown territory—my awful fear of abandonment raising its head. After such worriment, I would fall into fitful sleep, awaking to the usual sounds of a train running rapidly and smoothly along its tracks to its destination.

One evening there was much excitement as we were allowed to stay up later than usual. But why? "You'll hear, you'll hear!" is all Frieda would say, propping a shortwave radio atop the back of my seat as other passengers grinned. Looking at her watch several times, Frieda eventually turned on the radio, raised and twisted antennae back and forth while twirling dials in every direction. For moments there was nothing but static, as bored and sleepy, we wondered what all the fuss was about. Then, about nine o'clock, a voice, that wonderful voice still remembered by me, daddy's baritone! "Hello! Julia and Philippa! Daddy speaking here to send you a message from England! We hope to have you back with us soon . . ." static again took over no matter which way dials were twisted, antennae bent, the voice was gone. But I had heard Daddy, heard him after two long years, though the truncated message left me in limbo again, longing but not knowing what to do . . . perhaps it would have been better if I had not heard him speak, his voice so far away. Reality for us was a train plowing through the night to Maine. Years later I would learn daddy, with pull from friends at the Beeb as the BBC was affectionately called, had been able to say those few words during a delayed overseas broadcast of his own concert.

I have no memory of arriving at the house in Magnolia Beach near Glouchester. We frequented two beaches of several in the area: Magnolia in the morning, often rough and therefore more exciting as we ran in and out of on-coming waves trying to avoid crabs scuttling hither and yon, while at the far end of the beach waves smashed against rocks. The other was calmer, with a wonderful array of broken multicolored bottled glass, edges and colors softened by the endless to and fro, wear and tear of salt and sand, such pretty gifts from the sea which I gathered. As for Gloucester itself I remember driving through the village for errands sitting in the rumble seat of someone's 1939 Ford, wonderful fun yet always admonished to stay seated, keeping arms and legs within.

MAGNOLIA BEACH

In those mornings full of brilliant sunshine, Magnolia Beach was a-shimmer with wavelets ebbing and flowing, bigger undulating waves furling in on themselves as they worked their way to shore. With tide out they were not a threat as we crossed dunes with tall razor-sharp reed-like grasses buffeted by strong breeze blowing sand about as we made our way down to the beach trying to avoid splinters as we crossed small weather-beaten bridges. The jump from there to the hot sand seemed scorching, hot enough we felt to burn the soles of our tender feet, flip flops unknown in America until introduced in the 1950's from New Zealand, invented by the Japanese years before. Meanwhile and never-ending, seagulls screeched, wheeling on air currents above the seascape, stalked about or perched on rocks or posts to survey coastal waters for their next catch.

Always managing to race ahead of Frieda, carrying towels, tanning lotion, pails and spades, Flip and I tore over the dunes crossing the small bridges spanning four feet deep channels of run-off water mixed with tidal returns to the sea. Hopping across a bridge one morning, I glanced over its railing fascinated by the tiny crabs scuttling about below between seaweed fronds swaying gently as the water ebbed. Then, skipping on merrily, I assumed Flip with her shorter legs would soon catch up with me. When I turned to find her, she was nowhere in sight. Where was she, we who so needed to stay together? Running back to the little bridge, I found her at last lying prone on the rill's surface, unmoving and doll-like, drifting with arms outspread from her still chubby body, golden curls a halo around her head. Unable to swim, I didn't know what to do. A crowd began to gather: men on either side of the banks were shouting; nobody doing anything. Then, helpless and crying in despair, suddenly there was sixteen year-old John leaping across sand and railings, all six feet of him jumping in to grab Flip's foot before she floated away under the bridge. That this mean-spirited hulking teenager would save one of the greatest nuisances he had spent the past two years trying to avoid, seemed a miracle. Yet here he was, dragging her out of the water by her heel depositing this pest of his, none-too-gently on the bank at my feet. Resuscitation was hardly required for Flip told us, after a few sputtering coughs, she'd been holding her breath assuming even without a mask she would be able to scan oceans' floors at leisure, watching those cute little crabs scuttle about below. Soon Flip was her usual fearless self, running all over the beach, wondering what all the fuss had been about.

Daily we were rubbed down with baby oil to turn nut-brown while building sandcastles, splashing in the ocean or hunting for shells, and keeping an eye out for those nasty reddish crabs scrabbling sideways waving pincers in the air always ready to nip tender toes, or in a crab-grab, hang onto a finger. We had a book about these creatures, perhaps the very ones scuttling across Magnolia beach, certainly they were about the same size and just as redshelled, ready to nip unsuspecting naughty little boys and girls, so our book related. To prove its point, I got a nasty nip on my big toe, a big hurt, yet could think of no reason until remembering I had refused to finish my soggy cornflakes that very morning and being placed in the back yard until I did so. I didn't finish them after all, having been stung by a wasp and so allowed back in. It would be a two-nipper day! It seemed I was often being punished, was often guilty of a multitude of transgressions, and, so, often chastised and spanked, but seldom praised. In hindsight, yes, I was naughty, I lied, was spoilt, and I often swore like a Turk, as the expression then went; but whose fault was that?

Later in the summer I sensed something was in the wind as I began to pick up subtle vibes as sensitive children often do: looks, the sudden cessation of talk when entering a room, the "not-nows, laters," of Frieda or Carl. Unknown to us, plans were indeed in the works for our removal from their household, negotiations being agued back and forth, frantic wires between our parents, the Jacobs and Stantons, at first discussing the pros and cons of the Jacobs' back-out of their agreement for the duration; then, trying to find a solution. It seems the Jacobs had even gone so far as to refer us to a placement agency with thought of separating us, now six and four, for it was now more difficult to find a temporary home. Most American families were no longer willing to take on the responsibility of one child, let alone two, for an indefinite period, even with compensation.

So it was that once again the Stantons, with great benevolence and kindest sympathy, stepped in, more than anxious to see Keith's daughters happily resettled until such time as we could safely rejoin our parents. For all I knew that late summer of 1942, Flip would be joining me at the Country Day School under Mrs. Hencock's, sometimes, watchful eyes.

Fat and unhappy, for now

RETURN TO MADISON AVENUE

We may have returned to Red Wing Farm after that fun summer in Magnolia, that is, except for the crabs for I remember another long train journey to arrive in that vast complex of Grand Central Terminal—its official name and largest in the world for number of platforms and tracks. Located at the intersection of 42nd Street and Park Avenue, the imposing edifice was opened in 1913 to accommodate the heyday of long-distance travel. Within, no matter your age, you can't help but look up and about in awe, from its Beaux-Art architecture, its astronomy themed depicted ceiling, its clock, even the sheer number of people bustling about. Then there is the Oyster Bar on a lower level with the Italian architect Guastavino Moreno's interlocking terracotta tile vaults. By whatever means, we had indeed arrived back in New York City that late summer of 1942; returned to the more caring Stantons.

So indeed we found ourselves but with faint memory of these two kind understanding people: remember the flying orange juice? I suspect Aunt Dodie and Uncle Larry had no idea what they'd let themselves in for this time for we were no longer those two well-behaved children of two years before. But while astonished, they were lenient, realizing we had become drifters in a world not of our making. A few days of grace wouldn't hurt before obedience was expected, rules obeyed—no swearing aloud, decorum restored.

A photo shows us on a first outing to Central Park. What could I have been thinking that afternoon, for it shows a grumpy, resentful and overly chubby child staring back at the camera, not a glimmer of a smile, her four year-old sister trustingly clutching her hand while looking up as though to ask, "what's next?" If there was resentment, it was not for being here, rather that our lives had again been disrupted. As for Uncle Larry and Aunt Dodie, they were truly shocked, shocked at these almost unrecognizable children. Where were our manners, thoughtfulness, kindness to others, eagerness to learn?

A first question asked was whether we'd ever been read to? We had books, yes, but no one had taken the time to do so, though tales with morals had been told us ad nauseam, such as Aesop's *The Boy Who Cried Wolf*, a lesson in 'woe betide you if you lie!' which, to a large extent, we seem to have ignored. Next question: had we ever written to or colored a picture for our parents, been reminded of them, remembered them? The answers were no, no, no and only just. The Stantons immediately set about to remedy the situation: large Hollywood promotional stills of Keith now sat about in leather frames; his 78 rpm recordings played on their gramophone. A particular favorite was *King Charles* by Baroque composer Henry Purcell.

Beginning to settle I could not complain for I had Aunt Dodie's almost undivided attention as she tried to bring us up to a level of knowledge which would in the fall be augmented by attendance at Miss Summerville's School. In the meantime Aunt read and instructed, paid kind attention; leading, suggesting, advising and expecting results which she soon began to get. Her hands full, she also supervised our weekly letter-writing efforts to our parents, though most went to the bottom of the ocean. Only a few got safely across, our first-ever thrilling mummy: her reply happily reaching us read:

> Your first letter, [since] the children with you at last and my first letter from Julia in my life . . . nothing could give Keith and me greater happiness than to know the children are having a 'home life' with you. In England they were always part of us . . . Please keep them as close to you as you feel able . . . I remember in one of your first letters you stressed that you wanted them to feel secure and my heart warmed to you greatly because it is so essential in a youngster's life.

Dorothy Stanton was indeed our lifeline to the parents, while she undoubtedly came to care for us almost as deeply as they, never having had children of her own, and so it would prove. Flip was her poppet with her boundless energy and inquisitiveness, always everywhere and into everything, who she soon re-named Froggie, sometimes Scamp depending on what she had been up to. As for chubby me, I was put on a diet though both Stantons puzzled that only music and the gruesome fairy tales of the aptly named Brothers Grimm seemed to hold my attention. (Must I read you another fairy tale, he asked grimly?—my pun intended.) Where was the lively out-going child of 1940, they asked themselves?

Enrolled in Miss Summerville's School in Manhattan for Grades 2 and kindergarten, for school year 1942-1943 around the same time Churchill and Stalin were meeting in Moscow to discuss further war plans, I slowly began to find more interest in learning. Perhaps unwisely always trying to keep Mummy abreast of our progress, Aunt Dodie passed on this message:

> "Within weeks the headmistress took me aside to tell me
> Julia is not learning much and needs affection and attention
> from a great lack thereof . . . I'm doing what I can . . ."

Three thousand miles away Mother must have felt further sorrow, regretting she had not kept us with her and daddy for, after all, it had turned out our uprooting had been unnecessary but, who was to know that at the time? Though not doing well, I liked this new school. It was so different from the Country Day in Cincinnati, with its crowded classroom smelling of ham hocks, beans, chalk and noisy sweaty children. Classrooms at Miss Summerville's were roomier and, discounting the city's discordant klaxonic noises, quieter owing to better discipline. Light flooded in through tall east windows on sunny days, there was a large asphalt courtyard below, our playground for endless games of tag, Hop-Scotch, Mother-May-I, and the intricate steps of rope jumping. Also at our new home I was fascinated by and hearing lots of music, Mummy writing:

> . . . . it is lovely to hear of Julia's passionate interest in Music and of Keith's singing . . . Julia came and lay on the sofa during early mornings whilst Keith and I rehearsed and so imbibed a great deal . . . lovely too that she is interested in the piano [and] how good of the Doctor to play his cello for them . . .

Though not learning much, I was happier now. Certainly life was more interesting and enjoyable, the making of friends easier. We spent hours in Central Park at the zoo feeding peanuts to the monkeys, though eating more ourselves; at the Pond trying to save our top-heavy sail boat from tipping; hours at slides, jungle gyms and riding the merry-go-round with its endless playing of "Mairzy doats and dozy doats and liddle lambzy divey, A Kiddley divvy too, wooden shoe," written by Milton Drake in 1943, a great hit on the home front and with American servicemen overseas, the lyrics incidentally, often used as code during the war, or so 'twas said.

Although the Stantons opened our eyes and ears by taking us to a variety of pantomimes, concerts, circuses, zoos and museum trips, it was to libraries I went most eagerly, either the one at Turtle Bay or New York's Main Library, a wonderful edifice officially opened in May, 1911, at Fifth Avenue between 40th and 42nd Streets. Again in Beaux-Arts style, at the time it was the largest marble structure in America and contained seventy-five miles of shelving, its two famous stone lions guarding the entrance. Aunt Dodie read and read to us: the Arthur Ransome series, tales of *King Arthur and the Knights of the Round Table* illustrated by the marvelous Arthur Rackham, the Twain adventures, *Robinson Crusoe,* good old Rip Van Winkle by Washington Irving who slept off drink for twenty years; histories of civilizations, and poetry, and many more fascinating subjects. Soon I was avidly reading on my own, finding in books free range to imagination: you name it, I read it. I even began to write my own stories though recall only one in which I was determined to use the past participle of the verb "to have," able to produce: "after they 'had had' two cups of tea . . ." Really! How embarrassing! Another pleasure was stamp collecting, a rich experience, getting to know of different parts of the world, the fun of pasting into albums, the swapping and bargaining for ones most wanted.

Themselves avid readers, the Stantons pored over the *New York Times, The New Yorker, The Economist,* much as I do today, reading, discussing, even arguing over the news and discussing Franklin Delano Roosevelt's policies, they great fans of his. In their discussions I remember hearing of the exploits of the wonderful Tuskegee 332 Fighter Group created by Presidential order in June, 1941, the previous year. This was an all black unit known as the "Red Devils," who captured my imagination by their exploits, fighting not only the German Luftwaffe in protecting American B-24 bombers on the European front, but fighting prejudice at home.

At some point during these two years, I developed my third crush—my first, cousin John Keith in 1939, Dick, my valentine presenter in 1941, and now, sucker that I was for a good looker, Gordon F., my interest alas, not returned. Too late, on Valentine's Day, 1945, I did receive a card from him; he'd played it safe. A Gordon F. was, when last looked up some years ago, still residing in Manhattan. I wonder what his reaction would be if I should suddenly call? I won't! Still, nothing ventured . . .

CHRISTMAS

I was anticipating my seventh birthday in January, 1943, but first there was Christmas in New York. More sober this year than others because of the war, the lights on what had become the traditional Christmas tree were doused as part of the blackout of the Eastern seaboard which lasted until 1944. Originally the tree had been set up by workers constructing the massive Rockefeller Plaza complex which opened in 1939. The complex built by the Rockefeller family, designed in modern Art Deco, spanned twenty-two acres in midtown Manhattan, between Fifth 5 and Sixth Avenues, 48th and 51st Streets, to house nineteen commercial buildings, the whole declared to be a National Historic Landmark in1987. As for the Christmas tree, from 1945 onward it would be the biggest, brightest, and most famous evergreen in the United States, its 30,000 or so bulbs often lit by the current (pun) president.

Had Aunt Dodie been younger, we might have learned to skate at Rockefeller Plaza's skating rink. As it was, we watched as others twirled gracefully about, or in the learning, lost balance, tripped to find themselves abruptly sitting on the ice yet eager to try again. Watching all this, we drank hot chocolate piled with whipped cream, allowed such things again as I was no longer pudgy. Store windows along Fifth or Lexington Avenues were sights to behold, their windows decorated for the season: Bloomingdales, Macy's, Henri Bendel's, established in 1895, still with its original Lalique art glass windows; Altmans, Gimbels, Abraham & Straus, Saks, and Lord & Taylor with its enchanting décor, its Birdcage Restaurant and itsTea Room. We often went there with Aunt Dodie, enjoying a real treat of petit sandwiches and pastries, the outing adding to the party atmosphere. Before or after one such treat, we were off to see Walt Disney's *FANTASIA*, the first film released in stereophonic surround sound. Over two hours long with an intermission of fifteen minutes, the movie is still respected. It consists of animated segments set to classical music, performed by the Philadelphia Symphony orchestra conducted by Leopold Stokowski. It was an enchantment, though I was horrified by poor Mickey Mouse's ordeal with buckets and mops in the Sorcerer's Apprentice, though finding the dancing mushrooms in Dance of the Hours a pure delight. The proceeds from *FANTASIA's* opening in the Broadway Theater went to the British War Relief Society for its efforts in the Battle of Britain.

With one exception, all these steps leading to Christmas merely increased our anticipation. I'm not sure why particularly, but I had never liked sitting on Santa's lap in Cincinnati, yet here again we were urged to do so, to tell him our greatest desires of the moment. No Santa I had ever met had been a good representative of that jolly fellow from the North Pole, but then, everyone knew he'd been working overtime recently. Hadn't he? The puzzling thing was how could there be so many? Which the real one? Santa Claus might have made a good subject for panelists on television's "What's My Line," some years later, the panel to guess which out of three, the real personage. Not likely, however. A better way to spend the afternoon was to see a performance of Tchaikovsky's *Nutcracker Suite,* even though I have seen it so many times, I have become jaded despite that wonderful spectacle of an enormous decorated Christmas tree rising through the floor.

Christmas day finally, finally arrived after all the anticipation. The evening before, we had hung our stockings "by the chimney with care," from the dining room's mantle piece set above a roaring fire in its grate, a small decorated tree nearby, we leaving cookies and milk for, hopefully, the **real** Santa. Not long after dawn on the big day, Flip and I rushed downstairs to see what Santa had stuffed into our stockings, and were greeted by two sleepy "in loci parentis." In our night gowns we hurried to retrieve our stockings but only after sipping orange juice. There were to be no further spills on royal-blue carpet. Clasping our stockings from the mantle, we plunked ourselves before the fire to discover the contents: the inevitable lump of coal, an orange, a small toy or two, perhaps a pencil box, one or two candy canes, and, always, a small surprise. After dressing in our Christmas finery, green velvet with lace collar for me, red for Flip, and a quick but special breakfast, we were off to St. John's Episcopal Church.

In its simplicity, the Christmas church service contrasted beautifully with yuletide decorations of greenery with the reds, pinks and whites of poinsettias, variegated ivy; again, red, green, silver and gold ribbons woven throughout, the gleaming and flickering long white tapers in candelabras, crosses gleaming golden in reflected light, the unadorned elegant simplicity of small pine trees, their resinous scent perfuming the air. The crèche scene was off the nave and organ music, often accompanied by choir and laity in those wonderful Christmas hymns and carols, swelled to reverberate throughout. All this and more tantalized eyes and ears but not enough for fidgeting children anxious to get home for presents. At last the service was over but then adults seemed to have nothing better to do than greet and chat as they stood in the slowest of lines to the main portal where the minister greeted parishioners to offer his own seasonal greetings. The grownups seemed to think there was no hurry, while for us our return to 867 Madison couldn't come soon enough. It was not until after a pat on the head and good wishes that we were finally away. However, when we returned to 867 we found the doors to the salon firmly closed. Disappointed, we rushed to the dining room, thinking gifts must be there under the small tree, but not a one was to be seen.

We were rounded up for potties, juice, and snacks, our elders sipping champagne while we, having expected a different scene, could hardly bear the suspense. There had to be presents at sometime, somewhere, some place! When the suspense became almost unbearable, the Stantons, knowing full well how to draw out a child's anticipation, announced the magic moment had arrived. The salon doors at last swung open to take our breath away. Only lacking a fanfare of trumpets, there in this beautifully decorated room, stood a tall fir glistening, glowing and shimmering with lights, icicles and tinsel, while small candles of differing colors clipped to the tree's outlying branches had been lit in European fashion. Atop all, a gossamer angel; way below her feet, an array of presents wrapped in exquisite paper with colorful bows. Gifts, certainly not all for us, though fewer this year, had been carefully chosen, thought put into each one. I thrilled with my first stamp album and artist supplies. Sadly, we would not hear from Mummy and Daddy until after Christmas, only a letter from Daddy getting through to the Stantons in January:

> Thank you for your vivid description of the descent of the girls on Christmas morning with candles in the dining room for stockings hanging from the mantel piece [it] was joyful to read. It brought back to me how splendid you are to us and our girls . . .

That Christmas, our parents' joy must have been tempered with expectation the war in Europe might finally be winding down. 1943 would see Stalingrad freed. North Africa was liberated by the Allies in May and they also gained control of Atlantic sea lanes but not until the end of the year. In July the Allies captured Sicily, the Soviets advanced on the Eastern front in August, and the Italians surrendered in September. In November Berlin would be heavily bombed by the RAF, before it and the USAAF created carnage in Dresden, dropping more than 3,900 tons of high explosives and incendiary devices which resulted in a firestorm, death tolls reaching anywhere between 200,000 and 500,000. This, ordered by Sir Arthur Harris, known as "Bomber" or "Butcher" Harris, should have been considered a crime against humanity, as Dresden was known to be a cultural center; therefore, not an industrial target. As its perpetrator, Sir Arthur was just as guilty as any of our foes' atrocities. While war in Europe was easing, fighting still continued against Hitler's entrenchment there while appalling battles and tremendous losses continued against the Japanese in the Pacific.

After all the Christmas excitement, my 7th birthday in January, paled in comparison. I have no memory of it, and, of course, blissfully unaware of what was going on in Europe or Asia.

The endearingly constant Aunt Dodie

Pony rides in Cornwall with the Leach children

A CORNWALL SUMMER

Summer, 1943 we piled into Uncle Larry's big Buick, who, being a doctor I presume had that extra fuel allowance; otherwise tires and gasoline were strictly rationed for ordinary folk. On this longish drive to Connecticut, Flip and I, sitting in back, began to argue, as we often did. This time it was over two recently given and slightly different yet exquisite ivory bracelets carved from Asian elephant tusks, poaching of these long considered illegal. Back and forth we went over whose was prettiest, larger, smaller, whatever, the battle which, despite previous admonitions to stop, we continued, the argument un-winnable. Suddenly, Uncle Larry had had enough. In high dudgeon he slammed on the brakes, causing the big car and everyone in it to slew into a shallow ditch. Having lost his head or cool as we'd say today, he now lost his hat—men wore hats in those days—as we, shocked, hung our heads in stupefied silence, and were good as gold for the remaining miles.

Shame-faced, we finally arrived at Cornwall, namesake of the one or more in England. This one, settled in 1738, is surrounded by five other villages with all more or less the same name: North and West Cornwall, Cornwall Center, Bridge, and Hollow, all within Litchfield County in the Taconic Mountains area. For our purposes, these were for hikes and picnics on Mohawk or Breadloaf, now ski Meccas. Otherwise, the countryside consists, or did, of upland farms hemmed in by forests of pine and low time-worn stone walls. Aunt Dodie's brother Richard Leach, a prosperous farmer, lived nearby, as did other family members, so we had others to play with and, though shy in meeting other children, we loved riding their ponies or splashing together in swimming holes fed by cold crystal springs, where watercress grew by the handful on lower banks, harmless spider-like skaters known as Jesus Bugs, flicking across pond surfaces, harmless unless you were another insect, and the pretty multicolored dragon fly nesting near ponds swooping around garden and slow-moving streams. There were picnics galore that were usually held under those tall cool green pines on hillsides that tempered the heat of a late afternoon. All was laid out on those large and wonderfully smooth grey ice-age-worn boulders strewn haphazardly across the forest floor, itself carpeted with browning needles and pine cones fallen from older growths.

Daily we walked the few blocks to besiege Cornwall's tiny post office for that hoped for letter from England or to send one; then we went going on to search the small town library for books for that week's read. Just outside town, atop a nearby hill, was a building known appropriately as the ice house, which stored large blocks of ice cut and hauled up from the Housatonic during the winter, and stored in this weather beaten storage house. It was the only place to play on those hot afternoons as we leapt, jumped, and slid among great blocks covered in sawdust. Outside, growing along a fence, were purple and yellow flowers with small round prune-purple fruit ripening, as were green seed sacs. Thinking these pretty, I stooped to pick as my country playmates shouted not to touch, for this was the noxious weed Deadly Night Shade, also known as Devil's berries or cherries. The technical name is Adopa belladonna (Adopa, a Greek fate; belladonna, Italian for beautiful woman.) The foliage and berries, even though used as an anesthetic for surgery before the middle Ages, are highly toxic, causing delirium and hallucinations and, I suspect, death to children.

Near the ice house lived a formidable character named Miss Nancy Smith, not to be confused with my English godmother of the same name. It was the latter we stayed with when the Stantons returned to the City or needed a break, we spending part of the summer of 1943 with her. I loved riding in her bright red convertible with a klaxon, which Miss Smith always blasted when she whizzed through local villages, she and her car terribly "smart," making me determined to own my own one day. Young as I was, I knew Miss Smith was past her prime, for she had begun to lose what once must have been a luscious body and her hair dyed a vicious blond. Locally, she was considered a "fast woman," She had frequent male visitors. Sailors, soldiers, airmen; anyone at all in uniform, encamped anywhere nearby, all welcome in Miss Smith's home up the hill near the ice house. How many I wonder cooled their heads in there? With regularity, so long as they contributed food, jollity, tobacco, and brimming bottles, Miss Smith was amenable. Had Aunt Dodie known this, I'm sure she would have removed us from her premises then and there. However, no one spilled the beans. Why should we, for we were having fun riding around in that flamboyantly noisy car with its apparently unlimited supply of gasoline, makes you wonder where she bought her gas, we spoiled by all those kind servicemen with their endless supplies of Hershey bars. Why should we care what they got up to with our hostess; we who were too innocent to know or care anyway.

Miss Smith had joined the Civilian Auxiliary of the United States Air Force, (USAF) formed in 1941 to provide support for the Civilian Air Patrol doing air reconnaissance, search and rescue. Though I only remember a small cabin with maps, wall charts outlining the shapes of planes, both friend and foe, and most importantly, an emergency telephone, special towers had been built in some areas for plane spotting. Miss Smith often took us with her to gaze skyward, hoping of course to identify something, anything, flying over head. Aside from noisy insects buzzing among grass and field crops, rarely did we hear a plane, let alone see one. Though uneventful, these afternoons were long, languid, lazy and pleasant.

Even though Miss Smith was supplying on a smaller scale but no less important, her own style of good cheer and entertainment for servicemen in her own home, another job she might have undertaken and done well would have been to act as a hostess for the USO. The USO or, The United Service Organization was formed in 1940 as a "Link of compassion and reassurance from the ordinary citizen, that America cares, remembers and supports the service and sacrifice of those who defend her." In short, the USO would "deliver America to those far from home." From 1941 on the organization provided morale and recreation services to uniformed military personnel overseas, and was able to claim by the end of 1947 more than 1.5 million volunteers had worked on its behalf. From 1941 on Bob Hope, the British-born American comedian, began his long-time service with the organization, often appearing in or hosting shows with a galaxy of stars such as Dietrich, Garland, Grable, Hayworth, Miller and Flynn (my film favorite swashbuckler), to entertain the troops in some one hundred and ninety-nine shows during World War II, and afterward. It was often cracked in Bob Hope style, "Where there's death, there's Hope." For his service, an Act of Congress, passed in 1997 and signed by President Bill Clinton, proclaimed Mr. Hope an "Honorary Veteran," with Hope saying this award superseded all others received over the years, and was his most treasured.

Summer ending, we returned to the City to start thinking of school again. However, New York in late August is sweltering, seeming to belch suffocating heat from morning until early dusk and beyond as the sun blazed down on asphalt, and little air moving between surrounding skyscrapers. Into this stagnating air, exhausts from innumerable buses, cars and cabs combined to create noxious fumes that wafted their way up and into our fourth-floor bedroom. A breeze or even a storm brewing of an evening might bring a temporary refresher, but temperatures only moderated as summer began to cool, and the year slowly edged toward fall.

ELEANOR AND MISS CHITTENDEN

Before school started we spent time with two ladies so diverse you might not put them in the same room together. The first was Uncle Larry's secretary daily at 867; the other was the Doyenne of the music world in New York City, Miss Kate Sara Chittenden. I'll deal with Eleanor Francis first, she recently married to Roger, who was currently serving in the European theater. Eleanor was a rather washed out redhead who suffered acutely from asthma, had freckles on pallid translucent skin that dotted cheeks, nose, and upper chest, eyes a washed-out blue, making her pretty in a luminous, ethereal sort of way. When Eleanor's duties were light, she'd abscond with us and would take us to her walkup apartment somewhere on the Upper East Side where, just beyond her third-floor windows ran the noisy El. Built in 1868, the Third Avenue El was the earliest form of rapid transit erected on tracks above New York's avenues. Though blocking sunlight from reaching streets below and a noisy and dirty system, it provided a quick and cheap way for people to get about.

Though still baking in summer heat, it was a simpler life in this noisy non-air-conditioned apartment. On those torrid evenings, my hair and clothes sticking to my body, we sat on wrought iron fire escapes or climbed up to the roof hoping to catch a breeze or two free from toxic fumes, and watched the street scene below or waved at neighbors across the way. Always, always the noise of traffic, near or distant, even though blackouts had been imposed. All shore lights had been dimmed in hopes of preventing the silhouettes of US ships from being seen by enemy U-boats. These were still a massive nuisance in the north Atlantic. They had a nasty habit of popping up to destroy shipping from Maine to the Caribbean, to account for seventy percent of all allied shipping sunk in 1942. By May,

1943, it would take the small desk-bound fleet—never more than fifty people known as The Tenth Fleet within the Navy Department, to gain complete control of all aspects of the United States Navy's battle against U-Boats in the Atlantic. How, one wonders.

With no false modesty Eleanor was fun, the three of us often piling into her large claw-footed bath tub to scrub each others' backs. She had, I noticed, small pointy breasts, while I had none. Was this unusual? "No," Eleanor replied when I dared ask. "You'll have some, too, when you're a bit older, but yours may be a bit larger." "Me too?" Flip asked. "Yes, of course." It was Eleanor who took us to further visits of the New York Public Library and the Turtle Bay Library, whose conservancy and music school was generously supported by the Stantons.

There were further visits to everything of interest; particularly the dinosaurs in the natural history museum, and rides up and down Fifth Avenue in open air, double-decker buses. On rainy days Eleanor devised clever things to do: making glue out of flour, salt, and water for art projects, or something more interesting like baking cupcakes or cookies so we could fight over who got the mixing spoon or bowl for "lickings." We made ice cream too, that wonderful concoction we would miss if we ever returned to England. Sometimes, both in fall and winter of 1943, mid-Sunday morning with Eleanor or sometimes alone, I rode the double-decker to St. John's Episcopal, to robe up in red soutane with white starched collar, to join the choir as one of its youngest members. Where had this benefice come from, Daddy's fame or the Stantons themselves? Thinking all natural as a child, I took all in stride.

Now, back to Miss Chittenden, as I was instructed to call her. A rather austere and fierce elderly lady then in her eighties I think, a roly-poly, dressed in silky grays and blacks, shawls with austere hair-style. She was a prominent music educator and keyboard musician, serving as head of several prominent music schools; lecturer for the New York Board of Education and national music organizations: piano instructor, writer of books, hymns and, teaching pieces. A great friend of Aunt Dodie's who often invited her to tea, Miss Chittenden took me under her wing, evincing a keen interest in my future.

A great proponent of her own educational materials, focusing on children's understanding and ability, Miss Chittenden was eager to teach me piano in the salon. How much piano I learnt I don't recall, but she liked me and graced me with trinkets, including a silver brooch with two little hearts entwined with ivy, the last present a three-strand pearl bracelet which, now tighter, I can still wear. All these activities were duly reported to Mummy, who soon replied to Aunt Dodie:

> "You mention Miss Chittenden and the little book she has so kindly dedicated to 'Julia Christabel, the daughter of Keith Falkner, England's greatest singer.' You can imagine me just bursting with pride at my husband AND my daughter. I hope it is published." (I've never found this.)

So here you have two very diverse women, yet both enriched my life.

MEASLES AND A WINTER TRIP

That autumn, flushed of face, glands swollen and red of rash, Philippa was diagnosed by Uncle Larry to have rubella (German measles), a highly infectious disease, was promptly isolated into his large bedroom, shades drawn to protect sensitive eyes, attended by the devoted Aunt Dodie. Well, not on her life could I let Flip get away with this! Not only did I miss her, for, in our various upheavals, we had had to stick together, but she was now getting all the attention. So, on an afternoon when the grownups were otherwise occupied, I sneaked into her darkened room as she, glad to see me, flung her small arms around me in temperature-rated embrace. That should do it, I thought as I hugged her heated body, now we could recuperate together. I didn't realize there was a period of incubation before my symptoms appeared. When they did, I was the one isolated in darkened room, in the same great highly polished wooden sleigh-bed, where eons passed before I was allowed to read books and draw, feeling I had not received the same attention my sister had, but perhaps her symptoms had been worse than mine. While this had been a separation, at least it was under happier circumstances: isolation yes, not abandonment, though missing days at school.

Just after Christmas and before the New Year of 1944, Miss Smith was summoned to Madison Avenue to collect us on a deceptively spring-like day, and she drove into the City, complete with her menagerie of small dogs. All aboard by mid-afternoon in her red convertible with top down, we began the journey up Riverside Drive. The further northeast we went, the worse the weather, as it started to rain. As darkness descended, up came the canvas as rain turned to sleet with the wind picking up. Then, it was nothing but wind-driven snow, almost a white-out. Dogs in the back seat snuffled and yipped as Philippa dozed, while in front, I began to worry. In these blizzard-like conditions, the wind howling and buffeting the car, its insides barely warm, Miss Smith seemed if not exactly lost, then befogged and befuddled by her almost snow-covered headlights and warming nips. We saw no other car, for no person in his right mind would have been out on such a night. Several miles on, the road beginning to slope downward, we came upon a sign saying: "4 Miles . . ., but, to where? On what I think must have been the longest four miles of my life, the car slewing over ice and snow, we at last arrived at a largish town where lights glimmered dimly in the blizzard, not knowing whether we were we in Danbury, Waterbury or somewhere else in Connecticut.

Pulling off the highway we drove through snow-packed streets, Miss Smith heading for the nearest hotel, just managing to check in to the last available room. Then, just as she started to head out to collect her "doggies" and some luggage, the manager emerged from the front desk to announce no pets were allowed on the premises, adding he hoped she had none. Miss Smith replied: "No, of course not!" Taught not to lie, Flip and I immediately said "But, what about?" before being shushed. "Say nothing!" whispered Miss Smith. So we gathered such items as needed from the car and walked sedately across the lobby to the elevator, each of us with a blanket-covered basket and bag. The thing, Miss Smith had told us, was to keep the dogs quiet: this, the challenge.

Management must have been aware what Miss Smith was up to; maybe she had stayed here before? We rode up in the elevator amid an embarrassment of snorts and snuffles which I hoped the bell-hop did not think emanated from me. Then, aghast, I watched one small paw appear over the side of my supposed innocuous basket. Yet, nothing was said, not even the next morning when Miss Smith, with some arrogance, paraded her menagerie across the foyer, out through its frosty-front doors, on out to glistening snow banks for what she called her dogs' "walkies." So here we were temporarily snowbound for the next few days, the only excitement was to eat and take "walkies." Perhaps another evening of "civic duties" was taking, would take, or had taken place?

Two days later to everyone's blessed relief, the storm had passed. On this morning not a cloud was to be seen. For awhile, all was an enchantment before the rising sun exploded upon a landscape of pristine whiteness; a short-lived crystalline enchantment for, as we watched, its warming rays lit upon the powdery snow atop ice-encrusted pines as ice and snow began to melt, and trees began to shed their crystalline sheaths and, recover their shapes. Branches being unburdened, they shed tinkling sparking droplets onto the melting snow below as elsewhere from eaves, icicles dripped to drop. Finally, finally, we could leave, driving over cleared roads with highly banked drifts as we set out for Litchfield, where we found snow so deep as to almost obliterate surrounding hills and vales. At last we arrived at Mr. Leach's farm where Miss Smith deposited us to depart in haste, with yapping dogs, for her home nearby. All in all, she was good to us, sharing many happy hours, she who so loved a good time. In later years, I heard she had become an embittered alcoholic. Meanwhile, we stayed with the Leaches, a rambunctious family for the remainder of the holidays, our new playmates Aunt Dodie's niece "Muffy," and several older nephews. No doubt this was a heaven-sent break for our adopted aunt.

1944

The year 1944, while disastrous for Germany, brought good news enough so our parents could consider our longed-for return, perhaps even this very year. While full of happiness at the prospect, mother anxiously wrote Dodie in January:

> "I do hope I shall not be too great a disappointment to either of them. Somehow I do not feel a very exciting woman [for] living the life of a troglodyte does not make one glamorous. I so much incline towards our reunion that I am apt to forget the Atlantic is not cleared of all U-boats. But at any moment it may be!"

And again in February:
> "Suddenly oranges have appeared on market shelves—citrus has not been seen in Europe, particularly in Britain since the blockade, the cargo interspersed with bombs from Spain! We await the second front and wonder where it will be, there is a tense feeling in the air . . ."

To Mother's increasing anticipation, concern and worry over our return now four years older, Daddy wrote to console her:

> "The sooner we all four can be together again, the happier I shall be. You talk such arrogant nonsense about not being a good mother, I could shake you. You have been a wonderful mother to them. So you felt irritated by them

at times, isn't that natural? Don't those you love irritate and at the same time thrill you more than anything else? Go on, you are the most exciting woman for me and my daughters, and just remember it! Stick to me as close as possible!" (My, rather than our?)

Mid January had seen the Allied landing at Anzio just south of Rome where 110,000 troops surprised the Germans, though getting bogged down for some months. The intention of the Allied Battles for Monte Cassino was to link up with and liberate the army contained at Anzio, with its eventual success leading to the capture of Rome on June 4. This was overshadowed two days later by the Normandy invasion on the 6th. The second front had come at last, the public learning of the very secret plans put in effect for D-Day, the simultaneous landings by the British infantry and commandos on beaches *Sword* and *Gold*; the Canadians' Third Infantry on *Juno;* the Americans on *Omaha, Pointe du Hoc* with the Army Second Ranger Battalion and, on *Utah,* the Fourth Infantry. Germany retaliated by launching the first of many V-1 flying-bombs on Britain on June 13. Much was also occurring in the Pacific, but understandably our parents' concern was the European theatre and our reunion. As the year edged into high summer, the Allies plowed on, liberating Cherbourg, and Caen in France, and, in Italy, Florence. Finally, on August twenty-fifth, Paris.

Meanwhile our destination for the summer was a camp in Maine. Required uniforms and equipment had been bought and packed in duffle bags, everything from underwear to jackets, bedding to flashlights, all in white and green, my favorite color. The camp's name and our labels had been etched, printed or sewn onto everything going with us. We had been left in the care of Eleanor to get us to camp safely but were first to spend over a week with her parents in Massachusetts. Here, it seems, we caused general mayhem. Into this orderly household, long unused to small children, we breezed in and out of normally quiet rooms, noisy with chatter, tears, arguments, laughter, endless questions; bouncing on antique furniture and feather beds adding spills and breakage. Eleanor's mother tried to keep us under control with routines and tasks each day, a way to earn our keep. One of her problems turned out to be raids on hamburger. Who was the culprit? T'was I, I now confess, for an annoying wart had appeared on the outer edge of my left knee. Someone had secretly told me the remedy was to steal into the kitchen when no one was about and raid the refrigerator for hamburger. This had to be rubbed on the offending wart, the pilfered meat then buried in the garden. All this had to be done without being seen; only then would the cure work. Just to make sure it did, I stole hamburger whenever I could and rubbed some more. When the question arose as to the whereabouts of missing meat—I hadn't stolen that much had I—I professed innocence as did everyone else. Even so, I seemed to be suspect number one for whenever I lied, I blushed; this reddening remaining the bane of my existence for some years to come. What was extraordinary was the remedy actually worked; so I was able to arrive at camp sans ugly wart . . . only toads in fairytales had warts. What can I say?

On the nearby highway, not to be confused with our present-day interstates, few cars passed. Gasoline shortages were now acute, especially on the east coast as most petroleum was brought in by tankers which German U-Boats took delight in sinking. Gas rationing had gone into effect December,1942, and not lifted until August, 1945; having been rationed not so much for itself as to preserve rubber tires. The Japanese had cut off the supply of latex from the tropics, the United States' chief source. Tires became limited to five per car; more and they were confiscated by the government. Also 35mph became the speed limit in order to save tires and all pleasure driving outlawed for a time in 1943. With travel thus curbed, persons were given classifications: "A" entitled the holder to four gallons per week; a "B" gave up to eight gallons as did a "C," entitled by doctors and those involved in the war effort. There was also an "X" classification granting the rich and politicians, whose apparent survival depended on unlimited quantities.

On the aforementioned highway, a one-pump gas station did little business, so when a car did pass everyone ogled, especially if it stopped for its allotment. The main entertainment of a lazy afternoon rocking on the porch, was to watch for the fast approach and equally fast disappearance of a Greyhound bus on its way to or from the big city. As each passed, a cloud of sandy dust swirled along the roadbed, to gradually settle until the next vehicle drove by.

As the heat of the day waned and chores were done, in Rockwellian-style, the grown-ups rocked on porches to "natter," and to sip iced tea, lemonade or perhaps something stronger. This was the time when Philippa and I managed to escape surveillance to join other children heading for "The Pit," supposedly a no-go area. We had been warned of its risks, near disasters, even deaths of some children who had played there. We were drawn to its tempting and towering sand cliff anyway. Castles and forts were built, with much jumping about, strewing of sand mostly ending up in shoes, pockets, hair, ears. The big challenge was to see who could run higher and faster up or down the Pit's face before it collapsed in a sweeping landslide: the trick to keep your balance as you let your feet skid atop the shifting-sinking mass and so, hopefully, glide to the bottom without burial. We were without fear.

The days with Eleanor's parents were generally happy until our last Sunday, when I got a nasty shock. It was a beautiful day, a day of family celebration with everyone going to church. Afterwards, a small crowd returned to mount the steps of the shady porch to recover from the warm walk as, fanning themselves, the older folk sat upon squeaking porch swings or rocked in the white-painted high-backed slatted chairs chatting idly, sipping before dinner. On this day, the passing of cars and buses did not hold my attention for I was tense, made uneasy by a male family member always hovering nearby. He made me squirm. Sunday dinner finally over, we children were dismissed for the inevitable nap. On my bedside table was a half box of camphor crystals left from having helped Eleanor's mother put away woolen blankets for the summer. As I liked the smell, I occasionally sniffed at the remaining crystals.

My mind wandering, I waited for the long rest hour to end, when, suddenly a floorboard creaked in the passageway. I turned in that direction to find entering my room the very person who had made me so uncomfortable earlier. Closing the door gently but firmly behind him, he came towards me. I knew nothing of Uriah Heeps then or of their unctuous ways, but that is whom I think of when I recall the incident. With forefinger pressed to his lips "Mr. Heep" tiptoed toward me to sit beside me on the bed, with a sickly grin. My skin was already crawling as he put a hand on my bare knee whispering, whispering, always whispering, his hand slowly working its way up my thigh. I seemed unable to move as taught to respect and honor my elders, yet instinctively I knew this man was not one to trust. Then an instinct of self-preservation took over as, in a blur of movement, I jerked upright, snatched the box of crystals from the nightstand and flung them into Mr. Heep's face. Gone like a shot then, no doubt praying I would say nothing; he disappeared from my room and my life while I, unharmed, finished a wide-awake hour. I told no one of the incident, suspecting I would not be believed; who would take the word of an eight-year-old against that of an adult? I had trouble enough explaining camphor crystals all over the bed, bedside rug, and floor.

Flip and I continued to cause trouble one evening after we'd been put to bed for we discovered a bottle of nail polish in a bedside drawer. Garish in color, we tasted it, painted our fingernails crimson with it; then each other's toenails, and spilled the remaining shellac on our sheets. This wasn't as bad as when, supposedly, I swallowed a whole bottle of aspirin from another bedside drawer. I have no memory of this and at the time denied this vociferously, partly because I couldn't imagine doing so, the bitterness too horrible for a child to enjoy. Nevertheless, I was said to be guilty, adults accusing me of grogginess and furthermore, of lying. Had I in fact been blamed for someone else's over indulgence? Nevertheless, it was my penance to write one hundred times: "I will never lie or take aspirin again," a difficult order and, indeed, a bitter pill.

Flip and I were in trouble again one afternoon, when we spied a road crew paving a nearby street with that wonderful gooey black smelly stuff called tar. Fascinated, we watched a heavy steamroller with heavy weighted drums affixed in place of wheels, operated by steam. It was ponderously slow, a marvelous machine easing along, to squish and press tar onto the road bed as it traveled back and forth. The crew soon left for the day waving goodbye, telling us to go home but Flip and I just had to investigate this still sticky black mess. By the side of the road were wads of the black stuff, grass covered in inky spikes. Down we sat in it, trying to scoop up wads of it for we'd been told it could be chewed like gum: I hope we didn't. As dusk claimed the sky, we who now looked like Brer Rabbit's tar-babies, headed home for supper. Gasps and darker looks greeted us, we in tar-covered clothing glowered upon, getting a real "drubbing," clothes and shoes yanked off and discarded. Scrubbed until red-skinned—today peeling off tar would have been more gently handled, and in the standard punishment of the day, we were also put to bed without supper.

There had to be a last incident. This time we caused tidal waves in our bath when, hysterical with laughter over our invented words of "Bubble-bubble soapeens," we, bubbling away, sank, rose, sank and rose over and over again sloshing water all over the bathroom's tiled floor—a real mess. Indeed, we'd caused nothing but trouble the whole time, so I suspect Eleanor and her parents must have been very, very glad to see the last of us as off to camp we went.

CAMP MOY-MO-DA-YO
(EST. 1907-1971)
SUMMER ACTIVITIES; SURPRISE ENDING

In mid June "At last!" must have been the uttered sighs of our hosts as we left for Moy-Mo-Da-Yo, a camp for girls on Horne Lake near Limington, Maine. Summer camps had sprung up in the 1880's, the first of many institutions designed to educate and develop young healthy bodies. These goals remained much the same, though the way camps achieved them varied with changing ideas. For a background on camp life, the Schlesinger Library in Cambridge, Massachusetts has a collection of documents on camp life which

> shed light on important aspects of American and Women's history. The materials illustrate the ideals of the progressive Era [when most camps were born], the economic hardships of the Great Depression, the patriotism and sacrifices of the World War II era . . . these records also show camp life from the campers' perspective and document the evolution of girlhood during the 20th century.

Early campers at Moy-Mo-Da-Yo cooked, danced, sewed, swam, rode horses, canoed and played games. Waterskiing, wind-surfing, sailing and rock climbing would eventually be included, all to form a meaningful experience for the girls. And here it was that Philippa and I found ourselves living with girls of similar age housed in primitive modest cabins with assigned counselors. We went to bed with Taps and awoke to Reveille. The raising of the flag was followed by breakfast eaten in the long screened-in mess hall, where most meals were served. Other buildings housed arts and crafts, stables, pingpong tables, a stage for plays, in one of which I played Sneezy, or was it Doc in "Snow White and the Seven Dwarfs." There were numerous tennis courts, an archery range, and an oval for track meets.

The goals of the camp were sixfold:

1. To maintain and improve healthier minds and bodies;
2. To live democracy;
3. To develop individual capabilities;
4. To develop new skills;
5. To develop a spirit of adventure and exploration; and lastly,
6. To experience the personal satisfaction by making a worthwhile contribution to the group.

Our days were mostly outdoors, learning to groom and ride horses. The young groom was so handsome I nearly swooned when he adjusted a stirrup or my holding of the reins. We paddled canoes, rowed boats, shot arrows, ran races, and attempted tennis and swimming. I was thankful daddy was nowhere near when it came time for the last for, as an avid sportsman brought up in a different era, he would not have accepted qualms on my part. Any reluctance and he would have thrown me in to sink or swim, the way his father, his father's father and so on had been taught, that is if they had learned to swim at all. As it was, I was trying to learn under easier circumstances, though I didn't think they were at the time.

It was a calm sunny morning and our pathetic group was finishing another frustrating lesson amid shrieks, timidity, and splashing. The frustrated instructor called everyone out, shouting: "Now! I said everyone, and I do mean everyone! NOW!" Not me, I thought wading into clear water deep enough to caress my shoulders, sandy bottom underfoot.

Then, I saw it! Not three feet away, swimming speedily toward me, a large snapper! These were nothing to mess with. We had been told to get out of the water immediately on seeing one for lake turtles were apt to give nasty bites. Yet here I stood paralyzed in my own "sink-or-swim" situation. Suddenly I was moving, flailing and thrashing toward shore to arrive with the sudden and stunning realization I had just **swum** to shore. Exhilarated, at last I heard praise from my once despairing instructor; able now to learn different strokes. From then on, you couldn't keep this fish out of water or from showing off to those still struggling. While learning to swim had not exactly been a snap, at least it had been snap-less.

Hikes, many taken along on the lake's shoreline where we often saw the brilliant flash of the blue kingfisher with its tufted crest and heard its harsh cry as it swooped in to grab a small fish, a tiny frog or a wee insect. It was a cruel death, for this bird kills its meal by dropping it on a stone or beating it against a tree. Bird watching, known as "Twitching" in England, has always been a big thing in this area of Maine where twitchers have documented over one hundred and thirty-three species of birds. While fascinating, birds were only a temporary distraction to our hike's purpose which, aside from the exercise, was to gather woodland artifacts for collages made from such treasures as leaves, twigs, fungi, dropped egg shells, or pine-cones. Sometimes excursions ended in disaster like the time I stumbled over a rotting log on the forest's mossy floor. In an instant, an irate mob of hornets erupted from their hidden hive, attacking all within reach. Unable to outrun them, we returned to camp a sorry sight with tear-stained cheeks and all exposed flesh covered in welts. The infirmary soon had us plastered in white baking soda poultices.

On rainy days we sketched, learned songs, or mixed plaster of paris to pour into molds. When sufficiently dry and unmolded, we painted them to display for the supposed edification of all. Lanyards and lariats were made using the intricate art of braiding not just with three stands, but six, nine or twelve, all increasingly difficult. Some evenings there were movies, mostly black and white, usually Twentieth Century Fox films whose opening searchlights, then and now, tend to remind me of the warning wails of wartime sirens, search lights and the drone of planes I had heard before sailing from England in 1940. On clear evenings there were Weenie roasts around the campfire down by the shore where ghost stories enlivened evenings, smoky aromas lingering as they still do in memory.

One evening toward the end of summer our group set off to visit, so our counselor told us, a real, real Haunted House. As the sky turned to dusk, we with trepidation and apprehension, approached a house set well back in woods. The house, rotting for years, was dilapidated, weather-beaten and tilting off its foundation, standing un-bravely against the elements as did we, daring each other to be the first through the gate hanging from rusty hinges. Grasses and brambles had tightened their grip on a long overgrown garden among which cantilevered stone steps led to wooden tilting ones to the slanting porch. Did we dare? Egging each other on, we slowly edged our way along the path, up the steps which groaned under our weight, reaching the tilting, rotting front porch where shutters hung precariously from sashes, panes missing or jagged and grimy. Long deprived of paint and half off its hinges, the half-open front door loomed in the gloom as we inched toward it. Nearby, an owl hooted not once, but twice.

Clinging wispy cobwebs hung everywhere, their gossamer tendrils brushing our faces as we pushed each other forward, pushing to enter a small hall. A set of darkened stairs loomed before us, seeming to beckon. Daring each other, each in turn gingerly set foot on the creaking steps, each of us unable to ignore hanging strips of faded wallpaper splotched with rust-colored pigment. Blood? Halfway up the staircase we began to hear, ever louder, moans and groans before a blood-curdling screech rent the air echoing down the stairwell. Another followed. That was all it took, for now, spooked, screaming, we turned to race headlong down the stairs, through the cobwebs in the hall, out the dilapidated front door, on to and off the porch, over the rickety steps, trampling weeds, through the scratching clinging brambles until, at last, out through the lopsided gate, where still we didn't stop. On we ran down the narrow darkened lane, not stopping until we reached camp, an owl hooting over and over as the recently risen silvery sliver crescent of moon reflected off the blackness of Horne Lake. Munching Necco wafers a bit later, we unwound reliving the experience, its purpose so beautifully served: scary fun.

Summer was nearing its end, fellow campers beginning to pack in a flurry to return home, autograph books signed, camp photos taken with pledges to write and "see you next year." Our last evening was special with roaring bonfire, charring hotdogs impaled on long sticks, roasting gooey marshmallows as we sang around the campfire. As it grew darker, we took our handmade wooden boats, small candles affixed, down to the lake's edge. When all had been lit, we pushed these little barks out onto the lake's surface, there to bob in the gentle breeze, causing all to slowly drift away. At the same moment, the boys' camp across the lake released theirs so that the lake's surface was soon covered with twinkling lights: a perfectly magical way to say goodbye to new friends and summer.

Next day I was summoned to the camp's office. "I have news for you from Mrs. Stanton," said Mrs. Director: "First, you two won't be leaving with the others; you'll be staying a few more days with us. Your aunt has also informed us it is now safe for you to return to England. What do you think of that!" she enthused. Indeed, what did we think of that? We had grown used to America these four years, a place where we were now very happily settled in a country we had come to love and where, perhaps, we might want to stay. Who were our parents anyway; what did we know, remember of them? As though we had a choice in the matter, I said I'd talk with my sister, let the director know our decision soon—how cool can you get! That graying afternoon Flip and I sat swinging gently back and forth down by the quiet sandy shore, everyone else long gone as I asked: "Would you like to go back to England, see mummy and daddy again?" She, poor thing, would have had no memory of them but, plucky as always replied "Whatever you say is OK with me." Back in the camp office I said we might be willing to travel to our home of long-ago, but in all honesty said we didn't feel very enthusiastic at the idea. In reality of course, it was not our decision to make, we pawns on a chess board, or in this case, "The Pond." But perhaps more exciting adventures awaited us, too good to miss? With the excitement of travel in my blood now, possibilities of further trips were not to be missed. So "adventurously," I told the director we'd try returning home! The nerve of it!

GOING HOME

Home? What did we know of it, and returning, what would we make of it as we readjusted to parents stressed by war, we having lost contact and remembrance of our brief lives together? Perhaps they had thought as Churchill that everything eventually works out for the best though perhaps not looking so at the given moment. Time would tell.

In the meantime, we were back in school until early November when it would soon be goodbye again. It was a confusing time for mummy for in October she had received confusing cables from CORB indicating we were on our way, perhaps not, or would be soon. Which was it? The parents would not know until a final cable arrived to suggest it might be in their interest to turn up at the Liverpool docks early the morning of November 18, mummy's forty-second birthday.

But this was not our concern, ours were goodbye parties planned, held and given by parents of school mates and the school. The one put on by the Stanton's must have been the talk of the town among this younger set for some time for they gave us a truly fabulous farewell frolic in that large salon at 867. The room had been turned into an enchanting Turkish bazaar, complete with tents fluttering pennants, games, fishing wells, tumblers in harlequin, a clown, balloons hanging from everywhere, surprises inside each, though no one knew this until one popped, followed by a mad rush to pop the rest, with prizes for all. A juggler performed, and I cannot forget the magician with top hat and tails waving his magic wand to create wonderful illusions. Supper, set up on refectory-style tables, served the usual for the times, creamed chicken, green peas, mashed potatoes and gravy, followed by ice-cream and cake. Then the downside: excitable youngsters with upset stomachs. It was left to Miss Summerville's school to hold the final party. During the festivities, Flip and I were presented with a large wooden box, made by the school's older students who had sanded, planed, primed and painted it green, carefully put it together and labeled CABIN ONLY. Our instructions: to each day open the green box and withdraw some small carefully wrapped surprise from this magical box, one for each to help pass the time on our fourteen day journey.

We could not have been sent off in better style. For us and many others, America had opened not only her heart but her doors, another of this country's finest moments. We had been lucky in our placements, memories happiest with the Stantons in Cornwall and New York City whom we would be very sad to leave: Uncle Larry, a real "softy," and our ever so caring and doting Aunt Dodie, she who had made us feel so welcome with warmth, undivided attention, even love, yet with stern but kind discipline. We would miss her sorely though we would keep in close touch over the years.

I recall no great upheaval in our goodbyes that November day. The doctor and Dodie must have made our separation and departure as swift, smooth and as easy as possible, for I remember nothing of the day except that it was a coldly gray drizzly morning. Perhaps, once again I had slammed that portcullis of mine? Healthy or not, it served its purpose time and time again. Through the years though, Dodie was there, I often sought her wise advice and unending support. Until writ, I had not realized how much care, love and devotion she had spread over our years from babyhood into adulthood. I owe her love and deep gratitude, for time and again, Dodie was my saving grace.

So now we were going home, returning to parents at last but, who were they? Would we recognize them, would they us? Would we be able to retrieve some sort of relationship or remain at sea in unhappy reconciliation? Would my senses flood with memory, scent, anything from those early years? Vaguely, I remembered mummy, but would she be as besotted by me as she once claimed to have been? So many unknowns! Having been spoiled with the comforts in America, we would be returning to a war damaged country, but never mind for we were homeward bound at last, home to a country which had withstood Herr Hitler to the bitter end!

It had been Winston Churchill, the right man for the time, who inspired and pulled the nation together to fight off the Nazi threat, in the meantime instructing his six-month pregnant daughter-in-law at dinner one evening, "If the Hun come, I am counting on each of you to take one with you before you go." "But Papa," replied Pamela, "I don't have a gun, and even if I did, I wouldn't know how to use it." "But my dear," replied Churchill, "you may go to the kitchen and grab a carving knife." Given this sort of rhetoric, this incentive, the British would fight on until death for this man, this country.

On August 13, 1940, Hitler began the Luftwaffe's Blitz on London and other cities. Nancy Astor, then hostess and outspoken social critic writing in the *Washington Post,* following these recent bombings wrote:

"To see them, as I have, gazing at what was their home, now a heap of ashes, their neighbors dead, and sometimes their own families too, and yet they look at you with steadfast English eyes and say, 'Hitler won't beat us this way.'"

C. P. Snow, British author and physicist too wrote of that summer:

"There was a collective euphoria over the whole country. I don't know what we were thinking about. We were very busy. We had a purpose. We were living in constant excitement. In one's realistic moments it was difficult to see what chance we had. But I doubt if most of us had many realistic moments, or thought much at all. We were working like mad. We were sustained by a surge of national emotion, of which Churchill was both (sic) a symbol of essence, evacuator and voice."

In the end Hitler postponed "Sea Lion," his hoped for full-scale invasion on England in September, not having counted on Churchill and the British people to stand fast. Yet, the Blitz continued. In all, some forty thousand people were killed, five thousand of them children. Eventually, we would come to understand why our parents had sent us to safer shores. Sacrifices were made by many, yes, but one each Englishman owed his country, in its hour of need. So it had been, no matter the cost!

THE RETURN VOYAGE

Optimism had run high in 1944 that the worst was over even as bombs out of Peenemunde, the V-1 known as the Doodlebug, so named for a variety of insects, and later the V-2 rockets, kept harassing London. At the time, Pamela Churchill wrote to her ex-lover Averill Harriman:

> ". . . the foolish optimism of a few weeks ago seems to have died down & few people are resigned to the fact that they will have to grind their way through another long winter of war . . . London is as black as ever, one notices no difference."

Nonetheless, our parents with much optimism, managed to arrange our return following D-Day, June 6, 1944.

So here we were sailing out of New York harbor in early November aboard the Rangitiki to join a large convoy sailing for Europe and beyond. The typical size of such a flotilla was approximately five by six point two miles wide, by one point nine miles long, led by a Guide-on ship responsible for the execution of the "zig-zag." The ship, at predetermined varying lengths of time, changed routes at specific intervals of the clock rather than by visual or electronic devices which might be picked up by submarines. The last ship in the convoy was destined to rescue survivors of torpedoed vessels, the negative being, itself subject to attack. Destroyers, frigates, merchant ships, suppliers and chasers were escorts. These last went after U-Boats still occasionally to be found lurking beneath the waves, spotted by sonar, periscopes, or conning towers. Chasers then would converge on the scene to drop depth charges, also known as "ash cans." Aboard our ship, we children watched and awaited the tell-tale crump-thump as charges exploded in the distance to send a high plume of water surging skyward mixed, it was hoped, with black oil to indicate a "hit." Aside from the transport of troops, materiel, and returning passengers, some ships laid cable off their sterns, we left to wonder how any ship could haul enough to cover the floor of the three-thousand plus mile span of the Atlantic Ocean.

Eventually scrapped in 1962, the Rangitiki had been built in 1928 for service runs between Britain and New Zealand via the Panama Canal, in which, by odd coincidence, our parents sailed to New Zealand in 1956. We weren't the only children aboard the Rangitiki on this homeward bound voyage. Many were housed dormitory-style; others, like ourselves, escorted by temporary nannies, in cabins. Life aboard was busy: daily lifeboat drills in cumbersome life-vests made of kapok—a vegetable fiber from tropical tree pods—also known as Personal Flotation Devices (PFD) or, a "Mae West," so named by the U. S. Navy and others in the Pacific, for the well-endowed Hollywood actress. There were gas-mask drills and endless walks around decks singing "John Brown's Body Lies a-Moldering in His Grave," to end up at the "Tuck" shop to buy rich chocolate Hershey bars, which were nothing like the waxy product of today.

As I was never seasick, perhaps with my old-time Norse genes to the fore, and when not busy elsewhere, I was allowed to roam, loved watching the ocean with its unending spray and sparkle, swirling blue-green and white froth foaming from the stern or, leaning over railings, watching the surge, motion, swell of waves. On rough days waves were high enough to hide other ships as they, sliding down troughs, disappeared for moments at a time before clambering up the next mountainous wave only to disappear yet again with the never ending pitch and yaw in the wind-swept briny air. Gyroscopes, invented in 1852 by Leon Foucault, had been a lucky invention, the device enabling ships to maintain nautical orientation and stability.

Late one afternoon, U-Boat periscopes were detected near the fleet, so off sped the chasers to hunt and attack the menace. Immediately the convoy resumed a uniform "zig-zag" pattern, all passengers were ordered top-side in life jackets, thus given grandstand seats to what followed, as in precise synchronization, quite something to watch, the hundred or so vessels began their turn to new positions. That is, all except one. Owing to her "confused" captain, his ship charted a course to starboard instead of port like the rest, putting him in position to ram the left side of the *Rangitiki,* while she, having obeyed orders, was in his direct path. Spellbound we watched the two ships close, awaiting the imminent collision. When the massive jolt came, we were all clinging to anything we could grab as the vessels scrunched together with the awful screech of the rending metal. An eerie silence followed before being shattered by wailing sirens, blaring klaxons, ringing alarm bells calling all hands on deck. There was no panic, but to add to the general confusion, depth charges reverberated in the distance. Then, as the two ships' drift slowed, the 'disoriented' ship reversed her engines, easing from the jagged hole in the Rangitiki's side. A couple of supply/repair ships then plowed alongside to assess damage: a gaping hole near the water-line which had exposed one of the dormitories. A heavy tarp was temporarily spread and lashed down over the huge gash for the night, the damage hastily repaired, if temporarily the next day.

As the convoy neared the English Channel, ships veered off for European, Mediterranean or African ports, while others, like ours, headed in a more northerly direction to Southend-on-Sea, Portsmouth or Liverpool. At this last, the Rangitiki lay becalmed for a day or two as frustration mounted. What was the hang-up? Nobody seemed to know; marine personnel were uninformative. Finally, the Rangitiki was eased by tugs into her berth in the Albert Dock complex, the same from which we had sailed four years and five months previously, but it would be another twenty-four hours before we could disembark. In the meantime during daylight hours, our temporary nanny kept a sharp eye on the dock far below, soon spotting a red-headed RAF officer she was sure was our father, Squadron Leader Keith Falkner. Even at the distance of time and elevation, I knew this man was not he for he was neither tall nor handsome enough to be our daddy, nor did he pace like him . . . fancy remembering that!

Though I told nanny over and over it was not he, she continued to wave and shout, "Yoo-hoo, Yoo-hoo, Mr. Falkner!" It was so embarrassing! And so, the long day wore on.

The next morning we were up early, frustrated not to get breakfast over with quickly and be on our way. At last, like cattle, we began the long staggered descent down the gangplank to the dock below, ordered then to proceed into a cavernous warehouse. Inside we found huge letters swaying in a strong sea breeze as all were ordered to place themselves under the letter of their last name. Here we perched under the letter "F" where our previously unloaded suitcases sat, we to sit, sit, and sit some more, nanny becoming increasingly anxious. She had managed, somehow, to get us back safely, but where, she fussed, were our parents?

At long last, activity, as from the far side of the warehouse high-pitched screeches of metal upon curved metal tracks indicated the huge doors were gradually opening, allowing vetted families and friends to surge forward. Never ones to force their way, and leery of crowds, the parents let the mob stream ahead before calmly making their way to "F." The ever alert Philippa, watching all the activity with interested glee, suddenly turned to point at a couple hurrying in our general direction: "Look, look!" she giggled, "Don't they look funny!" And there, there they were, not funny at all, but our parents whom I vaguely remembered as Philippa could not: our mummy and daddy. We were indeed home, and on mother's birthday too!

Hugs and kisses, there may have been, though I remember none; perhaps the moment too overwhelming to remember more than smiles and grins. Our four years' absence had undoubtedly caused some restraint, yet here were the parents handsome and beautiful: daddy in mufti with his striking red hair, subtle smell of Bay Rum; Mother, blue eyes sparkling, wafting a faint scent of Chanel No. 5. There was also business to attend to: dismissing temporary nanny, sorting luggage and presenting documents before we could head into the future as a family again.

Finally, everything in order, we were on our way in that traditional black British taxi, luggage perched precariously on its open left-handed front platform where the driver, to our mind, should have been sitting. But this was England, every vehicle on the wrong side of the road or was it the right? Why is it we English drive on the so-called correct side, everyone else on the wrong?

The taxi headed for the Adelphi Hotel as Pip, as Pop called her, wriggled around on her seat staring out the taxi's windows, exclaiming over this or that. At one point having watched policemen directing traffic, she exclaimed in her American accent: "Gosh! Gee whiz! Guess all the cops around here must be pretty darn strict 'cause' o' the war!" The parents grinned as we drew up to the Adelphi where, wide-eyed, I stared up at yet another handsome cousin, daddy's eldest nephew: Alex Curror Falkner, Navigator in the Canadian Air Force assigned to Britain, who flew on many flights over the Hump.* At lunch in the hotel's restaurant we were served a weird concoction called an omelet, this made of powdered eggs imported from America. I, never having had the displeasure of eating such before for it was truly unappetizing, hoped never to do so again but would have to on occasion because of rationing. Then it was time to say goodbye to Alex of whom I was already smitten but would see again, we were off by train to London's Euston's Station. From there, during a bombing raid, we changed to another train to make our way to Berkhamstead, in Hertfordshire. It had been a long and exciting day.

---

* Flying the Hump—1942-1945—a five hundred and thirty mile flight flown by Americans and Canadians, our cousin often as Flight Engineer, over the Himalayan Mountains to supply troops on that side of the world. It was a costly endeavor: its toll nearly one thousand men and six-hundred planes.

Old Nettleden Farm House

OLD NETTLEDEN FARM

Warm loving greetings awaited us, in fact flowed not only from Gran, our one remaining grandparent whom I would come to adore, but also Annie. From an impoverished family in Hatfield, Annie had been hired at sixteen to be lady's maid to our widowed Gran, devoting over forty years to her employer. Their greetings, eyes sparkling by fire and candlelight, were full of pleasure, giving me such a warm feeling. Yet, realizing how exhausted we all were from the long exciting day, they kept their welcome short. After hot cocoa, Flip and I eagerly tumbled into bed this first night home, too tired to even dream.

Old Nettleden Farm, near the Anglo-Saxon village of Nettleden, meaning "Valley of Nettles," as I soon found out, is an historic town originally referred to as the terminating point of the Norman invasion in 1066, also listed in the Domesday Book, the town now affectionately known as "Berks," located some twenty seven miles from London. The long-ruined Berkhamstead castle, unique for its double moats, was once home to Thomas Becket, Archbishop of Canterbury from 1162 until his murder by order of King Henry II. In the fourteenth century it became the home of Edward the Black Prince, Prince of Wales eldest son of King Edward III and Philippa of Hainault. Throughout the current war these ruins housed the statue of the Black Prince on horseback easily seen by passengers as the train pulled into Berkhamstead station.

Old Nettleden Farm is a large sixteenth-century solid brick and stone farmhouse bought by father in 1937 for a few thousand pounds, quite a sum in those days, garnered from concert fees in the United States, and films made for Warner Brothers Studios, England.* At the same time he had bought and shipped back to England a wood-paneled Ford station wagon, yes, with steering wheel on the left, to be driven on English roads. I always begged for rides, daddy often taking me with him as I sat on a small stool on the front seat anchored by a belt twisted through its legs and strapped to the seat. Proper restraints for children would not be designed for years. On one of my early jaunts perched as described, a dog or perhaps a red fox dashed across the road, causing daddy to jam on the brakes. The stool lurched just so far, while three-year old me slid off the seat banging my head against the dashboard, shock rather than hurt making me cry while daddy, with little patience for cry-babies, told me to get over it: life sometimes gave you bumps and lumps!

During our occupancy, 1937-1946, the imposing yet ramshackle Elizabethan Tudor farm, once surrounded by acres of fields and forests, now contained but few. There was a large pasture, leased for grazing cows fenced in by 17 Century iron fencing an ancient orchard which was meagerly producing apples and the acre or so upon which the farmhouse sat. Large vegetable and rose gardens were nearby, a shed for garden tools. An ancient oak stood just to the west between house and pasture, daddy planting a new orchard to the south of the house with other varieties, his favorite dessert apple, Cox's Orange Pippin whose seeds, when ripe, rattled within the fruit. To the east he planted fast-growing poplars; up a hill to the north, a stand of pine, and he put in a driveway from the entrance gate to his new garage.

Ornate brick chimneys of the Elizabethan era decorated roof lines. Nesting within were families of jackdaws, smallest of the crow family, as they have for generations. Annoyed by their constant cawing and droppings, daddy occasionally took rifle in hand to blast away at them, a useless endeavor as there, firmly entrenched, they remained. In our time

---

* Keith Falkner Films for Warner Bros.: "Thistle Down," 1938; "Mayfair Melody," 1937; "The Singing Cop," 1937, the last two with Chili Boucher, all now lost.

and bearing in mind that the interior of this house had been untouched for more than a hundred years, it was hardly surprising to find ugly black drainpipes on outside walls of the building. Inside, upstairs were five bedrooms some with arched leaden windows; a bath and connecting sun deck over the new garage, a walk-in airing cupboard, a narrow room heated by hot water pipes with shelves for storing bedding. Downstairs: living room, dining room, guest bedroom, actually Gran's, long hallway with brass gong, mostly for show, to call people to table; a "cloakroom" for coats and wellies, with separate washroom, and finally, a large kitchen leading to a roomy coal coal-scuttle, mud room and garage. Except for the airing cupboard, the kitchen was the only other warm room, it with large coal-stoked Aga stove for cooking and heating water. Red flagstone floored the kitchen, larder and pantry. From this last worn ancient stone steps led down to vaulted alcoves in ancient brickwork for the storage of wine, root and fruit crops, some bottled, or canned. But perhaps, at a more swashbuckling time, these underground alcoves may have hidden contraband, or so we liked to think, stored in these alcoves which gave off a not unpleasant fungal muskiness from the damp loamy soil.

Downstairs, ceilings were at least twelve feet high in rooms without heat. To us just returned from America's central heating, everything seemed frigid that first winter, Flip and I dressing, playing, or simply keeping warm in the airing cupboard during a winter considered by many to be the harshest for many a year. Our clothing: vests (woolen tee-shirts), a blouse, two or three wool sweaters, knee-high hand-knit woolen socks and corduroy dungarees. Yet yet still we were cold. The only time of real comfort, aside from the airing cupboard and kitchen, was at bedtime when, after a hot bath, rubbed down with warm towels, we jumped into warmed pajamas and bed socks, making a dash along the hall to leap into beds heated by ceramic hot-water bottles. To warm their beds,—in those days husbands and wives seem to have slept separately, the small rug between the two either highly worn or less so, depending—their beds warmed by long wooden-handled brass or copper pans containing live coals, known as "Il Prete," Italian for "the Priest,"(I Preti, for two or more) for whatever reason! The mind boggles; a blessing or something more outré? One can but grin.

Heat was not the only deprivation. Since1940 England had become used to rationing, which, for some items lasted until 1956. Ration books with tokens were exchanged for food or clothing at particular shops. Before our return mother had written enthusiastically to her Squadron Leader, I assume what increase she mentions is per person, seeming poor pickings today: "Isn't it grand," she wrote in early November, "about the extra rations for Christmas: ½ lb. of margarine, 8 oz. extra meat, ½ lb. sweets for children and 1 oz. of tea for those over 70! Well, Well!" Upon our return, we disgustingly found ourselves privileged to receive daily doses, as all British children did, of fish oil mixed with orange juice, the occasional rare banana.

Though bread was still available, it was often in short supply. Queues formed early mornings at bakeries where, if lucky, you might find the occasional brown Hovis. So, when daddy was on leave and managing somehow to have found a source of flour high in wheat germ and whole meal, he took on the chore of making and baking loaves in the Aga, becoming as good a baker as his mother had ever been, enjoying the task which eventually became a hobby almost to his dying day fifty-years later. His bread dumplings were superb served with butter, when available, with Lyles Golden Treacle, inverted sugar cane syrup similar to honey and corn syrup but with more distinctive flavor.

That winter, everywhere and everything remained drably gray, dankly dismal and cold, yet the indomitable British spirit kept toughing it out. A black market existed but most locals bartered with neighbors in this time of Victory or War Gardens for Defense. Considered morale boosters, these gardens produced sprouts and winter cabbages, while spring and summer produced every vegetable known to man that would grow in the British climate, sprang up in gardens as creative cookbooks utilized the meanest of ingredients, even those dreadful powdered eggs! Carrot pudding was one, another, Woolten pie—nothing but vegetables with mashed potato topping, a bit of grated cheese, perhaps a sprinkle of parsley. Sultana and Sausage casserole was a favorite, though many including mummy, believed the sausage contained within its casings, nothing more than sawdust and spices. There was carrot fudge, carrot pudding, carrot and beetroot marmalade, carrots said to be increasingly good for the vision of night fighter pilots, therefore, the citizenry as well. In the meantime daddy did his best to lard the larder, so to speak, managing to buy a dozen or so hens who, if not eaten for Sunday dinners or grabbed by some wily fox overnight, laid eggs a-plenty, most candled for later use in baking, and stored in the cool pantry. Others raised bees whose honeycombs added much to drab meals.

If there was anything that winter and early spring 1944/45, it was the endless flights taking off in early evening hours, night after night, the setting sun glinting off the sleek bodies of Flying Fortresses, Liberators and planes towing gliders. Taking off from numerous airfields across Britain, they soared upward in a seemingly endless stream heading for Germany. Late night, early morning back they limped over Nettleden Farm, back to home base, many "on a wing and a prayer," while others had been forced to ditch on foreign soil or into the icy pre-dawn waters of the English Channel. The stamina and bravery of pilots, navigators, bombardiers and gunners in frigid aircraft, the endless readying and repair work of ground crews was extraordinary, for no matter how exhausted, teams continued to prepare and fly sorties night after night. Sequestered among these were many Americans and Canadians, of the former two Hollywood personalities stand out: Clark Gable at RAF Polebrook in Northhampshire, who flew five combat missions in B-17's earning a DFC; and James Stewart at RAF Tibenham in Norfolk, credited with many missions over Germany to earn two DFCs and the Croix de Guerre, the only person ever to move from lowly private to colonel in four years.

Another constant was the almost daily "Doodlebug," that V-I German rocket launched from Peenemunde primed for England. You could hear it coming closer as it zoomed along with its characteristic loud buzz, before it fell silent, lost altitude and hit the ground. Most exploded harmlessly creating great pits in open fields, long since covered with weeds and nettles. Folks, long inured to these noisy intrusions, ignored them as we would too, that is, after the first two or three.

Hoping to destroy America's ability to resupply herself, between late 1944 and January 1945, the Germans launched the Battle of the Bulge in the Ardennes, their last major offensive and, a lost cause. After D-Day, the war in Europe had been technically over; yet the Germans did not surrender until late April and May. It would take some time before military personnel were demobilized, and before daddy was, he was dispatched to Denmark to help mop up or clear pockets of Germans who had invaded the country in June 1940. On return, he often spoke of these poor ill-clad soldiers on the losing side of war, who with no assistance, had to make their pathetic way back to Germany mile after mile with little food or warm clothing, pushing their few belongings on any wheels they could find: a broken or abandoned bicycle, prams, furrowers or wheelbarrows. On daddy's return from these "mopping-up exercises," he always brought us small gifts hoping I suppose in some small way to help Denmark's economy get back on its feet. While daddy hated war, the gross inhumanity of it, his years in the RAF, despite temporary loss of career, were for him exhilarating ones.

This then, a brief picture of our surroundings upon return: what it was like to be back in a country which for some years had been threatened and survived attempts of invasion by the Third Reich, much helped by America thanks to Winston and Franklin's mutual friendship and understanding of the Nazi peril. Incidentally, by the 1980s, Nettleden farm, sold several times over since the mid 1940s, sold yet again much "tarted up," its price tag an astronomical three hundred thousand plus pounds, which today's exchange rate would be $600,000. How some things escalate over time!

We two, Home Again, Christmas 1944

SETTLING

Our first Christmas home we were agog with its pageantry yet found everything vastly different from American largesse. Britain was under austere rationing of most everything. Presents were carefully chosen, planned far in advance; much thought was given to cost and number of ration coupons available. Frivolous items were not on anyone's list: a bar of soap or something homemade was considered a wonderful gift if some knitted wooly, such as bed socks.

On leave before Christmas, daddy, with the help of the aging and endlessly pipe-smoking gardener, Mr. Cripps, dug up a fir with roots for later replanting. Unceremoniously they dragged all ten feet of it down the slope, in through the front door, down the hall and set it up in the living room. Appropriately enough our two cousins showed up to help, Alex and John Keith with another guest, Roger Francis husband of Eleanor, Uncle Larry's secretary. These energetic young men took over the chore of decorating the tree as Flip and I sat about ogling. The tree, had innumerable four-inch candles placed in attractive hand-painted tin holders clipped to the upper side of extended branches, never too close to the one above to avoid fire. There was little else in the way of decoration except shimmering glass baubles, a star far atop the tree. A ladder stood nearby for lighting candles, a lengthy process so not lit until Christmas Eve, a time of oohing and aahing.

Aunt Dodie and Uncle Larry had not forgotten us on this our first Christmas away from them, they probably missing us more than we at the moment. A large box arrived having survived the dangerous waters of the Atlantic, with presents for all: for me a book of elegantly fashionable paper dolls, not to be played with so much as to design their clothing—the hobby eventually leading me to create and make my clothes, just as smart and fashionable as any classy couturier's, if I do say so, and all on a minimal budget.

The Yule-time feast was not the fatted goose—did anyone have one that Christmas 1944 except perhaps literature's Scrooge, the family of Tiny Tim? Rather, I recall a large beef roast either affordable with extra ration coupons of visiting relatives or perhaps their donation—something mother treated with the utmost care, and, as in the old days "hung" it. I think to shock her daughters, she told us she'd buried the beef underground to age for a week. This I could hardly believe, but it had hung in the larder for about the same number of days to gain, she said, "aged tenderness." Certainly it was tender, if a bit high, but, when served with horseradish sauce, very palatable. It was accompanied by Yorkshire pudding, roast potatoes and an endless variety of winter vegetables, a veritable feast. A traditional Christmas plum pudding followed, at least a dozen made some years before had been steadily maturing over time on lower pantry shelves—the longer, the better. The pudding, served with brandy sauce: butter, sugar and brandy with a twig of holly and liberally doused with brandy, was set alight, everyone hoping their portion contained the lucky sixpence. The parents had managed, somehow to turn this Christmas into a happy feast not for four or six, but for nine. How did they manage this and all the other meals and drinks for guests?

My present from Gran was her hand-made and embroidered etui, a needle case. Inside there was a pocket for small scissors and thimble. The remaining space, stitched to other soft material, was a place to hold a variety of needles; even a bodkin or two. Gran had made each of us etuis with our initials embroidered on the outside in pink silk thread on a background of pale blue material the whole, rolled up and closed with button/loop closure. I still have mine.

SCHOOL

The holidays over, school loomed, my first and only venture into the British system; thank goodness, for it was rigorous. In those years children aged eleven had to take the Eleven Plus exam and, having studied for this, the results determined whether they were eligible to proceed to Grammar, Secondary Technical or Secondary Modern, this last indicating you were college material. It would be just my unhappy lot to take this exam at ten and a half. I would not do well, saved by, but that comes later. About my ninth birthday, January, 1945, I had been enrolled in the progressive Froebel school relocated from London during the blitz to Hertfordshire, in Little Gaddesden just up the long hill from Nettleden Village. I was apprehensive, having heard thoughts expressed about my apparent disinterest, and that what I had learned in the States was not up to Britain's advanced curriculum.

The Froebel's grounds were spacious with long expanses of lawn where grand cedars, imported from Lebanon during Queen Victoria's reign, though slow growing, were now tall, stretching out their lower boughs seeming to invite the young to climb aboard, then higher into aerial heights. All school buildings were draped in ivy or wisteria, their pendulous purple blooms so fragrant in late spring. Our fees were paid for by the parents' giving concerts at the school each term, something they continued to do off and on during our years of education. I came to like the Froebel, favorite subjects: botany, biology and history, when I enjoyed building an entire Celtic village, deciding then and there I'd be an archeologist when I grew up. It never happened. Music, as always, pulled me, so was pleased to join a class learning to play each band instrument and to conduct the various tempi. Ballet's eight basic steps were also taught, inflaming my class to aspire to become prima ballerinas. Seeing *The Red Shoes* starring Moira Shearer shortly after its premiere in 1948, only made me pine for the impossible, for by then I was too ungracefully tall. Flip would have been better suited, given her mother's build.

In school we were intimidated by Jennifer and Pamela, two sisters, who, like us, had been sent overseas during the war, and, like us, just back. These two chose to make our lives miserable; suggesting our sojourn in America had been far less acceptable than their place of haven, the Bahamas. Everywhere they sneered at us: at school parties pointing out we were deficient in whatever they could think up, snobby little bitches, who daily arrived at school driven by a chauffeur-driven Rolls Royce. But then, as suddenly as they had arrived, they disappeared, their father no doubt on to more important posts. We were not, I found out, the only ones offering sighs of relief.

The problem of how to get to school had been solved when I was given a fancy black, gold-trimmed Raleigh bicycle for my birthday. It gave me a sense of independence not only getting to and from school, but about the countryside in spite of endless winter and spring rains but that didn't matter for I was well protected in my yellow "Wellies," matching "Mac," and rain hat. Best were dry days when I often chose to bike home through nearby Ashridge Park with its copper-colored beech trees. It was either that route or coast down the long steep and curvy hill from Little Gaddsden to Nettleden Village. I often stopped here, leant my bike against the old brick and flint wall surrounding St. Lawrence church which was first mentioned in 1285 as part of the Ashridge monastery. Gate unlatched, I'd walk up the gravel pathway between the dark green yews with their brilliant red but poisonous berries; to St. Lawrence's ancient wooden door with its large heavy wrought-iron ring which turned to lift the heavy inside latch; then through the creaking door and step down onto the ancient stone-slabbed floor. In some awe, I'd tiptoe down the aisle overlooked by the church's wooden roof that was painted in a pagan red that seemed to match the poisonous red of the Yew berries. Reaching the organ, I clambered upon its seat my feet barely reaching the elongated wooden pedals. Hesitating only briefly, I'd pull out stops on various levels and begin to play, well play is not the right word, but trying to make a few harmonious sounds from this wondrous instrument with its assorted pipes. Surprisingly, no one ever marched in to tell me to stop, to tell me my small adventures at the organ were too dreadful, or barring that knowing Keith Falkner's daughter was supposed to be musical, my small attempts tolerated.

Churchill had celebrated his seventieth birthday in November, 1944, and by standards of the day was considered an old man, despite the endless cigars, beer shandies, whiskey and sodas, Remi Martins before, during and after attending the Yalta conference with Lenin and the ailing Roosevelt early February 1945, vibrancy remained. The three managed to establish and define the role of a United Nations, the division of Germany, Poland's independence, agreeing to Yugoslavia's independence, and Russia finally committed herself to declare war on Japan in a month or so.

In the meantime, we were more than happy to feel the gentle warmth of spring, 1945, during which Germany's unconditional surrender came on 8 May causing Britain to explode with exuberant rejoicing yet with sorrow for so much and so many lives lost. The day was glorious, a beautiful morning I remember well for there were the parents arm in arm dancing around the garden, later sharing a rare bottle of "champers," colloquial British for champagne, in celebration. The Japanese capitulation soon followed, another occasion for rejoicing: peace at last, or so everyone thought.

Daddy at forty-five was at his most dashing but was often still away on duty leaving mother in charge of the household, now with children, an ailing mother, a mostly absent husband, and Annie. Mother's experience for the past four years had been far more isolated and far more lonely than ours. She had been in the backwater of Inverness doing work about which she would never speak, not even to her dying day: spying, decoding, transcriptions? Who knew? And while her life was lonely, she was often asked to entertain Polish pilots at tea dances; they newly arrived from their overrun country. Mother loved to tell of the stilted conversations while dancing with these men, limiting herself to inquire about their homeland, families and children, hoping she said, to avoid any misunderstandings. One young pilot, in response to her question "Do you have a wife?" heard him reply: "I do, but she is impenetrable!" Chris, making her way back to her lonely flat, giggled all the way there. So here indeed may have been a woman "Hanging on in quiet desperation . . . the English Way." (Pink Floyd)

At forty-three mother was, or so we thought, all-knowing and beautiful despite the fact that her needs and desires were seldom expressed or met even to her dying day. She had, of her own volition, subjugated herself to Keith in a marriage that lasted sixty years, far longer than most today. With Mum so busy, the parents trying to pick up the pieces of Keith's career the war had interrupted, it is only natural we should turn to Gran. What are grandmothers for, anyway?

It was Gran who offered warmth and helped us to readjust, so it was early every morning I'd knock on her door to find her waiting, sitting up with bed shawl around her shoulders sipping her early morning "cuppa." "Come, my poppet," she'd say, patting a place next to her; "come sit just here, my love. Let me comb your hair. Now tell me, how you are this morning . . ." Soon, it was easy to pour out my small soul: my earlier and present childish worries, the fun and hurts of America, anything that occurred to me as she, listening, sometimes questioned, never judgmental as she gently soothed my aches, burnishing my auburn hair with endless brushing. Here was someone to love and who loved me without question. Back from school of an afternoon, I'd literally fling myself into Gran's room after tea for her warm hug, her soothing warmth. Ever patient and gentle, she taught me darning with that now old-fashioned wooden egg; to sew buttons that would never fall off again, to form my letters, and, being religious, taught me the traditional hymns, read me bible stories and retold those wonderful Grimm fairy tales.

Between our rooms Flip and I shared an archway which was just across the hall from the heated airing-cupboard where we could hibernate when necessary. Our bedtime schedule, considered early by today's standards, was seven p.m., the parents believing it best for us, while allowing adults to enjoy a quiet evening and later dinner after hectic days of separation, interviews and negotiations. One springtime evening after we'd been put to bed I heard the parents preparing to leave. I ran to window, waving, shouting and crying, fearing their departure might be another long term separation. They hadn't said they were going out, and given our history, I would often feel this fear, even anger in coming years.

Sometimes, though, when Pop was home, he'd let us stay up late to take us out after dark to view the heavens, name stars, galaxies, the Milky Way, the shape of the big and little dippers, and, occasionally have us wish upon a sudden falling star. Outside longer on a summer night, we might catch the shadowy glimpse of a local barn owl, Britain's favorite bird. Espying it was eerily spectacular; it with its white wide wingspan of some forty inches, never making a sound as it swept by overhead in long slow glides, hunting in darkness.

1945 SPRING/SUMMER VISITORS

Another cold winter set in but we didn't feel it as badly now, our visits to the airing cupboard less frequent, and another Christmas had come and gone with the much looked for visits of the handsome cousins still on duty in England. Flip and I were constantly arguing which one of us would marry which one of them as we checked the Book of Common of Prayer daily to see if there had been any changes to the rule about marrying first cousins. Both gave us presents: from John, a South African silver bangle with tiny elephants for me; from Alex a pair for each of us of wondrously soft leopard fur mittens brought from India on one of his trips over the "Hump." The parents gave us the best yet, a series of riding lessons from stables just up the road: we could hardly wait for spring weather.

Visitors included Aunt Nan, whose own chapter follows was but one of many visitors that summer. There was Schram, Dr. Emily Daymond, the first woman to earn a doctorate in Music from Oxford University, who had taken Keith under her wing as he began his career. Old now, she was very kind to me, often on a cold morning inviting me into her warm bed to enjoy our early morning "cuppas," talking about anything and everything. Another visitor was Dame Myra Hess, the world renowned pianist and great friend of the parents, mummy having studied with her in earlier years. Perhaps it was she who suggested mother start teaching me piano, though the venture was not a success. Parents seldom have the patience to teach their own children. Anyway, my main interest those days was rounders, similar to American baseball. Played in England since Tudor times, rounders remains popular with British school children to this day. Good at it, I was more interested in playing the game than learning how to play the piano! So much for that!

Uncle Phil and Auntie John often drove down from London in their posh Rolls bringing gifts: half a smoked salmon, a pot or two of caviar, wines, and, once or twice, a gallon of the Spanish or Portuguese olive oil that had not been seen in England for some years. This last gift had come about because our RAF air commodore uncle, owning a yacht anchored at Ramsgate in east Kent, had been assigned the task of sailing back and forth from the Iberian Peninsula to England to return downed allied flyers. These fellows had managed to make their way across war-torn Europe, across the Pyrenees into Portugal and to safe houses on its coast. Here they were picked up, along with the olive oil, by their Napoleonic, swashbuckling savior; our uncle and his yacht, to be sailed safely back to England. Olive oil was a new commodity to Britain in those days, only occasionally used in cooking, so mother determined instead to keep our wheels working, as she called them, by administering daily doses. Today, of course, it is the only oil I use.

As for our actress Auntie John, so named for a role once played on stage, though childless, she was great fun, spending time playing games, helping with homework, and reading stories, often acting out the different parts and voices. She also helped at bath time. One evening, as she dried my back and, liking her as much as I did, and perhaps still worried about our future, I asked her that if anything happened to mummy, would she please become our new one. She hugged me with tears in her eyes: "Yes, yes of course, my child!" Relieved, I hugged her back. It was taking awhile, but I was slowly regaining a sense of security, even thinking of alternatives, and always knowing too, there was my portcullis.

My Flapper god mother to be

In London 1972

NANCY BERNARD SMITH

Spring and summer had indeed brought visits from Aunt Nan, mother's dearest friend, and my dearest god-mother. I was enriched by her presence in so many ways. Her good fairy wishes, bestowed on me at birth, more than compensated for those bestowed by some unknown evil sprite. Seen or not, they were both present at my christening, Nan tickling my pinkly peeking toes, and twinkling at me when I was being held by my god-father Sir Adrian Boult, the blessing water thus leaving me quite unperturbed, no doubt to Uncle's blessed relief. Of course I didn't hear about all this until later and have always been amused that shortly after my birth, daddy who was away in America, singing at the Bach Bethlehem Festival, rang mother and quite forgetting about me, his infant daughter, inquired after the dog! But then, he never did know what to do with babies. In old age, whenever my father was shown a picture of someone's new arrival, he'd say with deep conviction, "Now THAT's a Baby!" This seemed to satisfy everyone present, while I had to busy myself elsewhere for fear of giggling.

Now, what can I _not_ tell you about this Aunt Nan of mine? She was a lively, ebullient, knowledgeable and intuitive woman with a background far different from mother's, yet they became best friends when attending the famous Rugby School, established in 1567 where, legend has it, the game of Rugby was invented, first played. Nan was the daughter of a Liverpudlian solicitor with older brothers who followed in the father's footsteps, all comfortably well off. I believe Nan became part of the business too, as assistant and superb typist. She read voraciously, taught herself any number of hobbies and crafts, and took in the family housekeeper known as "Birdie" who lived with her for years.

The whole atmosphere seemed to brighten when Nan came to visit with her boxes of homemade fudge and jars of marmalade. She must either have been hoarding sugar for months or had a friend in the Black Market! She had great fondness for children, delighting in making up fabulous stories for our entertainment. One told of a miniature lizard, who, with Liverpudlian accent, ran around creating havoc for the mean, with happy results for good children. This little geezer would slip down straws creating huge splashes to demolish something or other; leap from the bowls of long handled spoons to create chaos, or in a timed children's bicycle race where bikes had to maneuver between terracotta flower pots, our friend managed to squirrel his way underneath then move them when no one was looking, causing the nasty bully to lose, the good guy to win. He could create havoc on a skating rink, chaos on a trunk line whether for train or long-distance calls, his wanders through the Tower of London excruciatingly funny. In later years I begged and begged Nan to write the stories for publication: "No!" she said, "These were just for me and you to share. I had as much fun in their spontaneous creation as in the telling as you seem to have done, remembering them all these years." It was from Aunt Nan I got my first lessons in knitting, an activity I still enjoy. In later years, Nan was just as wonderful to my children, though they only met briefly on visits to England. Nan and I also kept up a riveting correspondence over the years and, I can say now, often pooh-poohing my mother's attitude to life observations with which I often heartily concurred. Nan also kept up with everything happening world-wide, passing on the news and especially events happening in and around Liverpool. She was one of the first to write me about the up-and-coming young group known as The Beatles. "Mark my word," she said, "they'll be world famous in no time!" How right she was.

PETS, RIDING LESSONS, AND
AN INCIDENT

Just before Squadron Leader Falkner was demobilized, that is, retired from military service, he was involved in closing down his RAF station. As personnel were sent home, a number of pets were found to be homeless, their owners having died in bombing raids over Germany. Dog lover daddy adopted two, a mongrel Flip renamed Sally and my inheritance, the brown and white-footed Spats, raised and trained on base. Hearing the word "transport," Spats would rush to find the nearest vehicle to leap aboard in a flash, or if a plane handy, it was said she'd sooner have jumped into it. She missed her master but soon accepted me: I loved her spunkiness, she and I going most places in the neighborhood together, often walking up the hill to the charming village of Potten End to its tiny post office which housed the only sweet (candy) shop around. The name of the village derives from an earlier form of *Pottern*, a place where pottery was made, and *End,* an old term defining a settlement in the far corner of a parish.

Finally the time came for our promised riding lessons with each of us envious of the other's equipment. Flip had a riding crop given by Uncle Phil; while I had mother's beautifully polished leather riding boots. They fit perfectly and I kept them in good condition with saddle soap, wax and polish. Of course, I had to make disparaging remarks about the cruelty of whipping horses, didn't I? With no spurs to my boots, Flip couldn't rebut. Thus did we begin our brief sorties into becoming equestriennes.

Eager to mount, we first had to be shown the boring basics: how to curry and comb, saddle, adjust reins and girth straps, how to sit, how to hold the reins, etc., for several sessions before we could be off riding. I loved it, even at a learner's pace. Then one day my horse, a beautiful black filly with white star in the middle of her forehead just like Anna Sewell's, *Black Beauty,* decided something a little more exciting was in order. Daydreaming as usual, without warning I found myself hanging over the horse's left flank, she having leapt over a fallen tree trunk. The instructor berated, suggested I quickly regain my "seat" and posture, and told me to remember it was best to pay attention when riding, just as much as it would be when driving.

After our sessions, we usually ambled home through swathes of magnificent ancient beech woodlands gloriously golden in autumn, their floors a-crunch of fallen leaves and nuts; in spring, carpets of bluebells. Down Cherry Bounce hill, the Cherry part so named for the wild and wildly blooming cherry trees in spring, the abundant fruit at harvest; while the "bounce," was said to be a reminder of the bumpy rides in farm carts of bygone years. The above recalls yet another Cherry Bounce, an ancient liquor for medicinal and enjoyment purposes, a recipe the Pilgrims sailing to America around 1620, took with them, their way of preserving fruit by soaking, in this case cherries, with sugar and healthy amounts of brandy, rum, whiskey or vodka, until Christmas. If cherries had been used, the drink concoction by now had turned a brilliant red and when decanted, much enjoyed at Yuletide; a heady brew; the preserved fruit must have been equally so.

The post war summer arrived and with most men away, fields around Britain were maintained by members of the Woman's Land Army, on site to care for the country's agriculture. First formed in WWI and revised for WWII, it would not be disbanded until 1950. Some sixty-seven thousand women joined to form this army of hardworking lasses who earned a mere pound, sixty pence per week, roughly $7.50, recognized by their green-gray jerseys (sweaters), brown armbands, trousers and berets, helping to keep England's farmlands in production. Several of these gals worked in nearby fields, one in the field next to Nettleden Farm. At teatime one afternoon, daddy, on leave, took a large mug of sweetened tea out to the gal plowing up and down the hillside; contour plowing apparently unknown yet in the United Kingdom. From the top of a hayrick I watched as the rather attractive lass noticed the very handsome Keith heading in her direction. Hastily, she jumped off her tractor and eagerly ran in his direction, eyelashes a-flutter in the breeze, thanking him a bit too profusely I thought, for a simple "cuppa." Amused in the watching, I suddenly felt a nip to my right pinky. Mouse or rat I wondered, as I caught a quick glimpse of the creature scampering away. If rat, I was done for, it was said to be deadly not only for bite, but fleas. If mouse, I might be spared.

At that very moment, movement in the field caught my eye. Initially tickled, I saw the gal's tractor begin to creep backwards down the hill only to gain momentum, heading for my haystack. Alarmed now, I called out: daddy looked up just as the lass turned for a fraction of a second looking bewildered, then it dawned on her as horrified, she thrust her mug at daddy and raced pell-mell, too late, after her machine. The tractor came to rest with un-gentle bump but little damage just below where I sat on a bale of straw. The only damage done was, I suspect, to the young WLA's pride. Oh, by the way, I didn't die but for awhile was apprehensive of imminent death, but didn't tell the parents of their imminent loss. It must have been a wee mouse which had caused my fears. I would continue to play on hayricks despite all, for after Spats came into my life, I had a great chaser of both rats and mice to keep me safe.

A DESPERATE AFTERNOON

And so time passed. In January 1946, the parents were away one afternoon. It was a gloomy and sleeting day as Annie gently reminded me the afternoon was beginning to darken, time to walk Spats. I'd best hurry said she, but what an afternoon for a walk! Finally, bundled up, Spats and I made our way down the driveway, the gravel, ice-covered, crunched under foot; best to stick to the grassy verges I thought, rather than the icy roadbed where we'd slip and slide. So off we carefully stepped, I with my best-est beastie-friend in the whole wide world.

This road, a country lane, was seldom traveled: the occasional car, farm carts, the odd bicycle and even rarer but scarier, Gypsy Caravans, sometimes travelling in convoy. We had been told to stay away from them unless we wanted to be stolen, or thrown into a Gypsy stew pot of an evening, a threat mummy thought dreadful enough to keep us away from them. Hah! I didn't believe a word of it, and in fact became quite fascinated with the few Romani I saw, they with their colorful hand-painted wagons.* Years after this present event, a charming Gypsy became a good friend, I finding Liz's beauty, freedom, sense of colors, nomadic travels, musical tastes, all fascinating leading her to re-settle in Moorish Spain, sorry our ways had to part. On a lark once, Liz and I placed bets on a horse named "Romany" running in one of England's many horse races. Despite the

---

* Gypsies, were said to have originated from the sub-continent of India traveling and traveled to most parts of Europe. During WWII, they were prosecuted by the Nazis as being inferior beings. Today, in many parts of the world and in England they travel in Vardos, highly painted gypsy caravans.

odds, we each won a bundle and so I consider the Romani lucky, certainly not "inferior beings," just people with different life-style.

Often I seemed to day-dream, a part of growing up I guess, certainly true for me, and I was doing it again, when I suddenly became aware that Spats had crossed to the other side of the road. At the same time, I heard the unmistakable sound of an approaching car, traveling far too fast given present conditions. What made me call Spats to heel at that moment I'll never know, for weighed down with unborn pups, she was slower. The car, sliding around the "T" junction at the end of the lane, swerved around the bend just as the driver spotted Spats in the middle of the road. Brakes, jammed on, only caused the car to swerve and skid, its driver the local doctor, who, unable to stop, created his own emergency on his way to another. Spats' and her pups' lives were snuffed out in one terribly horrible instant, the doctor leaping from his car, but with nothing he could do. It was left to the kindly, gentle, and sympathizing Italian prisoners in the nearby field, who rushed to help, picking up Spats' smashed body, burying all in the nearby field. I trudged slowly back along the miserable lane, cold, sad and guilty. On this dark afternoon in deep sorrow, I was unable to get warm despite the Aga's heat, and Annie's Cambric tea and biscuits. Had Gran been here, I would have sobbed my heart out, her arms around me; but she wasn't, nor was a parent present. Where are people when they are so desperately needed?

ANOTHER SUCH, BUT FAR WORSE

The early spring term,1946, continued miserably gray, raw and rainy. And on such a day, on an early Thursday morning during my half day at school, rain teamed down as late, I sped off to school, this morning of all mornings, failing to visit Gran. But why? Late, I had rushed out the back door into the garage, donned my Wellies, Mac, and hat; hopped on my bike; and sped down the country lanes to Water End, the routine on rainy days, there to catch a bus to Little Gaddesden. Back just after noon, I sped homeward along watery lanes, in a hurry to make amends, shucked my raingear; then, tore through the back entrance into the usually warmly welcoming kitchen, only to stop cold.

Before me, sobbing, sat mummy and Annie. Daddy was my immediate thought: something has happened to daddy! Never one to scream or shout, I quietly asked, "Is he dead? Where's Daddy, what has happened?" Mummy, wiping her eyes, said, "No, it's not your father, go wash up for lunch and I'll tell you. "No!" said I, "tell me now." "It's Gran," mum said, "she died this morning just after you left." Stunned, I was sure that had I paid my usual visit, Gran would still be here. Yes, I knew Gran not to be in the best of health recently, with a nurse on the premises, but nobody had prepared me for the fact she might die. And, too, no matter what she may have been suffering, Gran herself had always put on her calming, soothing ways, her face loving and kind. Heartbroken with loss and guilt, still I could not cry. My sister, back from school later that afternoon, wailed and sobbed, endlessly comforted. Apparently my outward composure made everyone think I had accepted Gran's death, while I suddenly realized no one had considered mummy's loss, after the kitchen episode, never to see her weep again. Perhaps she too had a portcullis; certainly mine had again slammed down on my ten-year-old broken heart.

The rain ended by mid-afternoon, the sun peeked out from swiftly moving and fast dissolving clouds, revealing glistening droplets on leaves, sodden grasses, newly opening wild flowers. Knowing Gran's pleasure with primrose, bluebell, and the late blooming snowdrop, I picked a bunch, tying them together with a green hair-ribbon Gran had once put in my auburn hair. When no one was around, I tiptoed down the hall to Gran's room, opened the door, and closed it quietly behind me. There she lay, this time there was no welcome, no one sitting up waiting for me to do any of the things we had shared: this time she lay still, arms folded across her chest, her blue eyes closed, as I tiptoed toward her. I had never seen a dead person before, but I instinctively knelt to gaze at her dear face, whose spirit, I quickly realized, was gone, nothing there for me anymore. Placing my posies on her bosom, I rose, kissed her pallid cold cheek and left the room, my goodbye said.

Sadly, this was not the end of the tale. That evening, as I took my bath, the door suddenly flew open to bang against a wall. In the doorway stood Gran's outraged nurse, arms akimbo, demanding to know what I had been doing in Mrs Fullard's room. "Er, nothing, nothing," I managed to stammer "just wanted to say goodbye, to leave . . ." "Never mind that!" the white-starched harridan spluttered: "Don't let me catch you in there again or you won't be the only one to hear of it." With that, grabbing the door knob, she slammed the door behind her, the noise echoing down the hall, leaving me to wonder what terrible crime I had committed. Miserable, I climbed out of the bath and went to bed, later to realize what a wonderful few years I had been able to share with Gran. Except for Gambu daddy's father whom I had known briefly, my other grandparents were gone before my time.

Gran was buried in St. Lawrence's churchyard, Nettleden village and so registered, but her grave, when I tried to find it in the 1990's, had long been left unattended, no longer to be found as, overgrown with weeds and brambles, no marker ever having been placed. Mother chose never to visit her own mother's grave, though I often asked when on visits, she made every excuse not to do so, telling me, "When you're dead, you're dead!" I could only respond, "Yes, and daffodils flower in the spring, die back only to flourish again the next year. She made no response, I was beginning to learn she could not deal with unhappiness or unpleasantness, having experienced much during the war. However, Daddy and I shared other thoughts and years later after his wife and my daughter Jocelyn's deaths occurred in the same year, we would prove that there is much more to life after the fact.

Flip and I were not allowed to attend Gran's funeral, adults at the time considering it unseemly for such rites to be attended by children. Instead, we were hi-jacked by neighbors across the field, the Langbrowns, for a picnic: not too bad a way to spend the day for with fish and chips in hand we settled in nearby woodlands overlooking the gentle green vales and dales of Hertfordshire, the woods awash in carpets of blue bells. My goodbyes already said, it was a wonderful spring atmosphere in which to remember Gran.

TO ITALY!

After the war which for the past five years had so disrupted his career, daddy had been looking for concertizing, teaching and anything else which would rejuvenate his career. After a meeting early that spring with the envoys of the British Council, Keith was offered the position of Music Officer in Rome which he eagerly accepted. We all were thrilled with his appointment, though we had to wonder what Italy would be like after the recent conflagration, and the possible difficulties in getting there. Too, we were still dealing with Gran's death, Annie being pensioned off to her old home in Hatfield; and the loss of Spats and Sally, with all seeming to have worked out for the best, so to move without worries.

Early in July, daddy departed, leaving mother to deal with selling the house, and storing or selling our household goods. We three in the meantime, tried to learn Italian from recordings about "La Famiglia Bianca" (the White family). It was August before we were free to travel to London, finding it less bleak, though war damage was still much in evidence: bombed out shells of buildings resembling large doll-houses, lacking stairs, plumbing visible, open to the elements. Uncle Phil came to see us off at Victoria Station for the boat train to Dover, presenting us with bunches of fragrant Parma violets, giving mummy a number of gold sovereigns for emergencies.

From Dover we sailed the twenty-odd miles to Calais to board the Simplon Orient Express for Paris. Since the introduction of Euro-Star in 1994, this connection has become less popular with people in a hurry, but the train-ferry still exists. We traveled to France, watching the White Cliffs of Dover slowly fade in the distance, wondering if and when we'd ever be home again. We were in Paris the next morning and de-trained to spend a couple of days visiting mother's old school friends from the 1920s, and see the sights. The ride up to and the view from the top of the Eiffel Tower were memorable, as was being taken to dine at a fancy restaurant. I had no idea what mother ordered for us as I knew no French at the time, but whatever it was, it was excellent, and I supposed it was some sort of chicken recipe. Afterward both Flip and I wanted to know what the delicious entree had been and were told, "jambe de grenouille," frog legs, if you please! What?! Ugh! Frog legs? Yes, yes, I know, frog legs are considered by some a delicacy, but not for children, the very idea repulsive; second only to eating a snail, which I now love; or having to kiss a toad, prospects of handsome prince or not!

The second evening, we re-boarded the "Simplon Orient," for Milan, the train to continue its last stop at Instanbul. Tracks being what they were through war-torn France and the overnight run through the Alps to Italy, there was no way to forecast time of arrival, though every mile took us that much closer to Italy, to Daddy, to our new life under the bluest of blue skies. At each station along the way, vendors sold fruit, biscotti, vino, pane e formaggio (bread and cheese), all negotiations handled through train windows. We arrived in Milano's Stazione Centrale in late afternoon where daddy, somehow having found out the approximate time of arrival, met us as the train drew up at the platform.

We spent the next day or so sight-seeing. With Italy probably having the largest number of churches per capita than any other country, it was inevitable we visit a few. One, Santa Maria delle Grazie housed Da Vinci's *Last Supper;* the Duomo, with its golden Madonna perched atop its spire, is the world's third largest church, the first and second being St. Peter's in Rome and St. Paul's Cathedral in London. We walked through La Galleria Vittorio Emanuale II, a covered arcade, said to be the world's oldest shopping center in a city renowned for design and fashion. The word "milliner" stems from the city's name. The galleria links the Duomo's piazza with the famous opera house, Il Teatro alla Scala.

Late the following evening, we returned to the station for the train to Rome and beyond, only to find an unruly mob trying to board the train all at once, pushing, shoving, gesticulating and shouting in malodorous fumes of garlic, new to our senses. Plowing into the melee, we, or rather Daddy, in uncharacteristic British fashion, valiantly tried to board and claim our sleeper accommodations amid this horde heaving bundles and baskets, cardboard valises tied with rope through windows and doors, all hoping to grab a seat. Finally, thanks to Daddy's efforts we gained our reserved wagon-lit for four only to find two men already in occupation. No amount of persuasion, coercion or argument would make them move. "Ci siamo arrivati prima di voi!" "We got here before you!" they gleefully announced. In other words, too bad for you! With language difficulties, the parents soon gave up all argument, and we were forced to bed down together; Flip curled up top-to-toe with Daddy in one bunk, Mum and I in the other, while the two strange men selfishly hogged the other two bunks, proceeding to snore the night away. What kind of country was this, anyway?

In the morning we were surprised to find more than half the train empty. Many passengers had decamped enroute, and so our early morning peaceful as the train edged, sometimes inched, its way over hastily and unreliably repaired tracks on its way down Italy's boot. We spent hours hanging out windows in sunshine so brilliant it hurt our eyes. Everywhere were the remnants of war: burnt-out tanks, overturned jeeps, supply trucks, helmets, guns, anti-tank bazookas, flame-throwers, while pockmarked buildings caused by shelling, were mere shells, a wall or two left standing or gaping, as did we at the stunning contrast of gorgeous scenery in the background as we passed from Umbria, across the rich sienna-colored soil of Tuscany with the sharp contrast of dark-green pencil-shaped cipressi (cypresses); further then into Lazio and Rome's Termini, arriving at last at our new home, a country I would come to love, learning its language and its people.

For the first month or so we were put up in the famous Excelsior Hotel on Via Veneto, the avenue just then becoming the center for Rome's social life, its two long blocks featuring outdoor cafes on either side of the avenue, where movie people had begun to gather and attract locals.

Everyone seemed to flock here, half the people either on the make, looking for anything from a job in the movies to just an espresso. A few years later, movie stars Elizabeth Taylor and Richard Burton among others, would sit here to be fawned over and bask in the attention of "La Dolce Vita." In comparison, our lives were tame struggling in late summer Mediterranean heat with the language. At least I had learned how to ask for a glass of iced water: "Un bicchere d'acqua ghiacciata, per piacere."

In those first weeks we were always on the move, being greeted, introduced, entertained or visiting innumerable ruins. The Porta Pinciana, a gateway through the old Roman wall near our hotel, leads into the famous Borghese Gardens, Barbarini Palace and at the far end, the zoo. The Forum and Colosseum were musts, not forgetting the Trevi Fountain, there to throw in a coin or two if you wished to return. There was St. Peter's, though I'd see more of it later on; the Appia Antica, the old Roman road, over 350 miles long all the way to Brindisi at Italy's Heel; the Spanish Steps which lead directly to Rome's fashion district on Via Condotti. There was the wedding-cake structure in Piazza Venezia, its name given by the former embassy of the Republic of Venice—a large altar-like monument to Vittorio Emanuele II, King of Italy from 1861 until his death in 1878, known as Father of the Fatherland.

We often found our lives in jeopardy crossing Rome's vie, for the "Topolino" (Mickey Mouse) car buzzed and skimmed through the streets as did Vespas (Hornets,) and Lambrettas (scooters) hustling, bustling, all honking as they wove through the "Vie." Female drivers were rarely seen then for this was still man's domain, and like frustrated race-car drivers, they sped unchallenged, forcing their way in whatever direction they chose to go. Policemen from their podia at intersections, tried in valiant theatricality to direct the chaotic traffic. These "Carabinieri," wore white jackets with golden epaulettes, black trousers with red stripes down the sides, highly polished black boots, gold-braided white kepis, their hands gloved in white as, arms waving, they tried to marshal the cacophonic traffic whizzing by in all directions; a grand opera of confusion! Several years later after Daddy bought a Fiat Mille-cento, we learned that on holidays or any day at all for that matter, a bottle of wine, a panettone (fruit bread) or box of chocolates was very much appreciated, indeed expected, dropped off at the feet of any one of these madly gesticulating carabinieri, especially those whom one passed regularly. The dropping off of gifts, in turn created further bottle-necks and increased the blaring of horns and toots, though nobody seemed to really mind. These "donations," often piled high enough around a policeman's feet to cover his boots; an intense competition, among these so-called directors-of-traffic, to see who was the most popular, the most "buffo," hence, the worthiest to receive more tributes than others.

The parents initially were taken aback by all this exuberance, love of life found everywhere, gradually adjusting amongst this Mediterranean ebullience, emotions spilling over at any given moment: such a change from the self-contained, cool, calm and collected Englishmen. In due time, I saw the parents ease into this more liberated existence, sensing changes in them: more sentient, sentimental loving, with occasional sadness in their interchanges. Mother, beautiful, was particularly vulnerable to Italian overt charm in this land of "l'amore," just as the Neopolitan song "Torna a Sorrento' claims. All of us, one way or another, would become smitten with this beautiful and seemingly chaotic country, and would have been, in father's words "quite happy to have spent the rest of our lives here."

EARLY DAYS

Those early weeks allowed a number of excursions out to the wonderful countryside, and though Daddy claimed he did not enjoy picnics, in Italy he seemed content to eat '*al fresco.*' There were great places around Rome unscathed by war: beaches at Ostia or Fregene, though occasionally a left-over mine might suddenly explode. There was Lago Bracciano, north of Rome, while a mere fifteen miles southeast of the city and overlooked by the papal summer villa Castel Gandolfo is Lago Albano, here where the blueness of sky is perfectly matched in the lake's reflection. Known to the Romans as "Albanus Lacus," it is the deepest lake in Lazio. Formed eons ago by the overlapping of two small volcanic craters, the lake in 1960 served as host for rowing events at that summer's Olympic Games. It was here we had our first picnic.

Nardone, a driver for the British Council, drove us that day. Probably in his thirties, with well-muscled torso, fierce-looking and swarthy with black hair tied with red neckerchief, wicked-looking eyes a-sparkle, he looked more like one of Sicily's mountain brigands, than a driver for the Council. He was, however, tame as a lamb. Parked on a hillside overlooking the lake, Nardone instructed the parents in the art of picnicking Italian/ English style, as he set up a primus to bring a pot of lake water to the boil, adding rice to be cooked just so, before adding oil, butter, garlic, cheeses, salt & pepper, known as "Riso al Burro." "Mangiate!" (eat!) Nardone ordered, helping the parents empty a bottle or two of local wine. After that, everyone lazed about in hot sunshine until Nardone leapt up, taking Flip and me down to the shore, wanting he said, to show us something. The "something," turned out to an antique shed, a site where once Romans had built and stored their pleasure galleys. Inside we found a small bireme sunk centuries earlier and recently dredged up from the bottom of the lake remarkably well-preserved. Picking up long iron nails beneath the galley with curved prow now stranded upon wooden girders, Nardone handed one to each of us, saying they were "originals." He ordered us to treasure them.

Another excursion took us to Anzio, some thirty miles south of Rome, site of the Allied landing on 22 January 1944, in an effort to establish a beachhead. In the four months between the landing and the Fifth Army's May offensive, this short stretch of coastline became known as one of the bloodiest, most courageous, and dramatic sites of the war. Braving mud, rain, and cold during an unusually harsh winter, Allied forces tried to scramble up precipitous mountain slopes where even mules struggled in an effort to penetrate German defenses. Just two and a half years later, on this beautiful calm day, we sat lunching at a simple waterfront café overlooking the port, trying not to think of the horrors, yet unable to ignore pockmarked walls, shelled buildings, destroyed piers, half-submerged landing craft, and supply ships rusting; all a-bloom with red-brown coats created by the briny air.

The beaches of Ostia Antica and Fregene became favorite spots. We would arrive mid-morning having passed endless fields of clove-scented multi-colored carnations; that is, if the old PU, army-issued pick-up truck similar to a jeep, could make it up the next incline, and the next. For whatever reason, this old PU lost power, and, with a nonfunctioning brake, began to roll backward, nobody seeming to know what the trouble was, though the locals agreed it had to be the carburetor, or lack of brakes. Huh? When we came to a rise Daddy would rev the engine, hoping thus to make it over the next crest, but more often than not we had to get out, to push the PU—with some help from the locals—up and over the slight rise only to have the PU suddenly come to life again on its way down hill, we girls often having to chase after it among the strong scent of petrol fumes mixed with the strong scent of eucalyptus trees. The old junker did fine, going home like an old nag eager for its oats, for the way was more or less downhill, along the flat Pontine Marshes, once mosquito-ridden, reclaimed in the 1930's by the Fascist Mussolini, who transformed them into an autostrada with separate lanes for cars and trucks.

It was on the way to Fregene that the PU needed the most pushing, so that we arrived "hot and bothered," immediately throwing ourselves into the cooling waters of the Mediterranean to swim and swim before picnicking. Daddy was getting adept at making riso or spaghetti al Burro, on the primus, beneath the shade of umbrella pines partially circling the beach. Afterwards, as parents dozed in shade, Flip and I, eager to return to the beach, faced a phalanx of deeply tanned parading Adonis' sashaying their way up and down the beach, gorgeous to behold in mini bikinis, manhood very much in evidence. We soon learned that a left or right pinkie's long fingernail indicated sexual preference, though in our innocence, were told it was for cleaning wax out of ears. An earring in left or right ear lobe indicated preference or availability. I don't know about Flip at eight, but Italy was certainly exposing me, at ten, to things I'd never thought about before.

It was Lago Bracciano, however, which became our favorite spot for weekend picnics. Some twenty-five miles northwest of Rome, the lake is dominated by the Orsini-Odescalchi fifteenth-century fortress, housing frescoes by Tuscan and Umbrian artists. Surrounded by farmland, the lake is a water reservoir for Rome, and, since 1986, under control to avoid pollution, then further protected by the "Parco Regionale del complesso lacuale di Bracciano Martignano, thus remaining one of the purest lakes in Italy." An important tourist attraction today, for us in the late 1940's it was an idyllic spot, quite undiscovered at the time, we never having to share the beach with anyone. All daddy had to do was produce a bottle of wine or a couple hundred lire, with the proviso we shut gates and leave no garbage, and the farmer allowed us to trespass through his fields down to the shore to the lake's clear refreshing cool waters gently lapping the black volcanic sand. In late summer, in nearby lanes, we could pick all the wild pink *ciclamini* we cared to, or buckets of blackberries from brambles overloaded with fruit, to return to Rome, where, tired and cranky, daddy and I made delicious batches of our favorite jam.

It was to this lake the parents often brought a gala's worth of world-renowned British artists, including the composer Ben Britten and his associate, tenor Peter Pears; the composer and conductor Eugene Goossens, a colossus in Australia; the composer William Walton; conductors Barbirolli, godfather Adrian Boult, and Malcolm Sergeant; among others. All were invited here to relax from heavy schedules, and all, no matter their fame, were just ordinary blokes, fun once you got to know them, which was easy to do amid the wonderfully relaxed climate.

AUTUMN, 1946

I heartily thank the parents for enrolling us in Villa Pacis just off Via Camilucia, up the hill from the villa we would be living in for the next two years. Run by Catholic nuns, the school offered us the quickest and easiest way to learn the language. We were thrown in with Italian children to learn or be damned! Unfortunately our challenge was doubled when we also had to learn French, only spoken at meal time. With classes not scheduled to start until October, and having moved from the hotel to the Villa Manzoni, we were off to Venice for the International Festival of New Music, daddy's attendance being required as Music Officer for the Council.

We flew to Venice in an antiquated propeller-driven plane, given a very bumpy ride in uncomfortable seats in a very cold unpressurized cabin with ears popping from varying pressures. In the loo, it was best not to sit, for below you was a gaping hole revealing the country-side far below as the plane overflew the poor sods below. Another unpleasantness was my sister's embarrassing ability to become air-sick upon landing. Who was this uncouth child? I didn't want to know her!

Our hotel in Venice was the famous Gritti Palace Hotel, located close to Piazza San Marco, overlooking the Grand Canal with incomparable views. The city, reawakening after the poison of war, was mending as so much of Italy was; but, having been protected by mainland Italy for nearly fourteen hundred years, the city had been mostly isolated from invasion. Considered "doers," the citizenry of Venice had long ago conquered the malaria-ridden swamps to build their city from almost nothing, enabling them, then, to look to the East to create their own opulent mercantile empire. There have been many famous residents, but one which caught my imagination, was the famous, some might say infamous, Lord Byron, with his reputation for lovers of which there seem to have been an infinite number, including his sister. T'was said the lord immersed himself nightly in love, dove in the Grand Canal at midnight, emerged to write until dawn, before falling into bed, not to rise again, pun intended, until late afternoon. But I digress.

The Festival was held mainly in the Caffe' Florian, or La Fenice, (the Phoenix) destroyed by fire in 1996, but risen again. The purpose of the festival this year was to present the latest avant-garde works in opera, ballet and concert. Luckily Flip and I only had to attend an occasional afternoon performance, while daddy had to attend all, most music found to be discordant, often to hear the Italian football-like crowds erupting with shouts of "Bravo!" or, "Basta!" While still attending all evening performances and safely leaving us in the hotel unsupervised, mummy soon joined us on our morning jaunts to the Lido. Music over, daddy joined us too, but careful with red hair and pale skin, while we rebelled against his imposed rule: no swimming for an endless-to-us hour after lunch. Some days we ate al fresco lunches on or near the hotel's pier on the Grand Canal; always, it seemed, in brilliant sunlight. Siestas necessarily followed.

Re-emerging, as did everyone else about five, it was time to sightsee: a first, Murano, "the Glass Island," where, for fear of fire, the works had been relocated from the city years before. From the seventh century, Murano's history and works have been influenced by Muslims and Asians, and, for many years, the Muranese were the only people in Europe who knew how to make mirrors, their monopoly lasting centuries. So respected did these artisans become, they were allowed to carry weapons, granted immunity from prosecution by the Venetian State, and, in the fourteenth century, their daughters were allowed to marry blue-bloods. Woe betided the glass maker who set up shop outside the Venice Lagoon, for he was subject to amputation of hands, or assassination. While a lot of kitsch is now made for the tourist, the isle of Murano still produces exquisite works of art.

There was the Duomo and Campanile to visit; and, the Doge's gothic Palazzo Ducale, which was the seat of government and venue of law courts, housing the city's jail until its relocation across the Bridge of Sighs. Late of an afternoon we'd be plied up and down famous waterways in a gondola poled by a sometimes singing gondolier dressed in unique style, often passing beneath this bridge. T'was said Lord Byron coined the name somehow sensing how felons must have felt as they headed for incarceration and were taking their last glimpse of Venice, of freedom. Local legend also has it that eternal love is granted to lovers if, in a gondola and under this very bridge at sunset, they kiss. While I was maturing, I was still too young to check this out though beginning to shed innocence in such matters, maturing in this rarified air! After gondola rides, we gathered as the sun set in San Marco's Piazza for an aperitif, Campari and Soda or, in our case. an almond Orzata, before dinner, returning afterwards to watch the demi-monde pass by. Too soon for me it was time to say goodbye to this captivating city and head back, as far as I was concerned then, to the belittling business of education. The flight back offered the same non-amenities; but, as the only children aboard, we were thrilled to be invited into the cockpit to meet the pilot and navigator, examine the controls, and peer out windshields. Then, predictably nearing Rome's old Fumicino airport, Flip up-chucked again no longer, at least on planes, a relative of mine! Holiday over, with some trepidation, off to school we went.

Near Tomba di Nerone, late summer 1946

VILLA MANZONI

The Villa Manzoni would be our home for the next two years; though as children we little realized the historical importance of the area. Located north of the city off the leafy Via Cassia that is the main route to Florence, and near Nero's tomb, Tomba di Nerone, church bells now echo across the area. The Villa built in the 1920's by Armondo Brasini, was on the site of the ancient one of emperor Lucio Verus. The new villa was named by the Manzoni counts, after their relative, the poet-novelist Alessandro, author of *I Promessi Sposi,* "The Betrothed," and the same Manzoni for whom Verdi composed his *Requiem Mass.*

In late August the massive rose-tinted villa with terra-cotta pan tiled roofs, overhung terraces and verandas, was more orange than usual. The Scirocco, with hot sandy winds, swept north-east out of Africa into the Mediterranean area, often with hurricane force, and blew over Rome to settle everywhere. On perfect days, the grounds were park-like, with broad graveled alley ways, overshadowed by those famous umbrella-shaped pines, "I Pini di Roma," described musically by Respighi; their pignoli (nuts) delicious to munch on in late summer as cones burst open. In the spring, an orchard of heavenly scented almond blossom had burst forth, so very white against an almost navy blue sky, to ripen in their turn to deliver a harvest of green kernels. South of the villa, hidden from view, a stone wall protected the Limonaia, the wall and hot sun hastening the ripening of lemon, grapefruit, orange, tangerine, and lime, while a little further on persimmons hung like Christmas baubles, their taste incomparable to any other, in my opinion. Fig trees tempted, both green and black, and where, early one afternoon, Alma, daughter of the head gardener and I perched, sating ourselves as several young farmhands passed by below. Thinking they might like a juicy fig or two and though my Italian was still pretty rough, shouted down: "Voi una fica?" This was received with enthusiastic shouts of "Si! Si!" and so I began to gather and throw figs from the tree, as in so doing, caught the look on Alma's face, noticeably red yet convulsed with laughter. What had I said? Somehow she made me understand that I had said "fica" when I should have said "fico." So? "Well," she explained, "you just asked those men," who had fortunately moved on, "whether they wanted a 'fuck!'" Not knowing the word, I was a bit confused but made it my business to find out, not physically of course, my turn for a red face!

Further west now, and backing into a large cave, was what was left of a large greenhouse once growing innumerable plants and seedlings. Useless now; glassless, shattered by earlier bombing, the cave acted as shelter and was used for cold storage. To the southeast, the farmer's house was open on the ground level, allowing farm animals to rove in and out at will. The farm also bred Schnauzers, one of which we'd soon buy. Rich brown fields were plowed, as had been done for centuries, by the yoked and ever patient grandly-horned white oxen. Further still, old and new plantings of olive and cork trees marched up and down sloping hillsides in orderly file. Large plots grew ripening tomatoes, which, when ripe enough, were plucked from their vines and laid out on huge chicken wire frames, there to ripen further and eventually dry in hot sunshine. Nearby, a stream where vines intermingled in an array of watermelon, cantaloupe, Persian, and honeydew melon, plus yellow squash, and in all stages of size and ripeness, green zucchini. There was a palate of color everywhere one looked: lemon, lime, orange, tangerine, to red, the thistle-like dusty gray-green artichoke, the blue/black eggplant, the yellow, red and green peppers, these and more which had nourished many during the war and would many more for some time to come.

Tall wrought iron gates faced north. From there, along an inner wall heading east, where little fuzzy yellow balls of Mimosa trees perfumed the air in early summer. Further, again under umbrella pines, planted between beds bordered by low fragrant varieties of rosemary bushes, were herbs of every description: the aromatics, such as basil, known as basilico; thyme (timo), marjoram similar to oregano, the heavenly verbena among them. Further east was the home of the head gardener; his wife, Giulia; head maid, and their children Silvano and Alma. Their house surrounded by tall mulberry trees which, when ripe, dripped sweet inky-blue juice on the ground, staining our fingers and lips as we popped them into our mouths.

Back to the main gate, as one entered from Via Cassia, a broad gravel drive passed on each side a phalanx of giant cacti before the drive curved out of sight beneath a large portico. It was, doubtful I suspect, but the tale was that these very cacti had been used as torture during the war: the victim being tied to the plant's fast-growing claw-like spine overnight, to be pierced or agonizingly impaled by morning. Be that as it may, from the portico gray granite steps led up to the grand entrance, where massive doors were opened by Pizzuti, the aging maggior-domo, impeccably dressed in uniform and white gloves. From there a large marble-floored foyer, two graceful marble staircases curving upward to the east and west wings of the villa. Between the stairs, ornate white and gold-painted doors opened onto an enormous marble-floored ballroom called a Salone (big room), suites to either side. In between, statuettes were ensconced in niches around the room, while the ceiling, painted with those chubby cherubs known as puti floated about among bouffant clouds in an azure sky, circling a grandly glistening chandelier. Floor to ceiling windows, heavily swaged in gold brocade, opened southward, leading down to yet another set of granite steps to the balustrade overlooking the orangery. This, then, an imperfect view of the grounds, as I remember them from 1947.

Rooms were sumptuous in décor. Ours were on two floors on the southwest side of the structure; the dining room and our bedroom were on the second floor as were the kitchens and large bathroom. On the third, mum and daddy had an antique elevator, from which they made their way down a white and black-tiled hall. On the left, an elongated Moorish sitting room resembled a harem with its carpets, draped drapes, divans, cushions and softest couches all in exotic colors. From there, double doors led out to two large terrazzi facing north and eastern skylines.

Somewhere in the middle of this opulent and to my mind over-stuffed room, stood a huge terracotta stove known as a *stuffa*, fed with pine logs. When home from school, the four of us would sit cozily around it awaiting tea. One winter afternoon, and every one thereafter during our two years of tenancy, just before four, as if on cue, a friend appeared. A minute or so later, tea arrived, brought up from the kitchens. As mother began to pour and to pass cakes, our small friend moved closer under the tea table to join the party, to expect a crumb or two. When they fell, often not accidentally, the wee mouse happily scooped them up nibbling away while keeping an eye on us and the floor, hoping, no doubt for more "crummy" behavior from above. Party over, still on its haunches, wee mousy cleaned his whiskers and with last look around, scurried off.

In this same elongated room were numbers of window seats piled with cushions. It was here that daddy, bless him, sat time and again to help me memorize multiplication tables. When alone, I'd page through huge tomes depicting the First World War in all its' horrors. If one could but take diplomacy out of war, as Will Smith once said, "the thing would fall flat in a week." War is a horrible waste of young men and women, fodder for the pleasure of rulers and generals.

Further along that black and white-tiled hall were the parents' bedroom and bath. The bedroom sported a tiled terrazzo which faced west to catch the setting sun. Many a cocktail party was held there in our time for famous musicians, none of them seeming to mind wandering through this exceptional room, decorated as it was, in Chinese décor of black lacquered cupboards and cabinets. The king-sized bed with headboard, and every other item, was inlaid with nacre. The room's tall mirrors and windows let in or reflected light as gentle zephyrs wafted, all creating an exotic, even romantic, ambiance. Any interruptions up there, could only have been caused by a maid, waiter, or children. The parents were isolated with no possible interruptions by telephone, for there was only one on the entire estate, and it was down in the foyer in an antique leather sedan chair under the west staircase.

We weren't the only ones who lived at the villa. There was the Contessa with her adopted niece Paolina, soon to be married to a German blue-blooded Nazi officer, so it was said. The administrator for the villa and his wife were there; he, horrible, always trying to hug me whenever we passed. I usually managed to avoid his clutches, only then to have my cheeks pinched in the passing: "Come sei carina!" he'd mutter before moving on. Another occupant was an American movie mogul though seldom seen by me; and, of course, ourselves. Gardeners, farmers, servants and hangers on, lived on the property too, the entire group fed by one fantastic chef named Ottorino, who had to prepare at least four separate meals three times a day, sometimes more, certainly more when guests visited, and staff to feed. His kitchen aides did the day-to-day making of breads and pasta, along with other prep work. All worked while being chased by this quasi-maniacal figure wielding a machete-like knife, a mad-man in his own kitchen, laughingly chasing his assistants, cooks, maids, even us, gaily around his vast kitchen in great fun. The daily great chore besides a smallish gas oven was to keep the bank of charcoal stoves ready on a far wall for anything needing cooking. It was fed hourly at differing temperatures all day varied menus being prepared.

Once a week, daddy drove this great chef to one of Rome's many markets where the chef, not daddy, haggled with the best of them for the best and cheapest, returning to create delicious meals from the simplest of ingredients: rice, pasta, fresh vegetables, fruit, olive oil, various cheeses, herbs, meat and fresh fish; all supplemented by huge sacks of sugar and flour provided us from both American and British supplies, war-time leftovers, along with the inevitable and questionable Spam: this last some contrast to the far better fare we were enjoying. Mother in an effort to spare Ottorino confusion, weekly handed him a menu for the week while giving him a fair portion of the above surplus supplies, all of which makes me wonder whether this arrangement was in partial lieu of rent.

Chef Ottorino, crazily delightful as he was, ruled his kitchen with an iron fist as most Napoleonic figures do, his creations in these austere times, magnificent. One of my favorite dishes was his Timbalo alla Macaroni;

my favorite dessert one which he only made for Christmas or birthdays, well mine in particular. His Mont Blanc was nothing more than a mound of riced chestnuts, chocolate, sugar and vanilla, all piled high and topped with sweetened whipped cream to emulate the Alpine Mont Blanc, which took forever to create. You can't help but wonder how Ottorino managed. On top of his many repasts and with little time for himself, he'd suddenly appear with dozens of fresh yeast doughnuts or, homemade ice cream with rolled cookie wafers, all gastronomic delights despite on-going shortages during a war barely over.

MOB SCENE

Shortly after moving to the Villa, Daddy on some other venture—probably golf—dropped wife and daughters off one hot mid-morning at the entrance to Piazza del Popolo. As do most in Rome, this piazza has a long history but appears it was not until the middle ages that pilgrims and travelers from the north, traveled down the Via Flaminia or Via Cassia into Rome via this Piazza. Lying within the northern gate of the Aurelian Walls, it once known as the Porta Flaminia, later Porta del Popolo, finally becoming Piazza del Popolo. Until 1826, the Piazza was a place for public executions. The obelisk in the center, known as the Flaminio, was brought to Rome from Egypt in 10 BC by order of Augustus.

We entered the Piazza, expecting to traverse it on foot with ease, only to find it crammed with mobs of people milling about, getting noisier by the minute. This horde was angry, pushing, shoving, waving and gesticulating and was beginning to look, if not yet unruly, close to it. The gathering seemed to be a demonstration of Fascists and the Communist party, the latter with their Bandiera Rossa, the Red Flag, a movement which had taken root among the working class during the resistance in defense of Rome in the 1940s. The meeting this day, from what I can learn, was an uprising of Roman disagreement between the two parties. So it was on this day, that we found ourselves having to make our way through those jostling warring parties. Normally, it was possible to skirt the whole area to avoid the traffic, but on this day, the entire Piazza was a sea of people, every inch of space covered. There was nothing to be done but plow into the melee.

Our demure and petite mother placed herself as a battering ram, had Flip hang on to her belt behind her, while I brought up the rear somehow clinging to my sister. As the last person in this push-shove environment, I had to suffer the indignity of having my bottom pinched several times. Forget politeness, no "scusate" or "perdono" here, as mother forced her way through the angry milling throng, a mere foot or two at a time. It was slow, agonizingly slow, crossing this vast piazza as occasional surges of panic caused the crowd to jostle, pushing us hither and yon: a fall, and we would have been trampled to death. The closeness of unwashed, un-deodorized male bodies in the heat of late morning was as overwhelming as the stench of garlic, our noses still unused to its use in the kitchen.

It took two hours or more in this kind of proximity, our own perspiration pouring from us, as mummy somehow managed to keep a sense of direction in this surging mass. Thanks to her, who must have been petrified with her great fear of crowds, neither Flip nor I felt any sense of the panic she must have been feeling. At long last, we reached the end of our trek across the Piazza to disgorge onto Via Babuino, where we sat exhausted cooling down with an Orzata, that wonderful almond drink. Later, I suspect mummy may have had a word or two to say to daddy over his carelessness in dropping us at the teeming Piazza without further thought.

It was about this time I began to hear of the massacre in the Fosse Ardeatine Caves, ancient Christian catacombs just outside Rome along the Appian Way. The massacre, orchestrated by the Nazis, was in retaliation for the partisan killing of thirty-three S.S. policemen in Rome's Via Rasella on March 1944. It became one of the most dramatic and bloodyest episodes of the Germanic occupation of Rome. A total of three hundred and thirty five, among them one hundred Jews were randomly rounded up, and shot. The caves which Angelina took me to, are a monument to those slaughtered.*

---

* For full story read: *The Battle for Rome: The Germans, The Allies, The Partisans, and the Pope, September1943-June 1944,* by Robert Katz. Simon & Shuster 2003. ISBN 0-7432-1642-3

VILLA PACIS
AND
A POSITANO CHRISTMAS

By now that fateful day in October of our first day at our new school had come and gone. We plodded from the villa early morning and ambled back along the rough path through the olive grove. What was left of a crusty loaf—it was so good—we handed in to Ottorino, as, seldom staying at school for supper, this was considered our portion of that meal.

That first day of school had been almost unbearable: so many questioning looks from new classmates, so much to adjust to and much to learn. Would we ever fit in, learn the language enough to absorb what was being taught; be understood, make new friends? Of course we did. Within two weeks we, at ten and eight, had picked up enough to do all the above, though declensions, inflections, pronunciations, nuances, innuendoes, and other subtleties would come later. To compound the issue, French and only French was spoken at meal time, from the simplest phrase of "please pass the bread," or "thank you:" "Passe moi le pain s'il vous plait," et "merci!"

Everything was new; from schedules, atmosphere, rules and regulations, to the wearing of uniforms: navy skirts, white blouses, navy knee socks, black shoes. Black aprons called "Grembiale" covered uniforms to protect us from ink's splatters and spills; old hat today. Each student wore a sash in the color for her grade, worn from left shoulder to right waistline, mine green and white. At the end of each month those brightest among us were awarded medals or pin-on ribbons, mine alas, only ever for comportment, something the nuns highly desired from students: obey, or be damned!

The nuns were not unkind; yet were demanding task masters, and, when not in the classroom, went about their business in silence. They seemed to be on call at any given moment, summoned from the foot of a massive wooden staircase by a nun ringing a large bell with muted clapper. Each nun hearing her distinctive number of clunks say, "clunkety clunk, clunkety clunk, clunk," would rush downstairs, often with wimple askew, to attend to whatever she was called for.

Mornings, all attended church as a "Sacerdote" performed mass, the altar server swinging a thurifer back and forth with its holey, (not to be confused with "holy" but, that too) exterior, incense wafting to purify and sanctify the proceedings. On very special Festa days with girls old enough to receive first communion, families gathered to watch their daughters in white become indoctrinated little brides of Christ. Not catholic, I envied them—oops, a sin right there—for the attention of doting families, their pretty dresses, veils and flowers. It was a feeling which died but slowly. Did I have doting parents? More often than not, it didn't seem so.

Flip and I had to learn proper Italian table manners starting with both arms resting on the table unless we were eating. Surprisingly, in this fashion I learned to peel an orange without touching it with fingers. Impossible, you say? With knife and fork it can be done. Another trick was learning how to twirl a forkful of spaghetti just so, and place it in the mouth without sauce and pasta dangling over the chin. An art yes, but much nicer than watching or hearing others sloppily slurping and sucking up strands of spaghetti, vermicelli, spaghettini, or tagliatele.

When the parents were away concertizing, we stayed a night or two at the nunnery. The dorms were long totally colorless rooms: row upon row of identical beds that were surrounded by everything in virginal white. The floors, walls, ceilings, window curtains and bed linens and bed curtains surrounded white painted iron bedsteads. Add to this, the chaste white nightgowns. The only colors were, a brown wooden crucifix affixed to the wall above each child's bed, the black hair of Italian girls, and a few rosy cheeks.

Time passed quickly and in no time it was La Festa di Natale: Christmas, and though Flip and I had miserable colds, we went ahead with plans to spend Christmas in Positano, after traversing war-ravaged Naples. We had been warned about this city, where vehicles were subject to assault by urchins and others, who were desperate to survive the harsh winters, harsher lives, and were stealing anything they could in the aftermath of war. Passing through the city, Philippa, smallest of us, was instructed by daddy to sit in the back of the PU to bash Fagan-ish knuckles with a stick, should any appear under the canvas tarp covering the tailgate. Navigating the streets was slow going as in the city center, daddy slowed further only to have Flip screech in horror: "Fingers!" then sat paralyzed as twenty or more small digits grabbed blindly for anything under the tarp; then, just as swiftly, disappeared. Ever our hero, daddy jammed on brakes and jumped out in hot pursuit, a waste of time for these demonic-gamins were long gone making off with daddy's RAF great coat. The commotion brought locals out like flies to gawk and guffaw; easy to tell which side they were on! It was time to move on, and quickly. Chagrined and somewhat embarrassed, daddy jumped back into the PU, to spend the rest of the journey happily relating horrific tales about the famous black African Brigade stationed in Italy and elsewhere during the war, who would sneak up on German outposts in dead of night, attacking silently to slit throats, hack off fingers, ears, heads, dismembering bodies as and when necessary. Daddy did enjoy the macabre.

And so to Positano, a small village on the Amalfi Coast (Costiera Amalfitana) south of Naples, the village positioned on steep cliffs, seeming poised at any moment to slide straight into to the sea. The area had prospered in the 16th and 17th centuries but hard times came in the 19th causing many to immigrate. By the 20th Positano was just a small fishing village, that is until 1953 when its image changed, thanks, depending on your point of view, to an article in *Harper's Bazaar* by John Steinbeck, causing masses to flock there, where tourism has become the major industry, though also well-known for its Limoncello, a lemon liqueur and

"L'Abertissimo, a famous tipple only to be found at L'Alternitiva, a stall at the harbor. Among other enthusiastic descriptions, Steinbeck wrote:

> "Positano bites deep. It is a dream place that isn't quite
> real when you're there and becomes beckoningly real after
> you have gone."

This Christmas of 1946, we arrived at this most vertical village along the Amalfi coast, overlooking a horseshoe-shaped bay on the Tyrranean Sea. The route was torturous, a one-lane gravelly road often with falling rocks, frightening and dangerously twisting and turning through terrifying hair-pin bends, sheer drops to the sea with nary a railing in sight. For upcoming traffic, those going downhill had to reverse to the nearest narrowest place to pass. It was not a trip for the timid but then, who in Italy was ever timid! In some surprise, we arrived safely.

It turned out we were the only guests at this small haven, the charming rustic hotel "Bucco di Bacco." (Mouth of Bacchus). The hotel's lowest floor was a Bacchanalian grotto, its sandy floor rinsed daily by tidal inundations. In summer, tide out, evening meals were served there. Bedrooms were on upper floors, where, as the only guests, we had the run of the place with meals served in our rooms. On the first evening and every one thereafter, Giovanni appeared about seven to ask what we'd like for dinner, the question always the same as he asked, rubbing his hands in intense anticipation, "Che cosa vogliamo per cena sta sera?" (What do we want for dinner this evening?) The question became a family joke, though we came to understand our dinner requests were a lottery for Giovanni and the cook. This being so, in consideration, the parents chose to be surprised: it was left up to the cook to choose and prepare what everyone ate on any given evening: always delicious.

The weather, however, was not so cooperative; ugly most of our stay: cold, windy and rainy, sea angry, gray and rough, waves sending plumes of spray skyward as they crashed, thundering, against boulders and shore. Free to roam anywhere, we walked through town in and out of shops selling sweet-smelling inverted tangerine-peel boxes most used as sachets, or the brightly painted miniature wooden plumed horses attached to tiny *carrozzi*, (carriages) buying both with Torone or Perugina Baci among other tempting things. We loved best to roam along *La Spiaggia*, the beach, to collect long razor clam shells, and pretty sand-buffed glass. Clambering over rocks, sloshing through small trapped pools, we often noticed they were ringed with white, salt, dried by the sun to produce a harvest of saline crystals.

One day, exploring further south down the beach, Flip and I came to a huge bastion of boulders with an opening facing away from the sea, a temptation which just begged to be explored, as waves gently ebbed and flowed in and out, to and from rocks and shore. Nothing to fear here, "Let's go!" we both said. Hand in hand we plunged through the opening to a fair-sized cavern. For some moments we explored before there was a tremendous roar, which I thought must be a terremoto (earthquake), except there was no shaking, no rocks falling, no fissures, but a cannonade from above, as a tremendous force of water smashed against overhead rocks. Seconds later, cauldrons of sea water poured in from every nook and cranny: overhead rocks, sides and in through the opening which had so tempted us in the first place as water rose, swirled across our feet on slippery rocks up to our knees in no time, and forced us back and back until we found ourselves up against a very cold wet stone wall down which water continued to pour. As we clung together, Flip and I could only stare, frightened, as water rose to our waists. Surely it had to ebb soon? A picture of weeping parents crossed my mind but everything soon reversed. The water swirled backward, out though a swift undertow threatened to take us with it as the churning sea ebbed faster now, out the way it had roared in only moments ago. The worst was over; we were safe but still in fear, without thinking twice, Flip and I were out of there faster than we had entered, never to venture in there again. Sopping wet, frigid with cold, and bedraggled, we struggled along the soggy beach, returning to Bucco di Bacco, managing to avoid the parents, vowing never to tell them of our narrow escape. Nor, did we.

AN ENGLISH SUMMER—1947

We flew back to England for the summer, daddy returning to the English musical scene; we to family and friends. Misty fog was our welcome and what little to be seen from the plane as we landed, was utterly gray and miserable after the vast blueness of Italian skies. A short drive and we were in London where everything was, or so it seemed, depressed, still dull, gray, rainy, with bombed ruins still in evidence. We did not stay here long.

"Redmoor Farm," near Rugby, where mother and Uncle Phil had gone to school, was owned by gentleman farmer, Uncle Will and his wife Aunt Margaret Parnell, Gran's sister. They soon departed leaving the farm in the care of the headman, us, the farmhouse with its spacious kitchen and large sunny gardens. That summer was almost torrid: bees humming, garden abloom with pastel and lightly scented sweet peas nodding in zephyr breezes. Children's naps and afternoon tea were taken in the roundabout sun house while on the lawn, pitiless games of croquet were played. The vegetable garden produced crops of peas, new potatoes, mint and baby carrots. Sunday dinners were either roast chicken with bread sauce, leg of lamb with mint sauce, or roast beef with horseradish sauce. Plums, pears, rhubarb, gooseberries, along with raspberries, white, red and black currants that were ripened to make jams, summer puddings, "Fools," or pies, were grown in abundance.

Rationing was still in effect but not at Red Moor. Everything was plentiful, the farm producing its own milk, cream, the clotted variety as well; chickens roamed the barnyard laying brown eggs, and well-matured fields produced plate-sized mushrooms. There were pigs, evidenced by the line of aging hams hanging up and down the back staircase. There was no lack of food here. Breakfasts consisted of porridge with cream and sugar, boiled eggs, toast slathered with butter, then smothered with homemade raspberry or blackberry jam, and topped off with dollops of clotted cream: so luscious, so caloric, so decadent. Bread, not rationed during the war, became so in 1946. A loaf of the ubiquitous Hovis, high in wheat germ and whole meal flour, could be bought daily at the local bakery. Strange to say, potato rationing began as well that year, the public being pressured into helping feed Europeans whose economies had been devastated by the war. What, we wondered, about England's? Uncle Will did his best to share his farm's riches with the locals who, as we, ate well that summer.

Occasionally daddy joined us, but, was more often away adjudicating for the Associated Board of Music, or arranging for the interchange of Italians to England for performances: Serafin, Molinari, Bellezza; tenors Gigli, Lauri-Volpi and Di Sefano. Conversely, English musicians to Italy for the coming year included composer Ben Britten with tenor Peter Pears; conductors Sir John Barbirolli, Sir Malcolm Sargent, Sir Adrian Boult, Eugene Goossens and Daddy's old friend Serge Koussevitsky with whom he had sung and recorded *The St. Matthew Passion* as Christus in 1939. On one visit, Koussvitsky came to Rome with young Leonard Bernstein in tow. I remember his sulking in the background, wanting his own moments of glory: yet having to attend to Koussevitsky's every move. One move included an invitation for me to sit on the old Maestro's lap much to my embarrassment at thirteen, as he talked with father while the old maestro hugged and patted me to my utter discomfort, he apparently attracted to young things. Tactfully, daddy managed to extricate me from these embraces, I having been too young, too in awe, to do much except feel uncomfortable.

Aunt Nan came to visit us at the farm, bringing her homemade butterscotch fudge, exciting tales, knitting lessons; still loving me as her own. Despite her great friendship with Mother, she and I some years later kept up a running correspondence; she, able to write about Mother's foibles and differences with equanimity and humor, while maintaining their life-long friendship. I have kept most of her letters, and I'm glad I have them now, as she died far too young; leaving me with some beautiful jewelry of the sort one keeps in bank vaults. Nan, Gran, and Aunt Dodie were the three older women from whom I most wanted approval, love, and respect; all of which I returned in full measure.

IL POGGIO IMPERIALE, S.S. ANNUNCIATA
(The Imperial Knoll of the Sainted Annunciation)

Hearing of this prestigious institution in Florence, the parents enrolled me for school year1947/1948, its students affectionately known as "Poggioline." Then known as the best school in Italy and renowned throughout Europe, its students were an interesting mix of girls from nobility to the plebian, the cost then still reasonable. I would be headed here in October age eleven through twelve.

Returned from that halcyon summer in England to Italy's sunny climes, presently with its Scirocco-driven winds, it was time to ready myself for the move to the Poggio, my fifth school in a gathering number I'd attend over the years, this one miles from Rome, while Flip became a border at Villa Pacis. Early October mother and I were on the way to Florence via the Rapido where she would commit me to my fate: incarceration behind those incarcerating walls of the Poggio Imperiale.

If nothing else, the Poggio was impressive in size, beauty and history. This grand ducal villa with obscure beginnings, came into the possession of the Medici family early in the 16th century, later home to the homicidal and unfaithful husband, one Paulo Orsini who murdered his wife Isabella de' Medici, hanging her in their bedroom, in order to marry his mistress. Maria Magdelena of Austria purchased the Villa in1618, she sister of the Holy roman Emperor, Ferdinand II, completely rebuilding and doubling the villa's size in 1622, and linking it to Florence by a long tree lined avenue, the "Viale Imperiale," The Imperial Way. In 1776 the Villa was again redesigned to become a summer home for Tuscany's ruling families, while later, it was given to Napoleon's sister, Elisa Bonaparte, the newly elevated

Grand Duchess of Tuscany, before being reclaimed by the hereditary rulers of Tuscany. In 1849 Florence became part of the *Risorgimento,* the reunification of Italy, with so many palaces Victor Enmmanuele II, the new King of Italy, had little use for the Poggio allowing it to fall into disrepair. In 1823, under the patronage of Leopold II and his wife Maria Anna of Saxony, this magnificent edifice became a school providing education for the daughters of Florentine nobility, a school ever since. More recently, a state-run school has been added, the Italian government granting both schools' use of the villa in perpetuity. It was unfortunate none of us, at least not during my two years, were told the history of this magnificent building. It would have been fascinatingly macabre to know, for instance, in which room Isabella de' Medici had met her end, and to learn of other misdeeds and machinations plotted within those very walls.

Into this historical and imposing edifice, Mother led me that October morn. "Oh God!" I dreading yet another agony of separation, as under the grand portico we ascended steps to the great portals of the Poggio. Mother rang the great bell, doors opened allowing us to walk up more steps to come face to face with a large ornate metal grill behind which sat the portiere (doorman). Necessary paperwork and luggage checked in previously, mummy and I stood around miserably in a small salon awaiting headmistress Signora Rosa Scopoli who soon arrived greeting mother, welcoming me. A few words and it was time to part, I barely able to kiss mummy without hanging on to her for dear life. But our family had never behaved that way and to ensure this was so, mum always dosed everyone with her homeopathic medicines kept for such occasions though they never seemed to help much. Older now, at least I realized what was happening, so different from our separation seven years before at age four, though I could not have been more miserable on hearing first, that metal grill door lock behind mummy—the school had its own form of portcullis—as I watched her descend the marble steps to the portals, which opened before her, she turning to wave a last time before the heavy portals closed solidly behind her. Running to a large window facing the outside world, I waved until she disappeared from sight, down the long

Viale Imperiale. Down now, came my own portcullis to stay down for those first few weeks as I began to weave my way through this newest of unknowns.

For some unknown reason, no classes were held until November so homesickness and boredom set in quickly, classmates and I spending endless days playing board games or outside under wintering gray skies as gray as my heart when writing anguished letters to Rome. Thinking about it now, these letters of mine must have been heart-rending for the parents, for if a tear fell while writing, I circled it saying "here's where a tear fell . . . Oh please, please come and take me home! I hate it here!" Poor, poor parents, yet they knew, once I settled, I would be getting the very best education.

Our classroom had immense windows from which I gazed for hours, the weather still autumnal (l'autunno), the Tuscan countryside, lovely to look at but I hardly noticed thinking myself in prison. Against cerulean skies, dark pencil-shaped cypress trees towered above huge-horned white oxen stolidly plowing their way, as they always had, up and down the gently sloping hills and though conjoined, were far freer than me, yoked inside. Resonating from small churches around the countryside, came the call of the Angelus, the peal of Florence's more distant campanile bells, often echoing in counterpoint with the smaller ones of the countryside.

Homesick or not, I found myself in this very cosmopolitan "institute" slowly adjusting, fellow students ranging in age from six to eighteen, the different classes generally kept apart. The following year when my sister joined me, I hardly ever saw her, she in a junior grade. We all looked the same dressed in uniforms, similar to "Madelines" of various heights, from our navy felt double capes, upturned wide-brimmed grey felt hats banded with navy streamers hanging down the back, elastic bands under our chin to anchor hats firmly to our heads. Grey pleated dresses with long sleeves either of heavy or light weight wool depending on time of year. Starched white pleated ruffs, shades of the ancient Elizabethan era, irritated our chins; our legs encased in grey knee socks and navy shoes in a style of one's choosing; so, with the beginnings of a shoe fetish, I chose the prettiest and most elegant I could find. Uniforms had slits on the skirt's right side, giving access to a pocket in a chemise underneath for handkerchief or treasure. Underwear, plain white cotton, though in winter months we wore grey woolen knickers over panties and long woolen socks, as well as fingerless mittens to ward off chilblains though we got them anyway with no fires or central heating in this vast building. Black pinafores were worn in class, again to keep ink splotches from uniforms. Aside from uniforms, all bedding was supplied from linen sheets to woolen blankets, all new and numbered by our personal number, "88" in my case. A special privilege, you had to earn this, allowed a student to line the inside of her desk and cover her text books with decorative Florentine paper.

A Catholic school, the establishment had but a small group of nuns who tended the chapel and infirmary. Staff was made up of teachers, church fathers for Christian history & catechism; servants, cooks, ground keepers, one of whom would create a scandal the next year by running off with a senior student; laundresses and seamstresses, to care for the volume of uniforms and linens, they slaving away below stairs where from inner courtyards, we could look down through gratings to see them daily toiling away, ironing everything from sheets to the tiny pleats of those horrible neck ruffs we had to wear, each stiff ruff, bleached, starched, pleated, and ironed "just-so," done with heavy old fashioned irons, heated on charcoal stoves.

As I settled into curriculum and routine, the powers that be, mainly head-mistress Rosa Scopoli and homeroom teacher Lea del'Amico, decided I should not have visitors until the second term in hopes I'd adjust more quickly to school life, internment was more like it! Although I had been allowed home for Christmas, it was well into the second term before I received a call to "The Parlors." When called, no mention was made of who the caller might be, so a lot of "by-guess and by-golly" went on with perhaps more than one lass hoping for "that special person" though visitors had been securely vetted by parents. So summoned, a "Poggiolina," was tempted to run down lengthy corridors to the Parlors but if caught doing so, sent back immediately to her classroom in disgrace. Most of us aware of the rule entered parlors with decorum. Six or so elaborately decorated rooms lead one into another with banquette seating, murals depicting rural scenes, cherubs floating above all. There was protocol to follow as one entered the Parlors, again no running through them until you found your visitor(s), rather, it was a slow dance in that a Poggiolina entered the first salon gracefully and if visitors were present but not hers, she still had to turn toward them, smile and execute the deepest of curtseys before rising slowly, only then allowed to proceed slowly to the next parlor. It could be slow-going especially if your visitor chose to await you in the furthest salon which was the one nearest the "portcullis." Visitor found, the Poggiolina still had dip into the curtsy routine but rose more hastily, to rush into a family embrace. It was a production whose time most students felt was unnecessary but taught manners and patience, self-control the order of the day! Mother loved to watch these performances from the furthest salon—she could be cruel—so she could watch the endless curtsying, the girls trying not to rush between rooms, their charming manners. My visitor that time was in fact mum, delighted to see me and my developing composure, as well she might!

Slowly I began to make friends: Renata Cosentino, from an important Sicilian family; Elena Panayotopulos from Greece; Tatia Volterra, of mixed Italian and Australian parentage, her father a famous pianist; and Dacia Maraini, whose father owned Salaparuta Vineyards in Sicily, she to become a writer and longtime amanuensis and lover of the famous Italian author Alberto Moravia. Our lives revolved around classroom activities, saints' days and educational outings. Once begun, classes included religion, Catholic of course and history; most of which seemed to be about the Romans and their endless Punic Wars, one hundred and eighteen years of them between 264 BC and 146 BC., then of Sparta and their remarkable women. There was geography, mostly Italian topography and of her conquests; reading, of course, and writing; also piano, dance, art, arithmetic, comportment, embroidery and the dreaded Latin over which I agonized translating *The Iliad* from Latin to Italian, later *The Odyssey*, both difficult chores. Proper conjugation of verbs had to be learned, and spelling, quickly learning Italian words were spelled exactly as pronounced, though there were exceptions. It helped too with the pronunciation of other languages, such as Japanese and Maori. I picked up the first from my missionary Aunt-in-law who spent eons in Japan as a missionary, and later when in New Zealand in 2002, such words Pukekohe were easy to pronounce.

Mother's "beanpole" daughter, for that is what she began to call me, had now shot up at twelve, to five feet nine inches though my brain seemed incapable of keeping up with my body. It was frustrating, a difficult time when I'd re-read paragraph after paragraph only to realize I had registered nothing. As the tallest in my class, I had to act as the male partner in dance class, not ballet but waltzes, polkas, minuets, above all, no unseemly sambas or rumbas for us! Some years later at high school proms, I tended quite unintentionally to lead my male partner to his: "You're leading again!" Another problem with my height was being the tallest girl, I was last in line, forever bringing up the rear as we marched single file throughout the Poggio the shortest leading. Therefore, it was always my duty to turn out the lights, the last to shut double doors of each salon one after another, as the class passed through, often to get way ahead of me down the long corridors. At night, it could be scary, these ancient rooms echoing with history, easy for one's imagination to get out of hand for, by the time I had done this seemingly easy task, I was almost in total darkness. As fast as I could, I at last reached the darkened staircase to race up the last steps to the safety of my dormitory bed.

Dormitories on the second floors, were large rooms with high ceilings, with cold marble floors, ornate frescos decorating the walls, grand windows overlooking the podere (farm) and gardens, (giardini), the hills beyond. Cubicles for personal belongings and one's bed, were contained behind pull-a-ble white curtains, each student responsible for making her bed and the changing linens weekly. Few mirrors allowed preening, though we could buy blue bottles of rose water from the school's shop to scent our pubescent bodies. In the inner hallways of these bedrooms, batteries of washbasins and toilet cubicles lined the walls. Opposite these were floor-to-ceiling windows overlooked inner courtyards. Each class had its assigned day for the weekly bath and after we had fetched our allotment of clean clothing from the Guardaroba (she who guards the clothes.) I liked the soft spoken accents of the Florentines with their soft "C's" instead of the harsher Roman ones: In stead of "O, Signorina, lei ha un bucco nelle calze," (Miss, you have a hole in your sock) the wardrobe mistress would say: "O signorina, lei ha un buho nelle halze." Fresh laundry picked up, we were escorted single file into the bowels of the Poggio, to immerse ourselves in individual gray marble baths surrounded by white drapery, were almost large enough to swim a few strokes. Hot towels awaited our exit to be, get this, rubbed down by a maid—it was wonderful. Hair was washed every two weeks, Italians believing natural oil in the hair is better than washing it out too often, yes, well . . .

In such a dorm, my first year, I awoke one spring morning to notice a small blister. "What's this?" I asked Matron who, almost before I could take in her words of "Avete la varicella!" found myself placed in the school's infirmary with chicken-pox, quarantined and medicated with others for some weeks. Fun, yes, well sort of, with special foods, no schoolwork, just games and the never-ending sighing of young girls over movie idols of the time: Clark Gable, whom I did not particularly care for—his ears, you know; the swash-buckler Errol Flynn whom I adored; Tyrone Power, not too shabby either though he and the rather fascinating William Holden were too short by my standards.

I was soon shipped home to recuperate for several weeks, something I did not mind at all for it was a mini vacation spent with Major Clive and Vera Robinson, he administrator for the British Council, both great family friends. With no children of their own, the Robinsons spoiled me rotten which suited me just fine, my days carefree, full of fun spent mostly at the beach, swimming, boating and picnicking while my sister, still at the Villa Pacis was green with envy. All very well, but by the time I returned to school, I had missed end of term exams. Nothing much was said at the time, and as summer was upon us, I did not worry about it thinking I'd manage somehow. Like Scarlett, I'd think about that tomorrow!

MONTE CIRCEO

The Parents felt no great need to return to England the summer of 1948 or indeed the next two. Instead, they chose to holiday in Monte Circeo, some sixty miles south of Rome on a promontory of the Mediterranean between Anzio and Terracina, there at a small seaside hotel. According to legend, this is where the enchantress Circe, after turning his men into swine, detained Odysseus for a year. The scenery justifies the claim of "Monte Circeo," being either a copy of Circe's face or her breasts, a topic much debated locally leaving those interested to wonder what Odysseus had thought during his year of captivity. For us, Monte Circeo was haven for six weeks, where the crystal almost non-tidal clear Tyrrhenian's aquamarine waters, from glassy green to deepest navy, reflected the sky's brilliant blueness.

We were not alone at "Capo Circeo" or "Cape of Circeo Hotel, which today is far grander. Now, as then, it is surrounded by Mediterranean scrubby trees, the usual pine, olive or fruit varieties, on a superb waterfront with private beach and views of the Pontine Islands: Palmarola, Ponza, Santo Stefano, Ventotene and Zannone though we never visited them. There were only two other sets of visitors during our stay; that is, until John and Emmie Tillett of Ibbs & Tillett, famous concert agents in London longtime friends and daddy's agents arrived as did the Robinsons. Other hotel guests were a pair of lovers; she a stunning lass from Australia; he, a handsomely rich Italian driving a red Alfa Romeo convertible. The other couple was a young family with adorable child with dark hair, the bluest of eyes. The father, obviously a trained diver, perhaps even an Olympiad, mid mornings would dive off the high "groin" into the blue waters below, twisting at right angles in mid-air as he did so land in a perfect shallow dive into a sea pool far below. Afternoons, at this couples request, I'd often play with their daughter. Once, after perching her on a low limb of an olive tree, she exclaimed: "Ci sta come gl'uccelini!" (I am like a little bird!) Indeed she was. As for the love-birds, one afternoon, they shared their exuberance of life insisting I join them on one of their sightseeing jaunts, all wonderful fun and made me think I wanted to grow up more quickly, that elusive need of mine to be loved.

Early each morning, Daddy and I stepped out onto a rock ledge and dove into silky blueness below, to swim to an outcropping of rocks where we were careful not to touch the long spiny dark brown sea urchins clinging there. Though good to eat, they were painful to touch, sometimes deadly.

Days were leisurely, mornings swimming and sunning, until one day we all sat up with a shock, a real surprise to see mother emerge from a palm-covered cabana in, heaven forfend, a blue and white polka dot bikini! Until then, she had hidden her body in a 1930's blue and orange triple piece woolen swim suit: I think, momentarily, we were all shocked to see so much more of her slender beauty at forty-six, she and daddy seeming to enjoy a new sense of freedom after the dullness and separation of war which mother had said, made her listless and uninteresting, yet here in Italy she blossomed. I also suspect that the ever-loving Latinos noticed her unique beauty. Certainly, the longer we were in Italy, the happier she seemed.

Late morning at Monte Circeo, the catch hauled in and sold, fishermen sat to repair nets and re-affix green-glass globes for flotation. I often sat with them on rocks rimed with salt, they teaching me to scale and de-gut fish for the the hotel. Meals at Circeo were simple and delicious; what could be better than the catch of the day provided by these locals? Have you ever heard of Fisherman's risotto? Fruit of the sea freshly caught and immediately served with simplicity could not have been better, served "al fresco" under a pergola overlooking the sea; large platters of smelts so tiny no cleaning necessary, dipped in batter and deep fried, to be served up with a smattering of garlic, salt, pepper, parsley, parmesan and lemon juice. So, so delicious! This followed by a pasta, salad, cheese and fruit accompanied by local white wines, after which, siestas were the order of the day.

I do not remember a gray day the whole time as we swam, basked, or hiked in the afternoon, the adults imbibing cocktails later, while we had our usual Orzata, and again in leisure, ate natures delicious fish, fruit and vegetables simply prepared towards sunset, as stars began to appear, daddy always able to point out which star was ascendant on any given evening.

While we enjoyed the summer, the Italian political scene was in chaos, what else has ever been new? The 1948 elections, the second ever that were democratic, had been held in April yet heavily influenced by the Cold War, and as it was feared Italy might be drawn into the Soviet's influence, the CIA stepped in to fund the election, then won by the Popular Democratic Front which, able to form the government, excluded the communists in power from June of 1944 until May 1947, the majority led by De Gasperi, the minority by Togliatti. The long finger of the CIA always seems to be meddling in some other country's affair to the undercover benefit of the USA. Perhaps I am naïve but I find this shocking.

Everything was perfect at Monte Circeo, until, horror of horrors, I was summoned to the Poggio for exams missed earlier in the year. For me, the summer was over. Leaving others to bask, daddy drove me to Rome to put me on the "rapido" to travel to Florence alone. There and somewhere between the station and crossing the Arno, a pickpocket in the crowd stole my purse carried under my left arm, fortunately my wallet was in my pocket, with such ease I was not even aware of it until time later when tramping up the Viale Imperiale. Striding up to the portico of the once dreaded Poggio, I found to my surprise, I was glad to be back even though my holiday had been cut short. For the next week as all studied and reviewed before exams on those last hot days of August.

As I studied at my desk one afternoon, sensing some disturbance, I looked up to find the rest of the room on its feet, many girls craning their necks trying to peer over the heads of others. I jumped up to find myself looking straight at, with eyes nearly popping out of my head, my idol, the very handsome Tyrone Power. Not five feet away and shockingly not much taller, "God!" I thought, "For such a 'romantic' on screen, he is rather puny." I discovered later Mr. Power overcame his shortness with an overabundance of ego, had many lovers for what beauty does not draw them; four marriages, a number of children, the last born after his death. Somehow I managed to curtsey without swooning, but, the question remained: what was he doing here? In 1949, he was still married to Linda Christian who, lovely herself, was standing with him. Apparently, they were checking out the school in hopes of pre-enrolling any daughter they might have in the near future. Romina was in fact born in 1951, after the couple had lost three babies and, while Romina was educated in Italy, I don't know if she attended The Poggio. The excitement of having a Hollywood presence in our midst that afternoon was slow to die, though my adoration of Tyrone Power had diminished in direct proportion to his size.

The dreaded examination day arrived, students gathering in a vast ornate salon with proctor who bade us sit and await individual summons when called for. Double doors led into the dreaded inner sanctum, an intimidating room where, behind a long ornate table covered with papers, sat the "judiciary" there to pronounce "pass", or "fail" upon us. This was to be an oral exam. As each Poggiolina was called, the rest whispered: "In bocca al'lupo!" (Into the mouth of the wolf!), to the immediate required reply from the so-called victim: "Crepi il Lupo!" (May the wolf die!) She then made her way, heart in mouth, to the examining room in hopes her brains had not become totally frazzled in the meantime. Our adjudicators were a stiff panel offering no smiles, no encouragement, and no sympathy; correct and rapid fire response from students was all that was required. Somehow, somehow, I managed to pass.

DISTURBING EVENTS AT THE POGGIO

By now I felt I was a true Poggiolina, and for this my second year, (1948/49), my sister joined me. I seldom saw her as my classroom was now on the western side of the villa. It was one of the better decorated ones always with white-painted woodwork outlined in gold, and frescos adorned with beautiful lolling personages who seemed to float upward to join the inevitable cherubs lolling about on puffy white clouds. French doors opened to magnificent gardens aglow and perfumed by highly scented roses and lemon verbena. There were fruit trees; my favorite the orange-ripening Kaki (Persimmon). To the south, a large gymnasium, while to the northwest, a small wooded grove spread cool shade amid the aroma of laurel.

Throughout these semesters, I was assigned a private tutor two afternoons a week to help me with Latin. She was a charming older lady more fascinated by gory stories than languages, for each time we met, she told me another story, in ever more vivid detail. I believed these to be true, that is until I took English literature in high school and discovered they had been written by Edgar Allen Poe's *Tales of the Rue Morgue*. I recall no stabs at Latin. Once she asked me how I saw my future and discovered just how frivolous a young girl can be. I wanted to marry an old man, I said, wear long black decollete dresses, drip with pearls, and have lots of lovers! Having said it, I wondered where that came from. Perhaps from one of the movies we were shown weekly? One of these desires did come true, which one, well that's for me to know. Meanwhile this school girl and another Poggiolina, Anna Maria Sargenti, vied to be the best in our class at timed foot races during gym class. Both of us, with long strong legs, either tied or bested each other alternately. So much for decollete dresses and dripping pearls!

Then, without warning, Philippa came down with Scarlatina, (Scarlet Fever) a streptococcus infection of the throat with high fever and rash spread by cough, which in some cases leads to kidney or heart problems. Flip was sent home, I was quarantined; a pretty dull existence on my own for two weeks, though I had no symptoms, nor did I get any. Quarantine lifted, I rejoined classmates while Flip was tended in Rome by Dottore Gagliardi for months, who, I believe, spared her from having all after effects by ordering a strict diet of bland rice and bananas and homeopathic medicine. It took some months, but Flip fully recovered to every one's great relief.

Because of our parents' professions, my friend Tatia and I often joined older girls at concerts, special performances, movies, art exhibits or plays, the latter often enacted in the famous Pitti Palace Boboli Gardens. We also rode to Prato to hear the then-eminent pianist Cortot play Chopin. One particular evening, we went to the Boboli with its artificial lake and island (L'Isolotto), to see a performance of Shakespeare's *Tempest*. The evening was magical with stars and moon shining upon us as we sat on risers on the western side of the lake. When the magician Prospero conjured up the tempest and Ariel danced, the island and nearby shore transformed itself into a towering shower of iridescent water spraying into the night air. Magical it may have been but to my mind, contained far too much emoting about the value of freedom, friendship, repentance, and forgiveness before the cast brought the long evening to a close. Tatia and I now began to make our weary way back to our bus over ancient cobble-stoned streets in almost total darkness, when I stumbled and fell. Instantly another person tripped to sprawl on top of me, followed by another. Managing to extricate myself from the heap, I apologized, dusted myself off, walked away with bloodied knees only to hear: "Eh! Queste Poggioline non sanno comme si puo comportarsi, mancano l'educazione!" "Eh! These Poggioline do not know how to behave. They lack manners!" Well, thank you very much!

Two more upsetting events occurred that semester: One evening as we attended a performance of Gluck's opera *Orfeo ed Oridice*. I was lucky to be seated in the front row of the balcony and could see the audience below gather for what should have been a pleasant evening. It would be anything but that. As the crowd made its way to seats in the front of the house, a handsome couple appeared, stopping often to chat with "I cognoscenti," before making their way down the aisle. They were beautiful. He was tall, red haired, and in full evening dress; she was slim, golden haired, divinely elegant in an off-the-shoulder brown moiré gown, and had the palest of pink camellias pinned to her dress. There was something so, so, familiar about them. But, of course! It was The Parents! It couldn't be, could it? Yes! Yes, it was! Without thinking, I leant over the balustrade waving: "Yoo-hoo! Mummy! Daddy! Up here! It's me! Julia! Up here!" They did not hear. It only took seconds for matron to grab my arm and lead me, struggling, to a seat in the rear of the balcony, there to sit and ponder the error of my ways. Shouting in public, much less in an opera house, was a definite no-no for a Poggiolina, never mind that adult Italians did so all the time, with their rude whistles, their "Bis'es", their cat-calls, and their "Bastas", "Bravos" and "Encores".

Ponder my manners I did not. Instead, questions flooded. What were the parents doing in Florence? Why hadn't they told me they were coming? Why hadn't they called, or come to the Poggio to take me out? Why, why, why? Had they only planned to visit the city and not me? When would I see them again? On and on went the torment throughout this agony of an opera. The only saving grace was that I might, just might, see them in the interval or, exiting the lobby following the performance, have all questions answered. As further punishment, no such meeting was allowed to take place; I was whisked away before the audience began to file out. This school with its often absurd rules and routines, many cruel and traumatizing, in fact taught us all to rebound from adversity with resilience, prodded by a "get over it" attitude or, in my case, to bring that everlasting "stiff upper lip" into play. I would survive and thrive. Of course I had the use of my old portcullis, which could be slammed down across the fortress of my emotions at any old time. Though hiding no less an ache, it was at least a "protective."

I was still upset the next day when I was called to the "Parlors." A visitor! I tore through the salons, another definite no-no, I didn't care though while still stopping to perform those endless curtsies, before I ran smack into the parents. "Get your cape!" they said "We're taking you out for the weekend!" I could not have been happier for those few hours of freedom and during lunch told them what had happened. They, of course, had already been informed of my "outrageous behavior" by Signora Scopoli. Upset over this unnecessary incident, partially their fault, from then on, they always let me know; well I think they did, when they would be in Florence.

While religious study for foreign students was not compulsory, we still had to attend services. Tatia and I, Episcopalians, found chapel pretty dull; with its endless Latin prayers, intoning, bell-ringing, wafting of incense. Tatia sat in the pew in front of me with her prized Bible. She perused it during services, occasionally passing it back to me, whispering: "I've just come across an interesting passage: Read this!" One such was "The Song of Solomon," my pre-teen mind agog that men and women thought about each other in this poetic way. Wow!

Student confessions were held on Friday afternoons, and, inquisitive as ever, I decided to find out what this was about and presented myself at one "confessional," kneeling before a wooden grill behind which I could just discern an elderly priest. I told him of my background; my interest. A lecture and a half later, I was dismissed, instructed to kneel at the altar, intone ten Hail Marys, and five Paternosters for the childish sins I had supposedly committed during the previous week, though I had admitted none, and so, pardoned, free to commit them all over again. What a comforting benefice!

To my mind, my piano teacher was an elderly, very religious woman who, while despairing for my Episcopalian soul, despaired even more over my piano-playing, the endless repetition and tedium of it all! In despair, she taught me to play arpeggios in every conceivable key, which I learned quickly to play in impressive style, or so I thought, fingers rippling up and down the keyboard with abandon. One day this devout teacher decided to take some students into chapel, I among them, thinking she hoped a few prayers might inspire us to perform better. I was wrong. No," she said. "We're here for spiritual communion. I want you to think of God, of Jesus, to pray to the Holy Spirit as though your very soul depends upon it. Then be still and listen!" In dead silence our group at this impressionable age, prayed as never before, then waited. Ah, the power of suggestion! Almost as one, we were enveloped with an overwhelming feeling. Of what? Heavenly grace, crossing a spiritual divide? One highly strung student fainted, others cried, the rest of us sat stunned in what can only be described as a feeling of "grace." Powerful in sensation, the intensity was overwhelming, enthralling, awesome, frightening, and almost orgiastic. When I managed to rise from my knees, I vowed never to repeat this type of religious fervency; nor have I.

During the school year some older students and I were, privileged to be taken to a meeting given by George C. Marshall, promoting the European Recovery Program, his Marshall Plan to help rebuild European cities destroyed during the war. The main focus of the so-called Marshall plan was to reduce hunger, homelessness, sickness, unemployment and political unrest, and to strengthen economic superstructures, e.g., iron-steel and power industries. It would be implemented for a maximum of four years; loans to be repaid. Many felt the plan was nothing more than American imperialism, an attempt to gain control of Western Europe as the Soviets had done in the East. Such critics rejected the whole idea as an effort by the United States to form a bulwark against communism. It was a long meeting at my age, boring in the extreme, but I can say, "I was there!"

With Dacia Maraini after performance of *Der Rosenkavalier*

ELBA
AND
EXIT TOMASINA

My last year at the Poggio was over, final exams passed, (Latin barely), this time with no Hollywood stars in the wings. Before leaving, older students were brought up to date on the news of India's independence, which had occurred in 1947 and had been brought about by leaders of the Indian Independence Movement, Mahatma Gandhi and Jawaharlal Nehru. Nehru became India's first prime minister. The first British outpost in India had been established in 1619, by the somewhat notorious East India Company, a monopoly of trade in the region. In 1857, following the Indian rebellion, power was transferred from that company to the British Crown, and India flourished. By 1945, however, anti-colonial movements were on the rise partout, the "wind of change" numbering British Empire days, while she, sensibly, adopted a policy of peaceful disengagement. Before pulling out altogether however, Britain partitioned India into two independent democratic nations: India and Pakistan. Since then, violence has increased between the Pakistani, Hindu and Afghanistani, that is still escalating to this day. Over the centuries, what the British have wrought!

For us Poggioline parting for the summer and fully expecting to return, would be either sad or a relief. Before we said our goodbyes, the entire student body participated in, I believe, *Der Rosenkavalier*, the comic opera in three acts by Richard Strauss, complete with imported soloists, and performed in the Poggio's Grand Salone for the public. My friend Dacia (Maraini) and I were partners dressed as peasants. I can only speak for females, but crushes often occur in single sex schools, be they male or female, forced into close proximity year after year.

At the turn of the nineteenth century in England it was acceptable for a girl with longings for an other, to leave a bunch of violets or a book in the room of her idol. It was said Eleanor Roosevelt had been a recipient of such "adoration" during her three years at Allenswood, a school near London run by Marie Souvestre, a lesbian feminist of bold conviction. Eleanor herself developed a crush on one "Jane." The Victorian era shows evidence of intense emotions between girls who often slept together, kissed, and hugged, practices that did not prevent them from becoming wives and mothers. This attitude was the same in Italy then I was there, it taken for granted that females of any nationality, could share intense emotions more freely than those expressed by or with men. A bond between two women, not sexual but intimate, is best described in *The Bostonians*, Henry James's novel of 1886 which dealt with what was called a "Boston Marriage."

These bonds happened to many at the Poggio, and, while crushes occurred, they were seen as harmless, easing as the girls aged to find the opposite sex of more interest, such as the seventeen and eighteen year-old's attraction to the school's handsome young gardener, or to the young men girls were now being introduced to in society. As for me, I was attracted not only to Dacia, but the witty and spirited Australian, Tatia, who, at my insistence, the parents invited to spend part of the summer with us on Elba. Over the long lazy summer days, Dacia and I kept up a loving correspondence, the intensity of school passions ending for me as the summer waned, as I was beginning to realize I had more interest in the opposite sex.

Tatia's mother drove us in her Alfa Romeo down Tuscany's coast to Piombino where daddy met us: he, mummy and Flip, now fully recovered from scarlet fever, already there. From Piombino, an old and dilapidated ferry chugged us into Porto Ferraio, (Iron Port,) so named for the red ferrous soil covering much of the island. Disembarking, we clambered aboard a row boat with our luggage as daddy showing off prowess with oars, propelled us in this antique wooden ark to the villa across the bay the parents had rented for the summer for little money. The villa, named Schiacia Pensieri (Scatter Unhappy Thoughts) was quaint and made up for lack of modernity with superb scenery overlooking and surrounded by sparkling sea. Mummy and Flip greeted us, as did an overweight cook named Tomasina, a red hibiscus bloom daily stuck behind her left ear in contrast to her jet-black hair; also, the plainer yet far more intelligent, attractive and interesting Elena, a temporary maid earning money for passage to Canada, where she was to marry her betrothed.

Elba is the largest island of the Tuscan Archipelago, sitting opposite, more or less, Corsica and Sardinia. In 1949 Elba had been made out of bounds by Mussolini for years, and without tourists, had remained pristine and a wonderful place to spend peaceful summers. Elba, as well known, is the basis for the English palindrome "Able was I ere I saw Elba," and is the island from which Napoleon escaped exile in 1815, to return to France and his eventual defeat at Waterloo, Belgium. On one of our treks around the island we did visit Napoleone's onetime abode but found it dilapidated, and over-grown with weeds and struggling eucalypti. Now the Island is spiffed up for tourists, its wines are highly regarded, and the population of Porto Ferraio is just over 12,000; soaring to three times that in summer.

The weather was perfect throughout our three month stay. We awakened to brilliant dawns, stroked by warm sun, dazzled by sunsets as stars and moon began to illuminate outdoor dinners. We took all meals from breakfast to dinner, al-fresco on a pine-shaded terrazzo overlooking the bay. For once, there were no snorts from daddy about "bugs and beetles." Gentle breezes would be wafting, night skies radiating, stars sparkling, all reflected on the gently ebb and flow of the inky-looking Tyrrhenian. The path to the beach led down a steep, rocky and sandy path strewn with vines, tangled brush, the occasional cactus and rock rose, to a small sandy beach where swimming was wonderful any time of day, and was particularly beautiful in moonlight.

Not bothering to drive the circuitous route around the bay to Porto Ferraio every morning daddy chose to row across it to fetch fresh milk, newspapers, and, more importantly, the mail. At first, at his request, I swam beside him; he, hoping I would become as good a swimmer as his own father who had been a member of Burton-on-Trent's Amateur Swimming Club, helping them to win the medal for England in water polo in 1889. Daddy tried hard to teach me, tempting me with a gold watch, if I would swim, swim, and swim every morning between the villa and the port, a round trip a distance of three miles. Thus did my father hope to train me to Olympian standard, but it was not to be, for I did not possess the necessary drive. I gave up long before summer ended, the gold watch not worth the effort, in my opinion.

We hiked and climbed most afternoons, up various elevations or smallish mountains on the island some, ruined fortifications. "Why," daddy demanded, as we girls slithered and tripped about, "don't any of you have proper walking shoes?" Of course, nobody had thought to bring anything more than sandals or espadrilles and, whose fault was that? One afternoon a photo was taken of Tatia and daddy as he tried to escort her down a particularly treacherous castellated incline, she leaning heavily on his arm lest she slip. In the photo, you can almost see daddy vibrating with annoyance at this female holdup to his usually energetic walks. Mother was not much of a climber either, nor were Flip and I though occasionally we "fell-into-step." It would take the likes of the Scottish cellist Joan Dickson (1921-1994) to accompany daddy very happily on his ramblings across the island. At the time Joan was 28, studying in Rome, eventually becoming a beloved teacher, renowned for her interpretation and recording of Elgar's cello concerto. Daddy had invited her to spend a couple of weeks and most days the two went off on their peregrinations, determined to climb every damned mountain on the island. Joan recalled in 1991:

> [there were] long walks up the very hilly terrain covered with rock-roses, fascinating conversations with Keith as we toiled up some of the very steep hills, clambering over rocks, climbing Monte Capanne. Somewhere on

the way I remember saying to Keith "You would make a wonderful director of the Royal College of Music!" I can picture that spot still. No one was more thrilled than I when his appointment as Director was finally announced some ten years later.

Meanwhile, Tatia, Flip, and I celebrated our freedom from these treacherous treks by going to Porto Ferraio's local market, loving those days for they were always boisterously loud, full of color, always supplying us with some pretty trinket or delicious pastry. Early afternoons, we might enter the dilapidated cinema, where, for a lira or two, you could watch, along with a sold-out crowd of screaming kids, *Tarzan and the Apes*, in Italian of course. That is where Flip and I were one afternoon, Tatia having returned home by then, as we "swinging through the jungle tendrils," felt the shudder, creaking, groaning, the building beginning to sway. "Terremoto! Il Terremoto!" screeched children hurling themselves from seats, climbing overflowing balcony railings through the push-and-shove down the wobbling staircase, to burst out into the relative safety of the piazza. Surprisingly, it was over almost before it had begun. In the same building a week or so later, I saw Alan Ladd in *Shane*, again in Italian, impressed until I learned he was barely five feet four inches tall, wore inserts in his shoes or, with taller actresses, stood on a band-box and so, no longer worthy of my attention!

Each night before sleep out on our balcony, Tatia and I would tie strings around each other's big toes. The first to wake, was to yank on it for a midnight raid. Tiptoeing in the semi darkness, it was never very dark with the moon peering through open windows and balconies, traipsing down to the kitchen often running into the parents on their own quest for a vino or two. One night, after one of these forays into the larder, Tatia and I decided to, shall we say put that mutual teenage crush to the test? Within seconds we, reduced to laughter, fell off the bed, tears rolling down our cheeks at the absurdity. It was of course, a time of growing, experimentation and learning, yet with a mother like mine, brought up in Victorian and Edwardian eras, (though there seemed to have been no restraint on Edward the VIII), she only occasionally made reference to "the birds and the bees," as she called the subject. So, I was left with little information, and much to learn. Mother undoubtedly thought there was still plenty of time for "all that," though I was past my thirteenth birthday, technically a woman. Having picked up quite a lot of "nonsense" along the way from equally ignorant classmates, I was learning!

As all summers do, this one waned, and had been one of the best of the four years we spent in Italy. We toured the entire island a last time, picnicking and swimming in secluded coves amid rocks and pines; driving to Porto Azzuro (Azure Port) with its brilliant aquamarine waters, its rugged cliffs, its stony beaches, and, further inland, olive groves and vineyards. In the distance, thank goodness, was Monte Capanne, all 3,340 feet of it, which Daddy and Joan had conquered. Too soon, it was time to pack, make the 120 mile drive after the ferry back to Piombino on the mainland, back to Rome, the whole trip truly operatic.

Dear Elena had already departed for Canada; the less dear Tomasina was another matter, her enriched summer diet having increased her girth proportionately. Daddy felt duty-bound to drive her back to Rome where mother, unfortunately, had hired her. So, when it came time to leave Elba, there was much pushing, heaving and shoving to somehow get all of us plus dog, piled into the Fiat, loaded and reloaded to daddy's increased exasperation. At last, taking a farewell look, depositing keys, we took off for Porto Ferraio, to catch the ferry back to Piombino.

Today's fancy ferries would come later: for us the ferry was just a battered leaky old tub plying back and forth as occasion demanded, hauling goods for the island, and at most, a car or two. Now the fun began. Two wooden planks, thrown higgledy-piggledy across the divide from shore to tub, were used to transfer goods and cars to the ferry, without, it was hoped, slippage of planks caused by sea movement. For safety reasons, with the exception of Tomasina who would not budge for any reason, no cajoling inveigling her to do so, we all got out of the car. She sat as we watched a bunch of gobs stand about shouting advice, whistling, gesticulating, trying to orchestrate and conduct our overloaded car over planks from the wharf at Porto Ferraio, up the incline and onto the bark. Of course, on the other side, at Piombino, the whole process would have to be reversed, the possibility of catastrophe ever present.

We made it to the mainland, when daddy, not trusting these over excitable tars, decided to drive his car across and down the planking to solid land. Immediately, it was evident from his somewhat erratic aim, his intense concentration and consternation, that he had no idea where his true aim should be during this risky "disembarking" business. With the up-tilted nose of the car, he was unable to see beyond the sky, before the car's descent to shore, and found it impossible to observe slippage as the craft bobbed up and down. Daddy being daddy, similar to Farragut, the Civil War commander, with his "Damn the torpedoes! Full speed ahead!" took a chance, and drove off. Meanwhile, fat Tomasina, still with red hibiscus, moaned, groaned, and crossed herself repeatedly in fervent prayer, as well she might, for she could have gone down with the ship, or, in this case the car.

By now daddy was quite used to Italian traffic. John Steinbeck, in his article for *Harper's Bazaar,* May, 1953, gave a wonderful description of what it was like to drive in Italy:

> ". . . Italian traffic is at first just down-right nonsense. It seems hysterical, it follows no rule. You cannot figure what the driver ahead or behind or beside you is going to do next and he usually does it. But there are other hazards . . . there are motor scooters, thousands of them, which buzz at you like mosquitoes. There is a tiny little automobile called 'Topolino' or 'Mouse' which hides in front of larger cars; there are gigantic trucks and tanks in which most of Italy's goods are moved; and finally there are assorted livestock, hay wagons, bicycles, lone horses and mules out for a stroll, and to top it all there

are pedestrians who walk blissfully on the highways never looking about. To give this madness more color, everyone blows the horn all the time. This deafening, screaming, milling, tire-screeching mess is ordinary Italian high- way traffic."

Of course, we too had initially been alarmed by Italian traffic and for our first trip out of the City, daddy you will recall, had hired Nardone to drive us to Lago Albano; Nardone who had behaved very much like the driver Steinbeck hired to drive him to Positano, one Signor Bassano:

"Signor Bassano was a remarkable man, he was capable of driving at a hundred kilometers an hour, blowing the horn, screeching the brakes, driving mules up trees, and at the same time turning around in the seat and using both hands to gesture, describing in loud tones, the beauties and antiquities of Italy . . ."

On this day and well acquainted with the hazards of driving, we made it to Rome without incident, until we arrived in the general vicinity of Tomasina's home near Piazza del Popolo. Daddy, pulling up to the curb, thanked the previously compensated Tomasina for her services during the past few months, telling her services were no longer required. "Arrivederci! Goodbye!" said daddy. There was no movement from the back seat. Again he asked Tomasina politely to get out of the car, yet she remained immobile, determined to remain where she was. Flip and I, embarrassed, cringed in the back seat, mummy saying nothing. Daddy with annoyance, shouted: "Get Out! Out at once!" "No! Non lo faccio! (No! No I won't!) shouted Tomasina. "Very well," said daddy opening his door and stepping out: "I'm going to get that 'carabiniere (policeman) over there to come help you." "Ah! No! No! Per carita! No! O Madre di Dio!" (No! No! Have Mercy! No! Oh Mother of God!") With that, she heaved her carcass up, squeezed out the back door, grabbed her cardboard suitcase and fled on foot despite her added kilos, to disappear around a corner with flesh, red hibiscus and suitcase a-flounce, thankfully never to be seen again. The opera buffa over, Tomasina was soon replaced by the gentle and motherly Angelina from Sardinia.

Too much sunshine!

THE SACRED HEART
By way of: I Bagni di Tivoli

We were headed now for our new school, the Sacred Heart, mere blocks from our apartment; again boarders, this to be our last school in Italy. Before summer was over, however, we often drove the twenty odd miles to the Tivoli Baths (Bagni di Tivoli) northwest of Rome, built by architect-emperor Hadrian near his villa Adriana in the second century AD. These whose waters continue to seep from sulphur springs, which, now as then, despite the awful rotten-egg stink, are said to be good for lungs and skin, as noses quickly adjust to odiferous vapors. There are numerous pools; even one for pets in our day. Jumping or diving into the warm opalescent water is like swimming in tepid skimmed milk, and when one is underwater, only the shadowy figures of other swimmers are visible. Getting out, rinsing off and toweling down, leaves one's skin in silky voluptuousness. Upon leaving, one is handed a small glass of this supposedly efficacious liquid to "cleanse the system." The Bagni now come with expensive spa treatments that are popular with today's jet-setters.

Rationing was still in effect in Britain as she, recovering from the war, was very much in penny-pinching mode. Cutbacks on her overseas councils, with the Arts as usual, the first to suffer, probably put daddy out of his job, despite his huge success in Italy. Though Flip and I had no notice of this, the handwriting on the wall, and the parents began to look to a future outside Italy. In the meantime, we were enrolled in the Sacred Heart in Rome, a reasonable cost-cutting venture, the Poggio now too costly.

So, here we were on a late September rainy morning entering through the heavy portals of Il Sacro Cuore, disgorging us into a black and white tiled marble lobby teeming with students. Then, a nice surprise, for there was my old Sicilian school chum from the Poggio, Renata Cosentino, her parents, too, probably having felt a financial pinch. It was so good to see a familiar face. The Sacred Heart, a nunnery strictly run with rules and regulations long established, was emphatically enforced by the then very rigid Mother Superior Immaculata, to be read about shortly.

The grounds of the convent were large and quite beautiful with many pines stretching umbrella-like overhead. Surprisingly, I enjoyed the year, though my studies as usual, were only fair. On still warmish autumn evenings, fireflies blinked and danced on soft zephyrs as we boarders played on seesaws and swings, daring each other ever higher, to, on the downward swing, tilt our heads backward, getting that almost exquisite jolt of quaking agony as our insides readjusted, realigning to gravity. Views from the gardens overlooked most of Rome; including the Vatican, the Stato della Citta del Vaticano (State of the Vatican City), that walled enclave of 110 acres, the smallest independent state in the world.

In the process of adding a new wing, the school had few boarders that year. Renata, Flip and I were three of about a dozen. The youngest was Katia, an exceptionally beautiful child, a three-year-old, who, missing her mama, often cried in the night, her parents like ours, public figures so I could understand her loneliness. As the eldest boarder with no nuns about to sooth the child, I often went to her cot when she cried. I'd pick up this little darling, set her on my knee, hold and rock her small warmly plump body: she comforting me as much as I did her. With her head on my shoulder, I made up fabulous tales to entice her back to sleep; then I tucked her safely back into bed and returned to my own.

MADRE IMMACULATA

Madre Immacolata was one mean Mother Superior! Her name alone reflects pristine purity, saintliness, and cleanliness of soul. On reflection, I remember her as petite, not a likeable woman but as Napoleonic, rigid, self-important and paranoid, with any number of chips on her small shoulders. I can see her now bustling about in her black robes, waist girded by well-burnished black beads, silver crucifix swinging from side to side as she hustled and bustled throughout the convent. Her black-and-white cowl and veil billowed behind her as she tore up and down corridors, in and out of classrooms, in and out of meetings, in and out of chapel, in and out of everything. Was her problem female frustration? Was it that the Italians had "disgracefully" lost the war; that her compatriots had, if not drawn and quartered "Il Duce" in 1945, assassinated him, this great friend of Pope Pius XII both of whom Mother Superior had so greatly admired? What else bothered her besides having it in for me, a non-CatholicAnglo, a burgeoning yet vulnerable teenager?

Far too often, late at night, rhapsodic piano music would drift from open windows across the street, over balconies, cross the avenue and, over convent walls to waft through open windows. The music was inescapable, luring me from bed to stand by my window, mesmerized, entranced with longing. How could this music have not tormented the young novitiate girls about to give up so much of life to become wives of Christ? Did they ever think twice about their choice? For myself, listening at those moments, I wished I could have been anywhere but in a convent, wondering who the brilliant pianist was, Rome at the time, full of flourishing artists from overseas.

In chapel, innumerable masses were held, even I getting to ring the tinkly bells during the Elevation of the Host. Otherwise, there were lessons, quiet contemplative studies, retreats, obligatory readings concerning the lives of Jesuits and often the unenviable lives of so-called saints. Even though I was now laboring in Terza Media with Latin III, the year passed quickly. In another year I would have to struggle with ancient Greek, which, I heard, was difficult in the extreme. There were other courses, too; my favorites always being art and music. I liked French but mathematics was an enigma. In art class another girl, Fiamma (Flame) and I, good at drawing, vied for best marks. It was the first time we saw and used ballpoints rather than fountain pens. Daddy, a calligraphy aficionado, was appalled at this outrage. All this went on while the bane of my existence was Mother Superior!

No sooner had my sister and I entered school and applied ourselves to our studies, Mother Superior, whom I shall herein refer to as MS, was hovering over me. There was always this or that she did not like about my attitude: I was not dutiful or submissive enough, did not apply myself enough, and did not sew a fine enough seam. Mother Immaculata despaired of my growth, singing inappropriate songs according to her standards, taught by my singer father. I ask you, what is wrong with Somervells's *Birds in the High Hall Garden*? Perhaps it was the minor key which disturbed her? My biggest failing was not being a Catholic. Too, I day-dreamed too much. How could I not have, at this impressionable age especially at night when that luscious romantic music poured out across the street? Because of all my failings, Mother Superior set out to save me and my soul; not so much for my sake, I think, as much as hers. For everyone "saved" from perdition in her faith, assured her of swifter ascension to heaven: "Nearer my God to Thee" and all that! So, the stage was set for a heavy bombardment of religious indoctrination and instruction. Heaven help me!

First, there were talks, consultations in her office: what did I think, feel or desire? Did I care whether I faced damnation in hell or a state higher up; that of purgatory or, better yet, sinless in heaven? All these queries began to wear on me. Never particularly religious, our family seldom attended services; though Daddy had been a chorister at New College in Oxford before his voice broke at thirteen, and was presently playing the organ for the Episcopal Church in Rome. In later years we only attend services for the wonderful music in British cathedrals, music that was often sung and played by graduates of the Royal College of Music.

Every other day or so I had an appointment with MS to discuss the latest book she had insisted I read. Be it of saint or Jesuit, I was expected to remember details of their blessed and saintly lives, what had brought about their "grace," when drawn to God and Jesus. Then there were the inevitable questions: Did I not feel a pull toward Him? Did I not feel a need for his blessed love, He my savior? And, had I prayed to His mother Mary for guidance, just as MS was praying for me? On and on it went, week after week; with, throughout the year, three-day retreats held with limited sustenance, endless hours of supposed "soulful" meditation, no conversation allowed unless you were in deep discussion with one of several priests. I noticed I was given special attention by these holy fathers, at MS's instigation, no doubt. Well, even though I was a lost cause, and while others sat in silence, I could at least talk with them! This "persistence" bore into my mind, my heart, my soul, so that my dreams became religious in tone. Then, finally, one such freed me forever from this "persecution," so that I could say loud and clear to MS, "BASTA!"

The dream had been too pastel, too innocently pure. I seemed to be standing on a gently sloping hillside, my feet resting on green grasses with carpets of English daisies. Lambkins were munching, and they frolicked as my eye wandered up the hillside. A few trees swayed there, leaves gently wafting on a light breeze against an azure sky, an occasional white puffy cloud sailing by as Jesus approached. Robed in purest white, blue of eye, pale of skin with no sign of the swarthier skin tones of the Middle-East and fortunately, not yet tortured. He stood on the hilltop looking down on me, beckoning, lovingly calling my name. Not impelled, I turned my back, never to look back, walking away, no doubt damned. I cannot deny that the dream was upsetting, but my choice was the right one for me. The moment I told MS my dream, was the moment Madre Immacolata threw up her arms, finally giving up on me; but not before one last try, taking me and a few others to the Vatican.

What the occasion was, I do not recall; though my sister says it was for the beatification of some saint; but, as she likes to embellish occasions, I'm not so sure. Certainly the rite was full of "pomp and circumstance," as Swiss Guards in their uniforms of orange, blue, black and red, their plumed shiny metal helmets and halberds, stood at attention before the great doors to the piazza, which was now thronged with people. With two nuns we had arrived early to sit in assigned seats just within the great vaulted room of St. Peter's. Eventually, dressed all in white and gold, Il Papa, Pope Pius XII, emerged holding the pastoral staff, the great triple-crown upon his head, seated on La Sedia (his sedan chair) supported by six men. As Il Papa processed down the aisle passing not three feet from us, he gazed directly upon our small group to give a special blessing, as he passed on and out through the portals, on out to the crowd awaiting their papal blessings. I could not help but feel this had been another of MS's ploys to lure me into the faith, and though moved by the Pope's blessing, it had failed once again to lure me.

Such a jolly-looking bunch!

EXCITEMENT IN ROME

The parents had now moved from Villa Manzoni to a large apartment on the third floor of Viale Bruno Buozzi no. 1, on a wide, tree lined street in the Parioli District in the northern part of Rome, its name deriving from the Latin "peraioli," once the site of pear orchards. Backed on the south by the Borghese Gardens from which we could hear the roar of lions from Rome's zoo, we were then just blocks from the apartment of the then disgraced Ingrid Bergman and her lover, the famed movie director Roberto Rossellini.

With the move to Parioli, and no longer attending the Poggio, as its cost for two was now prohibitive, Flip and I were headed, as previously noted, for yet another Italian-speaking school; this time the Sacro Cuore (Sacred Heart) just blocks from our apartment. Here we go again, I thought. Why did we have to be boarders when we lived so close? Not understanding, I chose to think of this arrangement as another lack of care on the part of our parents and was angry. They had shed us in war time, had us briefly with them in England; only to get rid of us again in boarding schools in Italy. Did they even want us around, or, were we just too troublesome; always in their way?

Often away, the parents left us in Angelina's care when we were on leave from school, with instructions where we could go, whom and what to see. On one such absence, they asked Angelina to take us to an afternoon performance of *Gone with the Wind*, being shown in Italy ten years after its 1939 release. Great crowds gathered to see it and, on the day we were supposed to go, performances were sold out except for the 9 p.m. showing. We didn't mind, for it would be exciting to stay up late. Maybe the parents wouldn't find out. Anyway, we didn't particularly care by then, for the movie had been spectacular with the beautiful Vivian Leigh as Scarlett in gorgeous costume, and Rhett played by, not my favorite, almost elephant-eared, Clark Gable.

Unexpectedly, the parents arrived home mid-morning the next day, to find us still in bed. It seems impossible to hide anything from parents who appear to have eyes in the back of their heads, to be accused of the same ability with my own children years later. So it was that I awoke to hear mummy confronting Angelina: "Why?" she wanted to know, "are the children still in bed?" Angelina, spluttering, muttered she had only been able to get tickets for the late show. "Then the girls should have gone another day! Our girls are always to be in bed, at the very latest, by eight o'clock, unless a very special occasion!" I liked Angelina's response: "Madam, this was a special occasion!" I heard no more.

I had begun to notice our "early" bed-time policy was at odds with the Italian child's "movable" bedtime, for having no "proper times." With indulgent grandparents, Italian children where allowed much later hours. The coolness of British parents compared to the overt warmth of Italians was an eye-opener, and I was finding the longer I remained in this beautiful, wonderfully exuberant yet chaotic country, I wished to remain, more native now than British. What had the parents wrought!

Most Saturday afternoons, Flip and I could be found at the Quirinale Theater. One movie in Italian was *Rebecca, La Seconda Moglie,* better known in America as *Rebecca.* Based on Daphne DuMaurier's novel and directed by Alfred Hitchcock in 1940, this film not released in Italy until 1949. Judith Anderson's portrayal of the disturbed Mrs. Danvers, was superb, as was that of my favorite villain, George Sanders. Sir Lawrence Olivier and Joan Fontaine were also excellent. The best foreign film for that year was the Italian *Ladri di Biciclette, The Bicycle Thief.* Generally, we were allowed to see any movie, whether suitable or not, including *Mayerling,* the story of the suicide (or murder) of Crown Prince Rudolf of Austria, which some maintain was the double suicide of himself and his mistress, Baroness Maria Vetsera the seventeen-year-old daughter of a diplomat at the Austrian Court. These sorts of films were perhaps not exactly suitable, yet the parents seemed unable to speak of life's blisses or tragedies, hoping by exposing us to such events, we'd become aware of the vicissitudes of life. So, what was I to think of their telling me that all films were make-believe? Were they or weren't they?

For being so uptight about bedtime, the parents were extraordinarily lax in allowing us complete freedom to roam about, to explore Rome on our own. Some may know of the lascivious and lustful attitude of Mediterranean men, be they young or old. Now a developed thirteen-year-old, this was all new to me, and, while I was initially flattered, nobody told me how to deal with it, causing me much embarrassment and redness of face. One late summer afternoon left me particularly rosy of cheek as, walking up the Spanish steps to a side street for my weekly drawing lesson with Professore Leone Rosa where I spent hours drawing, in charcoal, fat puti (little angels) floating on clouds. So, walking to my lesson, a middle-aged man passed me to mumble: "Beato l' uomo che ti avra!" What does a girl of my age do with that except blush? Flip, at eleven, was having her own "swoon" over one charming young Nino who lived in the apartment above us. For her, there was much peering out of windows and walking of dogs so the two could accidentally meet on purpose.

VUOI SPOSARMI?

One morning, carrying one of those large denomination bills of millions of lira that were products of post war inflation, I was sent to market several streets away. Perhaps it was the Viale Parioli, in my time a food market but which now also offers household goods. Or, it could have been the Magnagrecia (Greater Greece) or even the ancient and picturesque Roman Campo di Fiori (Field of Flowers). Whichever it was, it was incredible to think such activities had been going on throughout Italy for centuries; awesome to find oneself standing where Romans, be they famous, infamous, or less important personages had trod! Stalls in markets are laden daily with fresh fruit and vegetables of every variety, every scent and color: a veritable palette for the palate. Too, the briny scent of the day's catch of seafood is displayed on trays of chipped ice, including the much loved sea urchins and squid. Never ending shouts of competing merchants vibrated in cacophonic chorus, each salesman trying to outdo the other. Despite crowds, the pushing, shoving, and haggling over prices, by mid-afternoon there is not a single sign to indicate a large and vibrant market had been there that morning, for now all was gone, only to be set up all over again on the morrow.

Apart from shopping at the market, we had the weekly visit of an old—well, she looked old—crone dressed in voluminous black. Her ring at the door answered, she'd step into the foyer amid rustles and clucks from within her robes to bring forth live chickens and fresh eggs. Which did we want on any given week? I believe we mostly settled for the eggs, Angelina only occasionally caring to deal with a live chicken.

Otherwise when Angelina was too busy to shop, which soon became almost daily, when home, I performed that task. There were no fridges, though one might have a small ice-box for milk products, and the iceman delivered a small block every other day or so. On this particular day, having bought the items I needed, I stopped at a bakery for a slice of foccaccia, my so-called reward for having gone to the trouble. This wonderful flat baked yeasty bread, sprinkled with garlic, rosemary, parmesan, sea salt, black pepper and olive oil, was available by the slice. As I ambled home, though mother had told me it was unseemly to eat on the street, I could not wait, happily munching as I went.

One day, on one of my ventures to market, and, as I was about to turn into the driveway leading to our apartment, two young men passed me whistling, one saying, sotto voce, "Vuoi sposarmi?" With cheeks aflame I walked faster, having been told never to talk to strangers, and I dashed into the safety of the apartments' private drive, to soon forget the incident. That is, until several days later when once again I was asked to go to market, and where, once again outside the wrought-iron gates, stood this persistent fellow, saying he wanted to talk with me. I kept walking, doing my best to ignore him, hoping to shake him in the market. Yet, everywhere I went, there he was. Finally, I turned, demanding he leave me alone. He just grinned and kept following me everywhere, and back to our gates. This went on for some weeks, he persisted in walking me back and forth to market or to wherever else I happened to be going alone, always asking if I wanted to marry him. Couldn't we meet somewhere, anywhere, to talk . . . blah, blah, blah. If anyone wonders why I didn't refuse to go to market, didn't tell mother of this pursuit, I only remember thinking she wouldn't understand and would probably think I had somehow invited this attention. I would be proven right about this attitude of hers about five years later when she accused me of flagrant but false behavior.

After several weeks of this pursuit, I began to relax despite all, even liking him a bit. He was a sort of new-found friend, as he no longer asked, "Vuoi sposarmi?" In case anyone wonders why a young man would be following a thirteen year old, I was already five-nine, looked older than my few years, too, and thanks to being educated in Italian schools, I spoke the language fluently, even slang, to the point of thinking and dreaming in Italian. I appeared to be a native, especially when I wore my long dark hair in braids curled atop my head, corona-style.

Do I blame Angelina for the weekly purchase that I often read in her kitchen, that trashy Italian weekly magazine "Il Grande Hotel," often with pictures of Jane Russell voluptuously draped across its pages. Was it that, or just curiosity which one day made me agree to meet this fellow? Who knows, but to my peril one afternoon, I agreed to meet him at a local cinema. I wonder what kind of excuse I made for my absence from the apartment. When I think about it, whatever excuse I gave for my absence must have been an obvious lie to mummy.

Entering the cinema, let's call him Enrico, greeted me by snatching me by the arm to lead me not to seats on the main floor, nor to seats in the balcony, but to the very last row of the upper, upper balcony. No sooner did we sit when Enrico was trying to kiss me. Not at all interested, wanting to see the film, I gently slapped at him naively thinking we had arranged to see this movie together. How stupid; how naïve! What movie was playing that day, I shall never know nor care. All I remember is being too busy fending off roving hands to my breasts, even lower. Shocked, mortified, I fought him, but he was more powerfully ardent than I. Gaining advantage at some point with no great damage done, I jumped up, ran down staircases and out into the street, and home. From then on the parents seemed to need me to be somewhere with them, and so, thankfully, never had to run into that creep Enrico again.

THE COLTISHNESS OF YOUTH

In the Parioli apartment my sister and I were often asked to greet, meet and help entertain musicians and diplomats at cocktail parties, luncheons, or dinners. Does every budding teen suffer through an awkward, coltish stage? I certainly did, tripping over my feet as though legs did not know in which directions they should be going, creating if not mayhem which it usually turned out to be, then embarrassment and annoyance for all concerned. While Flip passed a bowl of nuts, I was asked to serve drinks on a silver salver, when it was known I would trip, the tray would tip, glasses would slide, martinis would splash, and crash to the floor. This happened too often; yet I was always asked to serve. In shame at my father's annoyance, when these disasters happened, I would bang the tray down on the serving cart and flee to my room in absolute misery, having failed yet again. Yet, wonder of wonders, I was never chastised for ineptness, perhaps a way of teaching me to cope. Yet, I eventually met a man who would teach me in no uncertain terms, that "coping" was never good enough; you had to go out there and solve the problem, whatever it might be. Amen to that, for I soon outgrew "coltishness" to become a poised, most of the time, young lady who could serve and chat, if not exactly with ease.

Flip and I were also at that awful stage when it was impossible not to giggle at some guests our parents invited for lunch. Sitting opposite each other and noticing some visitor's amusing habit or idiosyncrasy, we'd kick each other under the table and giggle. One visitor in particular, who often lunched, was often the cause of our dismissal from table. He was a portly Irish friar; I believe the music master of a Franciscan monastery. This poor rotund and unpleasantly fragrant Fra with his Irish brogue, his unwashed brown soutane sporting previous meals over a protruding stomach, would send us into gales. Excused from table, we rushed from the dining room to our room, where we'd burst in howls of hilarity. We were awful! In return for the parents' hospitality, daddy was often asked to dine at the priest's refectory and once, with no warning, asked to give the blessing. With aplomb daddy arose to intone in deep bass voice, "Benedicat Benedictum" (bless this blessing) and sat, causing laughter among the brotherhood, as they too, sat to dine.

We were also expected to be sports enthusiasts. Daddy of course loved cricket, having learned to play on Sawston's Village Green in Cambridgeshire, following his father, also an avid cricketer as so many in the family have been. Cricket, traced back into the mists of time, is a game certainly played before the 13th century; by the 18th, it was played more by the leisure classes, with the Marylebone Cricket Club formed by Thomas Lord in 1787, now Lord's Cricket Ground north of London. Daddy was so proud of his membership number 475, the club's members now numbering in the many thousands. So, on rare occasions in Italy, he, when he could gather enough players, eleven each side, promoted a match.

A natural at all sports, daddy was also good at tennis, though he preferred golf. His friend and mentor Sir Adrian bemoaned the fact, accusing him of great stupidity. "How can you," Adrian demanded, "be so daft as to hit a little white ball off a tee; then chase after it for eighteen holes? Are you insane?" I came to agree with my uncle after daddy roped me into being his caddy when the American and British ambassadors and great friend Clive Robinson paired off to chase these "silly little white balls" up and down fairways, over hills, onto greens, always aiming for the illusive tiny cup in the ground, be it nine or eighteen holes later. They, and I, only got excited when one or another managed a hole-in-one. At thirteen, it was a heavy burden for my young shoulders carrying daddy's ancient canvas and leather bag with its odd assortment of old-fashioned hickory-shafted clubs. Sports bring back fond memories now.

Madrigal group: Christabel Falkner pianist and alto; James Eagleston, tenor; Vera Terry, mezzo; Joy Hoodless, Soprano and Bass-baritone, Keith Falkner.

JOY

A new person now entered our lives, the Aussie Joy Hoodless, with lovely figure, soprano voice. Recent winner of a scholarship to study in Italy, the parents invited her into our lives, daddy having taken her under his wing to help her career. As we were mostly away at Sacro Cuore, she was free to rent our double room, which meant on return we were rather crowded. Joy at twenty-two, despite the strong Australian jaw and prominent nose, shades of ancestors sent to penal colonies from England, was glamorous, with gorgeous figure, green eyes, and piles of red hair.

Recently having formed a madrigal group to tour up and down Italy, daddy invited Joy, who's recent performance in Puccini's *Madame Butterfly*, had impressed him, to sing with the group, joining the American mezzo Vera Terry and tenor, James Eagleson, both studying in Rome; the bass-baritone of the group, daddy; mother accompanist, occasional alto. Up and down the land they toured, Joy always a major attraction garnering whistles, shouts, the stomping of feet from males in the audience ever appreciative of beauty and voice. A knock-out, Joy brought in the crowds. There was also general acclaim for the quintet as nothing like it had been heard in Italy before. Not only was the group remarkable for their madrigal singing, but for their calmness during earthquakes for as shudders and quakes shook to cause chandeliers to sway, buildings to creak, floors and seating to quiver, the tendency for panicking Italian audiences to bolt outdoors. However, often as lights swayed and dimmed to go out during such events, daddy kept the group singing, they slowly backtracking to stand under nearby stage-doors hoping the cross beams would stand, the only light coming occasionally from the flick of Jim's cigarette lighter.

As the artists remained calm, so too did the audience, filing out calmly, stampedes thus avoided.

Equally immensely popular in Rome, Joy drew every male aware of her presence to her, she invited by both available and unavailable men. In the course of "hot pursuit" the Latin Romeo is relentless until he either persuades the lady to succumb or, she shakes him off. Said would be lover, is never offended; just shaking his head to move on to other more susceptible conquests. So, it would be, just for awhile, Joy was safe.

MY FIRST GROWNUP PARTY

A statuesque fourteen, I too began to find myself admired. (Witness the unpleasant young man previously referred to.) Pretty heady stuff, this, given no guidance by parents, who, I presume still thought me a child, they, back in the dark ages of their own up-bringing when even the word "sex" was verboten! It was now, as the 1950 New Year approached, that Joy asked the parents if she could take me to my first grown-up party. Oh, Joy!

The party was to be held in a large apartment of two prominent, operatic, in every sense of the word, Italians. But, what was I to wear? Joy, who loved Italian couture, needed no persuasion to take me shopping, and so daddy paid up, and off we two hurried from dress shop to dress shop, shoe shop after shoe shop until we found just the right outfit in my favorite color. It was an emerald green moiré cocktail dress with a silvery-green wrap, silver slippers, and a matching bag. All wonderful, so what did I care about Christmas? It went by in a blur, my only thoughts, "The Party" to come.

Finally, after one of the longest afternoons in my life, it was time to dress for "The Party." My almost waist-length auburn hair was braided and woven around my head as a tiara, the lightest makeup, applied by Joy, a trace of lipstick and powder. Mummy supervised, of course, and, pleased, presented me with a pair of dangling earrings made of silver and green crystals to match my outfit. I felt grown up, certainly looked older than my years, and the color of the evening was the same for my sister; she now green with envy.

The party was in full swing when we arrived about ten; teeming with personages, people of all ages, music, conversation, food, dancing, the ebb and flow, roaming throughout rooms, onto balconies for it was a balmy December evening, all incredibly noisy. Of course, Joy, on arrival, became the focus of attention as I had expected, she too in green with her gorgeous red hair, leaving me far behind. I was shy, and I still do fight shyness, which people often mistake for aloofness. Now, older, I try to make others comfortable rather than worry about myself, but back then I felt awkward. Not for long, however, for any shyness was quickly dispelled by one whom my mother would have called "a nice young man." Paolo was his name, and the more we talked, the more relaxed I became, a little light imbibing helping too. Then we danced. I liked him and besides, he taught me to Samba amid this swirling noisy throng. All such fun.

Sitting by an open window, trying to cool down and to catch my breath from recent dances, suddenly it was seconds before midnight as the count-down started: "Dieci, nove, otto, sette, sei, cinque, quattro, tre, due, uno, zero!" Auguri, Auguri! Buon Nuov'Anno!" as lights all over the city blinked, then went out for ten minutes, every church bell pealing and fireworks blasting skyward, as our boisterous party slowly melted into silence. What was going on? Then startled, with no time to react, I was kissed by my "nice young man," albeit sloppily; certainly nothing to get excited about. Then Joy's somewhat muffled Australian "twang" echoed across the rooms: "Julia! 'Arr right?" Of course, but I was wondering whether it was she who needed to be asked that question, for when the lights came back on, a number of people, including her, seemed to be somewhat the worse for wear and not just from "il vino." All too soon, as far as I was concerned, Joy announced it was time to leave; but why? Having such a good time, I wanted to stay, my first real party coming to an end far too early; yet, as I later drifted off to sleep, I recalled the evening in detail: it had been such fun. When was the next one going to be?

A DRIVE TO NAPLES

The next gathering was hardly a party, but rather an agonizingly long day, a drive to the American Consulate in Naples for visas and permanent residency certificates necessary for entry into the United States. It was already warm at 6:00 am that summer morning, as we left after a breakfast of peaches and black coffee. It was torrid by the time we reached Naples, though fresh breezes were blowing in from the bay. The bay, an arm of the Tyrrenian, is a ten mile-wide expanse; in the west the Mediterranean, bordered by Naples, one of the largest seaports in Italy, certainly the busiest cargo port, and Pozzuoli, once home to Sophia Loren; on the east by Vesuvius; and, on the south, by the Sorrentino peninsula, main town Sorrento. As we drove along the waterfront, fortunately with no more attacks by street urchins, I was thrilled to see the United States Navy in port, sailors ashore looking handsome in their dress whites, and jaunty sailor caps. However, no time for swooning was allowed, as, after a quick lunch in a café overlooking the blue waters, we were expected to appear at various places for inductions, physicals, and the swearing-in, during which we would vow not to overthrow the American Government.

It was the physical part of the ordeal which was upsetting, as all females, and there were a large number, were herded cattle-like into various cavernous rooms, forced to disrobe to our waists, removing bras to expose chests for x-ray. I, who had only seen Eleanor Francis' small breasts, was overwhelmed by "an embarrassment of bosoms." It was impossible not to notice the divergent shapes and sizes: from the pert to the pendulous. The last belonged mostly to older Italian peasant women hoping to immigrate to the States, all of whom who found this exposure demeaning and devoid of modesty. All of us bided our time, mere ciphers to be processed like a herd of milch cows. Mother, so modest, could hardly stand the ordeal, maintaining a fixed smile all the time, while I was more than embarrassed by my budding chest. Flip, prepubescent, was merely embarrassed by all this pulchritude while other young women seemed to flaunt their "wares," or what they thought to be their best asset. Of the peasant women, always dressed in black, it was difficult to ignore the scents of their all too un-deodorized sweaty bodies, long-unwashed hair, the oil of both considered to keep both healthy. Most of these women and families would find passage in steerage at some future date; we, with tickets, would sail in early September, on the, freighter the "Maria C," Costa Line, recently remodeled for fourteen passengers.

Eventually the long and wearisome day drew to a close, and, with final oath sworn, papers in hand, we drove the 120 long miles back to Rome. I wished I had had the time to see more of those handsome Navy men! Through the lush poderi we drove, oranges and lemons ripening in profusion; olive farms, their trees ripening green and black varieties, all flourishing against the darkening sky that now was cooling the day's heat. It was late when we got back; we, looking to the future and at the same time, regretting the move, for we had become enamored with Italy, the land, people, cuisine, long history, and its art.

CIRCE? AT MY AGE? HARDLY!

The previous summer, we had spent our holiday in Monte Circeo where there had been much debate as to whether the mountain's shape was a breast, or a nose. Circe was said by Homer to have been the loveliest of all Greek deities; known alternately as nymph, witch, enchantress and sorceress. I, then a nymphet, hope to be forgiven for any comparisons to my romanticized fantasies. Too, after the episode with Enrico, I had become more cautious somehow managing to avoid the daily jaunt to market and, therefore, Enrico. However, this restraint had only given my imaginative fancies about the future further scope.

In our third floor apartment, most windows faced away from south and west, but a number did not, and so received the full brunt of the midday sun. These half dozen windows, one of which belonged to our bathroom, overlooked the tall hedge which hid the gravel driveway that led up from that notorious wrought iron front gate from Via Bertoloni. Across the drive was a beautiful garden belonging to the villa next door. It too was surrounded by high shrubbery and overlooked by our bathroom window. Entered from the far end of the parents' bedroom, "il bagnio" (bath), its main feature a large ceramic tub, had exquisite tiling covering walls in blues, greens and assorted shells. There were, of course, the other necessities: the toilet, and, between it and the large shell-shaped pedestal basin or sink, a bidet placed inches below the window sill. Flip and I had wanted to know what this was for and were told it was for the washing of feet. I didn't believe for a minute the parents didn't know its true purpose.

For some no doubt well-reasoned schedule devised by the parents, my bath time was fixed for five every afternoon: its timing, no doubt allowing

193

the rest of the family to refresh in timely manner for concerts and evening adventures. The bathroom was the only place in the apartment where you could have complete privacy, at least for a little while. It had been here, shortly after a return visit to Villa Manzoni that I read a note, badly written and lurid in detail, suggesting I join the writer, the gardener's son, in behavior I had never thought nor heard of before. My face had suffused with shame and disgust. So there, in the privacy of that bathroom, I shredded the note, which, after several attempts, flushed away down into Rome's ancient sewer system, where it rightfully belonged.

In Italy, from meanest abodes to fanciest villas, windows have casements called "Persiane di finestre," a shutter but not the type known here. In Italy, these are usually metal frames inserted into the outside edges of windows. Depending on time of day, the shutter may remain closed or raised, clattering noisily up or down as it's adjusted to different levels. Or, in late afternoon, when it's lowered, it can still be opened by pushing out the lower part of the metal base, allowing the immediate outside views to be seen and to catch the late afternoon or evening's cooling breezes. What was left of the heat of day, was kept at bay. A fine invention!

Thanks to the Italians and their more southern climate, children mature earlier than their more northern or western cousins, who are, at the same age, still in junior grades in school. I had overheard remarks as I approached maturity that I was becoming an attractive young thing and, hence, a subject of interest. I can remember only too well the embarrassment, agony, and conflicts between mother and daughter as we shopped for my first bras. Where I had wanted lace, mother had bought plain cotton!

At home we were expected to behave more or less as adults. Therefore, we were seldom praised, remonstrations given for bad grades or over emoting. This seeming lack of interest or caring on the parents' part, had only increased my yearning for attention and love, the lack of which not so long ago, had concerned a headmistress, and Aunt Dodie. There were few shows of affection, rarely a hug or praise, it being taken for granted that overt signs of emotion, while felt, were quite unnecessary. The mores of a previous generation or two, and a life focused on music were considered the best way to raise children. This is not to say we weren't loved; just that it was not demonstrative, yet any undue emoting or disgruntlement on our part brought mutterings of "pull yourself together," or, "pull up your socks!"

Perhaps partly for what I experienced as a lack of love and care, my fantasies and romanticism began to flourish in earnest given the wonderful Grecian and Roman tales; not to mention those pale ladies fawned over by unrequited lovers from afar. The highly romantic and oh so Grimm fairy tales I had read had made me unconsciously more aware of instinctive impulses, full of curiosity as I was, with an appetite and thirst for life, as my budding body blossomed, "coming of age" in a centuries-old environment, with all its beguiling attractions, invitations and possible pitfalls.

So it was, with all this and more in my head, that I exited my bath on one particular afternoon, pretending to be Circe, in that gorgeous 1891 Pre-Raphaelite painting by John William Waterhouse: that dark-haired beauty, red-lipped, diaphanously-clad Circe, left breast barely covered, roseate nipple half in evidence, where, seated before a large round mirror, she offers a chalice-like cup to Ulysses distantly reflected in the round mirror behind her, thus tempting him to fall under her spell. Well, better Circe, I thought, than that rather pure "Venus on the half shell," as others and I call Botticelli's "Primavera." It wasn't always Circe I pretended to be, however. There was Aphrodite, Venus in Roman mythology with her myriad lovers, who alas comes down to us as De Milo sans arms. There is Bethsheba, who bewitched King David; Diane de Poitier; and any number of other great beauties, who beguiled as they bathed or exited the bath. Such were the fantasies and imagination in the mind of a growing juvenile, rampant, but with little understanding of the nature of such involvements. However, I was not thinking about these ladies as I took my bath on this particular pre-dusk evening.

The shutter had indeed been lowered; yet I had pushed out the lower part to gain what few breezes there were that July afternoon as I emerged, damsel-like from a cooling bath scented by the heady scent of Lemon Verbena, that delicious smelling deciduous plant, to my mind, the most erotic and blissful of scents. So, here I was emerging, lemon-scented, more Botticellian than I'd care to admit, stepping out onto the bathmat to dry what mother unkindly referred to as my beanpole figure.

Gazing into the bathroom's full length mirror, there was nothing "beanpole" about me that I could see: yes, I was tall, taller by some four inches than mother's five-foot five. I tried to compare myself with some of the Roman statues of so-called idealized-perfection, and could only think I was not all that bad looking; rounding out nicely in all the right places. But then, I had nothing to compare myself with except statues and a mother with a far more delicate figure, which I was never, it seemed to me on pain of death, ever permitted to see. Anyway, there I was, staring at myself, seductively draping a towel this way and that about my body looking for best effect, when, from the corner of my eye, I saw movement.

Turning toward the opened "persiana," I was momentarily stunned and highly embarrassed to find I had been caught in an act of vainglory for there, three stories below and on the other side of the villa's hedge, stood a young man, watering flower beds, his gaze firmly fixed in my direction! Unless he had x-ray vision or a wonderful imagination, I could only guess at what he might think to have seen. So, there I stood, blushing, while he over-watered, drowning the flowers, the inference now implicit.

I continued to have my lemon-scented bath each afternoon precisely at five, knowing, even without looking out the "persiana," my admirer awaited, waiting to catch the merest suggestion of rounded breast, bare shoulder, long leg raised, as I bent to dry my toes on the bidet. I'm not ashamed to say I tried to invent varying poses each afternoon, this to further entice my admirer's interest: rather like playing a game of hide and seek, but far more provocative: "now you see me, now you don't," safe and, unattainable. Italy had taught me a lot by flirtatious observation; so, here I was at fourteen, playing not only with fantasy, but also with seduction. But suddenly, these pulchritudinous "excursions" came to a stop when the parents announced we were off on holiday, this time to Austria, for the next three weeks. So, it would be "Ciao" for now, to my voyeur, knowing he'd be there: same place, same time, on return.

LAST MONTHS

Our departure from Italy had come about because early in 1950 Sir Adrian, daddy's great friend and mentor, had seen the direction funding for British Councils was headed and so took it upon himself to suggest to Cornell's Music Department, looking for an Associate Professor of voice, that they might be interested in talking to the eminent singer, Keith Falkner. Cornell jumped, and daddy's appointment was confirmed for the coming fall. With that, Adrian handed daddy one thousand pounds sterling toward the move. Could one have had a better benefactor? It turned out to be an interesting coincidence that Andrew D. White, co-founder with Ezra Cornell of Cornell University in April of 1865, had at one point been United States ambassador to Russia, his secretary none other than mother's father to be, Thomas Fletcher Fullard. Is it not a small world?

Meanwhile, owing to the British Council's Music Officer's continuing arrangements, both Italian and British musicians continued to perform in each other's countries: of the British in Italy, most notably were again Ben Britten and Peter Pears; William Walton, composer of, among other works, *Façade*, which daddy would perform innumerable times and record at Cornell in the late 1950s. All this was going on as things began to wind down toward our departure. Flip and I managed to ease our way out of Sacred Heart with the help of a tutor, to pass final exams, even me with flying colors for third-year Latin. No one was more surprised than I! The tutor, an English graduate student studying in Rome, had been hired primarily to teach us the "correct" history of the British Empire, focusing particularly on British and American confrontations, including the Boston Tea Party and the burning of the White House. Perhaps the only good thing about leaving Italy was that I'd not have to study Greek in following years. More's the pity, for it might have been as invaluable as Latin, which has stood me in good stead over the years.

Time now for one last holiday, thinking the parents might have chosen some special place in Italy. But no, for after poring over music festivals, maps and train schedules, daddy decided on Austria, the very place where he and mother had spent their honeymoon twenty years previously. So, from Rome we made our way to Venice; re-boarded a train to Bolzano, to travel up steep inclines through rocky slopes and pine forests into Tyrolian Austria, to Innsbruck, capital of Austria since 1429.

Innsbruck was home to the first non-court opera house funded by Ferdinand the II, Archduke of Austria with Antonio Cesti its court-appointed Italian composer of Baroque music. Daddy was scheduled to attend the "International Festival of Early Music, 1500 to 1750" something not to be missed, but I feel sure he enjoyed the renowned "Choral Festival" more. Late suppers followed performances, where once, at a round table I was thrilled to sit near Kirsten Flagstad, the great Norwegian Wagnerian singer of the twentieth century. Daddy had sung with her at May Festivals in Cincinnati in the late 1930s, once telling me he had wondered whether he would be drowned out by her rich tones, but having no such problem. Sitting there, that wonderful evening, I thought Miss Flagstad, at fifty-five, the epitome of a Valkyrie; not so young, but still quite lovely, her golden hair plaited and woven atop her strong forehead. Others were at these late suppers whom I should remember, but with the talk which seemed to go on forever, and tired, I do not, always glad for bed, eager for the holiday to come.

At last, festivals over, we boarded the funicular, a train with few cars, to slowly inch its way up inclines, engine huffing and puffing, up through strongly scented pine forests, eventually to reach Reutte. The journey reminded me of *The Little Engine That Could*, except no big and important engines had roared past. A short drive in the area known as Trentino, Alto Adige, or Bavarian Alps, near the border with Germany, took us to Lake Planzee, where, as mentioned, the parents had honeymooned. Nestled in these lower western Alps, the lake is spectacularly beautiful, its waters of incredible clarity and blueness. And here we settled for three weeks, our fellow guests international: I spoke Italian with Italians, managed "un peu de Francais" while flirting with fellows from Belgium; relaxed speaking English with the British and one or two Americans, and, being a quick learner, began to utter German phrases mostly forgotten now, except for daddy's ordering of: "Ein dunklas bier, danke." The languages did get a bit confusing at times: why was cold in German "kalt" instead of hot which I thought would have meant, as in Italian "caldo," cold being "freddo." Then there was the French "chaud" for hot, "froid" for cold, more akin to the Latin base.

At the time, would it have made any difference had I known the area near Reutte had once had a Dachau sub-camp? Probably not, for as yet I had little interest in the war. Except for daddy's tales of his RAF exploits and the blood-thirsty Africans, the atrocities of the war had never been discussed in my presence. It was much later that I learned Dachau had been the first concentration camp for political prisoners, an oft heard jingle at the time being "Dear God, make me dumb, that I may not to Dachau come," the concentration camp the model for all others, housing over 200,000 prisoners from thirty countries, a third of whom were Jews, thousands more to die in Dachau sub-camps like the one near Reutte; here, where we were now enjoying a holiday. The contrast seems appalling. It had been a mere five years since the end of the war; yet nothing about the existence of this nearby camp was mentioned in my presence either then or later. It is hard to believe no one in the area knew of the goings on behind locked gates not so far away: the locals in denial, or just blocking such knowledge?

"Good Morning Girls!" Daddy shouted soon after dawn each morning as he flung open our door. "Rise and shine!" as he tore off our eiderdowns and sheets. "Everyone in the lake in five minutes!" We scrambled to meet this deadline while mother stayed snuggled in bed. As we donned bathing suits, we noticed a herd of sedately swaying cows, muted brass bells worn on leather straps around their soft brown necks clanking softly in the misty air, as they plodded along an ancient pathway to high alpine meadows.

They returned late afternoon to be unburdened of their "udderly" rich milk, only to faithfully repeat the process, day after day. Twenty days of such rude awakenings might very well have been enough; yet we came to enjoy these early forays where the air was colder than the water, the fog so dense at times, it was impossible to know in which direction you were heading. After these more than refreshing swims, hot baths and sumptuous breakfasts awaited, before we were off on uphill-and-down-dale hikes. Daddy would have been far happier to go off on his own; yet was again frustrated that neither his wife nor daughters showed any real interest in becoming alpine hikers. Even if we had, we never seemed to have the right shoes for the purpose. Whether this was accidental or not, I never knew, though I feel Mother had a hand in it; certainly it was not up to us to equip ourselves for such ventures! Anyway, at the time, I was more interested in red strappy sandals!

One of our excursions took us to the base of the 9,721 foot Zugspitze, an impressive massive bulwark of stone jutting straight out of the earth, site of the 1936 Winter Olympic Games. Fortunately we did not have to climb it. Instead, we took a gently swaying cable car up to its peak, where the air was so rarified, so brilliant, everything seemed etched in vivid clarity. It was a sight I would not see again until years later, when driving up to Santa Fe from Albuquerque near the Sancre de Cristo Mountains. But now, at the peak of the Zugspitze, in this almost too brilliant crystalline sunshine, we munched sandwiches and Dunklas Biers, with sunshine and glare almost too vivid against the contrast of a blue-iced glacier creeping inexorable down the mountain. As mist and fog began to gather, we took a last cable car to ground level, quite a trip, for winds had begun to pick up, buffeting the car, and causing it to sway alarmingly. It was not pleasant, in fact, frightening, but we landed safely, and with relief we re-boarded the last bus for Reutte.

Most afternoons we plodded uphill paths to alpine meadows, stepping over cow patties, seeing Alpine Ibexes, the wild goats that lived in the European Alps. Excellent climbers, their habitat is the rocky area along the snowline above forests where they roam at elevations of 6,500 to 15,000 feet. Also in the distance were flocks of sheep tended by Maremma, Italian sheep dogs native to the Alps, able to work independently at high altitudes. Otherwise, on the many sunny slopes, we admired multicolored bell-like columbines bobbing in the breeze, ready, so it seemed, to peal gentle "pings," that is, if heard in fairyland. There were the blues of gentians, pinks of primrose, the golden yellow Triglav Hawksbeard, the pale blues of the Alpine forget-me-not, sometimes the Carnelian lily with its inverted orange velvety petals, the white and green of Edelweiss among lichen and limestone on outcroppings of rock, and back, once more, to the astounding blue of the Gentian, all in glorious profusion.

Clearings in woodlands further up the slope, revealed large patches of wild strawberries, their sweet scent perfuming the air, so far superior to the common garden variety. In Rome markets, punnets (small boxes) of these little gems are available in season, and, when rinsed in a sprinkling of fresh orange juice, touch of sugar, even a splash of orange brandy, are truly sublime. Known to have been consumed by Stone Age man, it was interesting later to learn this was the very area where, in 1991, a well-preserved mummy dating to 3300 BC, was discovered in a glacier between the Italo-Austrian borders. Named Otiz for the area in which he was found, said Otiz was a Neolithic man of about forty-five and just over five feet tall. He, too, may have indulged in cramming his mouth with these delectable gems, though it is known that Otiz's last meal was not strawberries, but rather fire-cooked flatbread, herbs and ibex meat; before he was killed with an arrow to his back.

Aside from harvesting strawberries, our walks in the Tyrol could be exciting or dull. On dull days, daddy ran us through multiplication tables up to thirteen times thirteen,(169) or have us list every state in the Union in alphabetical order. We did wonder though, as I suppose most children do, why the difference in pronunciation of Arkansas and Kansas? Daddy did not know and nobody has been able to tell me since. Must be some big secret!

On another walk in thick woodland one day, as I jumped from one side of a stream to another, I was a shocked to discern poking out from piles of underbrush, a spiked and rusting helmet, complete with steel bowl and visor. After daddy and I had consulted, we agreed it appeared dated to the Austro-Prussian war of 1866, its purpose to expel Austria from the German Confederation. What I had found was the place of death of a cavalry officer, so we decided to leave the helmet where it was, doubtless near its fallen owner's bones. We resumed our walk, a bit stunned, talking of war, helmets, bones lying about not only from previous wars but, time immemorial, the awful futility. Apropos of this, on one misty rainy afternoon's walk, we came within inches of the border of Austria and Germany. Flip and I looked at each other, and having no kind feelings from what little we knew of the latter, gleefully spat upon that vile country. "There! That should take care of the beastly Boche!" We were not allowed to say "Bloody."

On our last glorious afternoon, Flip and I were happy to be at the Planzee lido, pleased not to be climbing yet another mountain. Fresh from a swim and lying on a beach towel, I watched a man of beautiful physique proudly maneuver his way across the crowded sand, hop up tall steps to the wooden diving platform, and, balancing himself, stretch out his arms, and so, beautifully positioned, leap out into a perfect swan dive. It was perfect indeed, except that he had stumps for legs. It was my first and shocking observation of what war can inflict on body and soul. A further tragedy in those benighted days was that those so handicapped, were often hidden either by the sufferer's own volition, or, more likely by the family, thinking to hide such a person from sight, from embarrassment. How brave was this man of wounded body! Flouting the norms, the willpower to overcome prejudice, to be as normal as possible, in an age just beginning to wake up to the fact that no matter one's position in life, state of body or mind, all are human, subject to feelings. It was an eye-opener. See? I wasn't all frivolous!

PACKING AND GOODBYES

August was waning as we back-tracked to Rome, bath times again on schedule, my voyeuristic gardener with grin happily waved his watering hose. In the meantime, the time became a flurry of packing, of goodbyes. Over the years, mother had learned to pare everything from the Falkner baggage; everything that, in her opinion, was not worth saving. Her attitude was "when in doubt, throw it out!" Away went my favorite books, other articles, all my artwork laboriously done in school and under the respected art teacher Professore Leone Rosa. I would not discover this until I began to unpack in Ithaca, late that October, whereupon I could have happily killed her! I was livid! How dare she! But, Mother's life revolved totally around daddy's and their necessary economies, while we suffered. Mother's job was to make her husband's life as easy and comfortable as possible. So, out went our "stuff." It was hard to forgive her.

While our English furniture had been stored in Maples in London when we left for Italy, somehow we had acquired enough goods for three large crates, all winched aboard the "Maria 'C'", the freighter which would transport us from Genoa to America. Despite our regret in leaving, we began to get excited about this new venture, the sailing, our return to the fondly remembered and exciting United States. Meanwhile, daddy, male that he was, and never one to be involved in unpleasant or difficult arrangements, escaped to England for several concerts. One in particular, arranged by Benjamin Britten at his Aldeburgh Festival in East Anglia, where Keith was booked to sing Bach's solo cantata No. 56: *Ich will den Kreuzst gerne tragen*. The reviews were very satisfying, speaking of the privilege of hearing this famous bass-baritone again, the *East Anglia Times* wrote:

"his control and phrasing are as fine as ever and his singing has, above all, that spiritual quality which makes him an interpreter of Bach's music par excellence."

Or, from Frank Howes, music critic for the London Times:

"[he] had his own but now uncommon warmth of tone and firm line and another rare combination [that] of flexibility and certainty of intonation."

Fine praise yes, but daddy had to make a living. Lamentations from Italian musical quarters now began to pour in from all sides that this fine musician should leave their shores. Keith wrote of parting that August night of the 31rst:

"I was very moved as members of the British Council staff and many friends came to see us off, a host of regrets and well-wishing with much correspondence from critics and musicians all over Italy. We were sad to go as we would have been quite happy to spend the rest of our lives here."

"The Italians liked the unfamiliar mixture of honest English-Man and sensitive artist, or cricket and music, so to speak. The chance visitor from England who saw them, [The Falkners] at work could be proud that his country was represented by two such personable and proficient ambassadors."

So wrote Frank Howes of the *Musical Times*, sometime later.

THE SAD DEPARTURE

Ever so sadly, we were about to leave Italy, to miss this beautiful country, its people, its chaotic laws, regulations, not to mention its traffic, all of which we had come to know, sometimes to enjoy, sometimes irritated, during four mostly pleasurable years. This time t'would be as a family we'd cross the Atlantic, returning to a country which before and during the war, had been generous and kind. Our destination, this time, Ithaca's Cornell University, in upstate New York.

There would be several weeks before we had to say our final goodbyes, and of course, once back from Austria, I had resumed my bath routine, my voyeuristic but thankfully distant viewer always at his post. It was on August 31st that I took my last lemon-perfumed scented bath in this beautiful flat at No. 1, Viale Bruno Buozzi, Apt. 3, Roma. For this last performance—for this was what it was—I decided to act a little more provocatively, and so, accidentally-on-purpose, dropped my towel from pubescent breast only to grab it again in haste. My reward? He raised to his lips the five fingers not attached to the watering hose, kissed them; then, blew the kiss heaven-ward before turning to me, offering the same tribute. What does a very young woman, having lacked so much love in early youth, make of that? It goes to her head, at least for awhile. Then, robed, I raised the "persiana" for the last time, beginning to smell the sweetest fragrance of all, the white night-blooming Jasmines wafting up from the garden, as I waved and disappeared from his view forever. I wonder if he ever missed our late afternoon "trysts." Certainly, there can never have been complaints from the villa, for the flowers had thrived under this young man's "watch," flowering beautifully as so well watered during the hot summer. I, on the other hand, with our upcoming move, soon forgot all about him: so frivolous is youth!

It would be on return to the United States that I'd be rudely awakened from all those god-like erotic creatures and come down to earth with a bump, flung backward into juvenilia without the enchanting, erotic and sensual environment for as previously mentioned you grow up faster in southern climes. I now found myself in a totally different and immature climate, an uncultured world, I ahead of my peers in many ways. But, I had little time to wonder about that now, for the next morning we arrived in Genoa, and traveled directly to nearby Portofino, then an attractive and unspoiled small port and fishing village, now, a tourist mecca. At the time, Sir Francis Toye, Director of the British Institute in Florence, had a retreat there, and on this day he and wife Nina gave Keith, and the rest of us a farewell luncheon.

At the time, The British Institute and Sir Francis's home were located in Florence, which had once been the home of the controversial, some thought heretical, astronomer of the fourteenth and fifteenth centuries, one Galileo Galilei. Here, it was said, eerie events often occurred. On one of daddy's visits to the Toyes', he was put up in the "Galileo suite." After a superb lunch and plenty of good vino, everyone retired for the siesta hours. Several hours later, daddy awoke to find himself standing in the middle of the room, talking with his parents, dead ten and twenty years earlier, finding the occurrence comforting. Weird indeed, but daddy was fey, as am I.

Sometime during the luncheon in Portofino, Sir Francis asked Keith what he would like to do following his two year stint at Cornell: "Oh," replied Keith, "I should love to someday become director of the Royal College of Music." "It'll never happen." spluttered Sir Francis, "they only hire organists!" As it was, daddy would be at Cornell a full ten years, ending as full professor before taking up duties as, indeed, director of the RCM in 1960, enjoying tenure of fourteen years. Known primarily as a singer, he had also been an organ scholar at the RCM in the 1920's and played the organ at All Saints in Rome. With his appointment, Keith was considered to have broken the "tyranny of the organ loft!"

BACK TO AMERICA

So here we were on a beautiful September morning at the Genoa docks prepared to board the 'Maria C' of the Italian Costa Line, also known as the "Linea C." Their ships had been sailing since 1924, the "Maria C" primarily a freighter until 1947, when temporary quarters were installed to accommodate fourteen or so passengers. She would be scrapped after 28 years service. For our trip, the "Maria C" with port-of-call Naples, was carrying a full crew and officers. From Naples, she would sail across the Mediterranean to and into the Atlantic, a voyage of some fourteen days.

On the way south from Genoa, we passed Elba, site of the previous summer's holiday, and the lovely isles of Capri and Ischia in the Naples area, the ship berthing to pick up further cargo. During the three day lay-over, we were free to roam the city, Pompeii, and Herculaneum. Daddy and I went to Pompeii, while Flip, with some bug or other, remained on board with mummy. I found Pompeii fascinating, frozen in time since the eruption of Vesuvius in 79 AD, where recent excavations had uncovered much from the inundation of ash, lava and pyroclastics, those fast-moving currents of gas and rock with temperatures of 1,800 degrees Fahrenheit sweeping down the mountain to kill all before it. Digs had revealed raised streets and stepping stones over gutters, erotic murals and phallic symbols which, at the time held me in some thrall bringing to the fore tales of gods and goddesses indulging in the likes of which I had never seen before. Meanwhile, I was constantly being urged to move along when I wanted to look, and look, learn more. It was hard, though try as I might as I walked through its' aftermath 1,870 years later, to visualize what that long-ago day of destruction and death must have been like, though before me lay the encrusted forms of people and animals, people who had existed so long ago, the long dead. Not so distant, the gentle-looking slopes of Vesuvius remain, "that peak of hell rising out of paradise" as one historian, Pliny, I believe, put it. Today one is led to think all is calm, but Mount Vesuvius has never been that, and though its hillsides are again draped with vineyards and new housing, another catastrophe is building within the mount in the form of a huge magma chamber, this according to latest volcanologist readings. The Vesuvius eruption of 79 AD had occurred on a day similar to this September day of 1950, as gentle breezes had ruffled wavelets as the Mediterranean sparkling in the near distance. Then, with little warning, the earth had exploded, erupting in chaos and death. I soon found I had had enough though illuminating, excursion, and later that afternoon, pleased to step with daddy, more safely aboard the "Maria C," she to sail the next morning.

The "Maria C" indeed pulled anchor to make her way across the Mediterranean toward the straits of Gibraltar, once known as the *Pillars of Hercules,* said to have been split by him into the exit portal between promontories separating Spain and Africa: "The Rock," on the European side; "Jebel Musa" on the African. Rollicking dolphins joyfully escorted us along the way, playing alongside the ship, traveling through clear aquamarine waters. According to Greek and Roman mythology, dolphins were symbols of harmony, and, as in history and art, murals and other art forms depict a boy riding a pair, described by Apollo to be the embodiment of peaceful virtue.

A family of Poles, sans father, were fellow passengers; several men, and two young American women who spent most of their time when in perfect weather, sunning top-side top-less, or else entertaining the captain, who was seldom thereafter, seen at his helm. "Che vergogna!" "For shame," muttered the crew, as did the bo'sun, oddly enough. Another passenger was our miniature Schnauzer, and though the ship's "manifesto" had listed her as a "canarino"(canary), we were still able to have our "cagnolina" (little dog) Liza, in our cabin. The crew loved her as she dashed around decks under my supervision several times a day, her "poop" scooped overboard. In great exuberance, she would often take flying leaps across hatches which, often to her great surprise, were open. One minute she was there, gone the next, to drop like a stone several decks below, splatting unceremoniously, yet unharmed, on piles of corn or wheat. Why was the ship transporting this commodity to America, it with its great fields of grain? The crew got used to Liza's interruptive mishaps as one or another would climb several flights of iron ladders, bearing Liza in his arms, to gently deposit her safely onto more solid decking.

As Liza and others were doing, Flip and I roved everywhere, for no place was off limits except, of course, the captain's quarters. From wheelhouse to engine room where near naked stokers, heads bound in bandanas, blackened olive-colored skins and sweating muscles rippled in endless toil as they heaved huge shovels full of coal into the gaping maws of six or more voracious furnaces. The generated steam caused giant pistons to thrum up and down in deafening noise, to rotate gigantic propellers which in turn, propelled the ship across the ocean.

A favorite spot of mine was the radio room, located on an upper deck, where the middle-aged operator showed how he sent and received messages. Surprisingly, when not busy, he thought it wise to teach me how to iron men's shirts and trousers: "Someday," he said, "it might be useful for you to know." It was, but that was long ago, for I soon gave up that awful chore. I also hung around the galley with the cooks, wanting to learn, but soon found they considered me to be a pest. Toward the end of the voyage, the chef had had enough of me, and cajoled me into the giant freezer, only to slam the door behind me. I refused to panic, knowing full well someone, at sometime, would need something from said freezer. Just so, to eventually be released to emerge colder, and chastened. Fortunately, the experience did not chill my future culinary adventures in the kitchen.

Though Flip and I shared a double cabin with the parents, we saw little of them. Were they seasick or just talking, making love, planning, or thinking about their new life to come? P and I were never seasick, despite her airplane landings, though the parents suffered, sometimes unable to appear for lunch. On one very rough day we were lunching on liver to suddenly hear: "Oh perduto il mio fegato" "(I've lost my liver!), to gales of laughter as, indeed her serving had slid off her plate to the floor.

It was the time of year when storms are spawned off the western coast of Africa making their way across the Atlantic, some to increase in enough intensity to turn into hurricanes as they churned westward. Our time of voyage coincided with this season, seawater temperature and winds ripe enough for us to run into one. It was hurricane "Dog," that year, which turned out to be the nastiest of that year, blowing strongest winds, spawning waves over one hundred feet high as our little freighter ran headlong into it, as both made their way westwards. Could we outrun it?

Wind shear swept off wave tops as they, rising ever higher, created great billows of foamy spray to cascade and crash onto the foredeck. Water rushed and foamed across decks as the plucky freighter plowed downward into deepening troughs, to climb the face of yet another towering over her as she righted herself again and again from side rolls. The captain, perforce now, spent hours at the wheel, while Flip and I found the storm exhilarating as we watched the ship play and roll in the maelstrom. It was then we had a great idea: with the "Maria C" momentarily on an even keel, we dashed across the deck to starboard and there clung to its railings. As an even greater wave crashed over her, the ship reeled, shuddered, tilted further and further toward the ocean's floor. How much further could she roll before righting herself, I wondered, as, clinging for dear life now, we stared vertically into the ocean's depths. Finally, the motion began to reverse itself, we finding ourselves traveling skyward, up, up to stare into the grey, boiling, roiling, billowing rain-drenched clouds. Briefly suspended there, we then began to tilt in the opposite direction which, if this had ever been fun, was no longer. Scared now, yet exhilarated as the freighter temporarily righted herself, I grabbed Flip's arm, running to the safety of the main cabin; not daring to venture deck side again until the sea calmed somewhat.

Two of the crew preoccupied me: one, the bo'sun; the other, the very handsome second engineer. The first, a burly man probably in his mid-forties, took a fancy to me; yet made me squirm every time he came near. I disliked him intensely. As the journey neared its end, he told me he wished to marry me. Me? I was not yet fifteen! He would take me back to Italy he said, as he handed me some little white pills. Leaving to go about his duties, I had enough sense to drop whatever these were, into the ocean, somehow out-smarting his unwanted enticements. Had I succumbed, he, having grown tired of this young thing, would probably have sold me to others, for, in hindsight, I see him that sort of guy. My parents, if not too preoccupied, would have been too protective to let this happen, unless, of course, I had been spirited away, nowhere to be found. In the meantime, everywhere I set foot on this ship, except for the dear "old" radio operator and the handsome second engineer, I heard whispers always said with a smile: "Pero Tant'e!" What did this mean? Nobody would tell me. Eventually, I coerced the second engineer to do so, but that was later.

ILARIO

I couldn't have been more smitten, that is the only word I can think of to describe what happened to me when I came face to face with the Second Engineer on board the "Maria 'C'". He was yes, handsome, in fact to my eyes, an Adonis, this Ilario Navarini, especially when in dress whites with naval insignia. He became my all consuming infatuation, my first BIG crush. And though thirty to my fourteen years, the difference in age didn't dissuade me from pursuit, which must have been disturbing, annoying, even embarrassing for him.

Flirting in Italy seems to be a national pastime, and, ever observant, I had picked up a few pointers during our stay. There was a certain tilt of head, a sly glance, the walk, look of eye, bat of lash, just so, all of which I now brought into play. I must have looked idiotic emulating this unsubtle behavior for Ilario's, or, more hopefully, my benefit. As he paced decks performing his duties, I would brazenly step into his path, forcing him therefore to be polite and acknowledge a passenger. But gradually he began to relax, and I sensed a mutual attraction as he too, with brown eyes sparkling, began to flirt, sparks in his dark eyes.

As we sailed across the Mediterranean, the evenings were balmy. Desert scents wafted from Morocco; Gibraltar loomed in the distance. On those too few nights when the moon's bright path almost obliterated the brilliant phosphorescence lapping the prow and sides of the ship, I danced in Ilario's arms, my romance ripening, or so I hoped, as moon and stars washed over us and others, as we danced on the upper deck to an old Victrola spinning forties' platters. I was often silent, swept away just gazing up at him, he once asking in poetic form, another reason to fall in love with him more: Perche mi guarda ma non favelli? (Why are you looking at me without speaking?) rather than using "parlare." Why? Why, because, I was smitten. So young, so in love, with no idea what I was yearning for, for what did I know of ardent bliss? Would the promise I thought I had felt in Ilario's arms ever be fulfilled, yet not knowing what that might be? Yet, writing years later, I can but laugh at that silly goose of a girl.

Yet, indeed! Into the Atlantic now, and well acquainted with the ship as passengers had been allowed to rove everywhere except captain's quarters, one day I got up the nerve to ask Ilario if he'd show me his cabin. He agreed. As we entered his tidy quarters mid-deck, my heart raced. Alone at last; with no prying eyes. Now surely . . . Taking a deep breath, I turned to him. Had I been older; more mature, I'd probably have thrown myself into his arms, to be loved and to possibly rue the day I'd ever met him. Instead, I nervously looked around his cabin, chatting madly; only then to look up at him. What I saw was a man whose dark eyes were blazing: fixated on mine, with a look of such longing that I suddenly realized what I had unleashed from Pandora's Box.

It was Ilario who broke the spell, forcefully wrestling with his conscience, duty, regulations and obligations. I had never bothered to ask about any of these, supposing a sailor free from such things at sea, and if he had a wife or girl friend in every port, why was he bothering with me? Foolish girl! Grabbing me by an arm, he flung open the cabin door, pulled me unceremoniously behind him, and rushed on deck to sobering salt air. And there he left me, broken-hearted; yet, with the memory of his, almost, capitulation. Maybe, just maybe, another time?

Those awful coal-stoked engines, pushing us ever closer to America's shore, were now unwanted destinations, for what did I care about being back here to see again the New York skyline, the Statue of Liberty, the Empire State Building? Nothing, for all I could think of was having to part from Ilario, my heart crying with despair. Too soon, the dreaded day of debarkation arrived, the ship having pulled into dock over night, and was now busy disgorging passengers and freight. Soon, all had left the ship, and were presently going through customs, while I tarried, the parents, patient to a point, becoming increasingly annoyed, and rightly so. Yet I hated to say goodbye, it was an agony as I struggled with my emotions, as I begged Ilario to keep me in his heart. Remember, I was more Italian than anything else, expressing myself just as they did—to write, to please write, kiss me goodbye. As the crew watched, even cheered, he did so but chastely, as unobserved, he gave me a special pinch with these last words of advice: "Don't forget La Bella Italia and its ways. Love life, be happy, enjoy. Mind your manners, be kindhearted, keep it simple" and, he stressed, "do not become part of that brittle," as he saw it, "hard sell of the American way of life." I have, I hope, lived up to all these injunctions.

Could anyone have had a better fellow for a young crush? Though flirtatious, Ilario, gentleness personified, had behaved impeccably, as he, playing the game; though tempted, never once had taken advantage of this girl who wished nothing more than to throw herself into his arms? To have had this adventure in my young life was highly flattering, and an awakening. And so it was that sorrowfully, tears in my eyes, I walked down the gangplank, turning constantly to wave; heart crushed. Blowing Ilario a kiss, I turned and disappeared from his sight, mine from him. The ache was extraordinary, my only consolation Ilario's promise to write; and so he did; often. I have kept two:

Cara Piccola Mona Giulietta:

> I'm keeping the promise wrenched from me from two splendid and limpidly imploring eyes. Yours was a rosy dream, but now that you are far away, I can confess that many times I felt the desire to hold you in my arms, steal a kiss. So you can see that I too fell, the only difference is that I am a man of an age where I can overcome my impulses and feelings, while you are a dear and naïve girl who allows what's in her heart to show in her eyes. Perhaps one day I may find myself again with you when I may see those eyes, your mouth, smell the fragrance of

your body. But, what am I saying! I am only your friend and have no business talking like this.

Now, as all women, you are curious, wanting to know what "Pero' Tant'e'" means. I would prefer not to tell you but since you insist, I will. More or less, "Tant'e' means: "E oncora un po giovane, pero' mi lo papperei egualmente!" Now your face is red but the expression is a compliment which goes to show that despite your fourteen years, you are already desirable. Are you happy now that I've told you? I send you a little kiss, would to God it was in moonlight!
Pero' Tant'e'! Ilario

Ah, Gli Italiani! Could one have had a better introduction to love? A shame I never answered that last letter, perhaps too alarmed by the sentiments expressed, either that or by then, too involved with the machinations of high school, its cliques, an experience more of boys than of men, a totally new coed experience for me.

I can't help but wonder what happened to "my" Ilario: Did he have a good life? Ever think of me? If still alive today, he'd be an old man, he who had so selflessly and gently indulged a young girl in her first big crush, with kindness and understanding.

Dovungue tu sei, con grazie ed amore, ti abbraccio.
Addio, Giulietta.

Part of Ilario's last letter

RETURN TO USA

The glorious colors of a crisp fall afternoon spread before us, somehow accentuating my heartache for Ilario, so wanting to share this with him as we made our way through the Hudson Valley by car to upstate New York. John Kirkpatrick, that eminent player of Charles Ives' and Carl Ruggles' music, then Dean of the Music School at Cornell, was driving us to Ithaca at the southern end of Cayuga, the longest of the Finger Lakes. The lake, once home to the Cayuga tribe, is situated between two of the five lakes: the Onondaga to the east, Seneca to the west; the other two the Keuka and Canandaigua, all home to these tribes. The Cornell campus, "High above Cayuga's Waters," as its alma mater goes, sprawls across the eastern hill, hell in winter, to face the western one, the lake extending northward from Ithaca. It is here, as the sun slides west over that further hill, that the campus is lit in a golden glow, the town below sinking into dusk. Such evenings are impressive; especially in winter when snow storms often unfurl, drifting down the lake to blend with fading light, enfolding the town and hillsides in a blanket of white, only the warning flash of the red beacon barely visible near the lake's breakwater.

It was late in the day, after cheeseburgers and coffee milkshakes, a novelty for us, when we arrived in Ithaca. As all others would be, this first house in Renwick Heights was leased from a professor on sabbatical. The house was small, dated and rather unattractive, of brick and mortar, looking especially gloomy on this late afternoon, a cold misty rain falling. As we walked the slippery slate steps to the front door, keys in hand, brown shriveled leaves dripped drearily, such a contrast to the vibrant colors of the Mediterranean. This return to America seemed dismal, my heart already half broken, to this ugly small house, our new home away from home. For

217

too long home had been wherever we laid our heads, however briefly, and we felt we had lived out of suitcases most of our lives.

Father's focus was the music department, and his confreres were introduced at a welcome party: the noted musicologist, Donald Grout ("When in doubt, consult Grout"); Bill Campbell, band director; William Austin, musicologist; and composer Robert Palmer. A little later Thomas Sokol joined the faculty as choir director to become a great friend of daddy's. In 1954, Karel Husa, the famous Czech composer, joined the department. Thanks to Keith's friendship with the composer, another on campus that year, was the eminent Ralph Vaughn Williams, known to friends as Uncle Rafe, who came for a full semester. There was also the music librarian "Sherry" Sheresheftsky from Austria, whose wife was a superlative pastry cook. At that time students and faculty in music shared lessons in a rather homespun and antiquated house at 320 Wait Avenue. Today though today the music department is housed in the renovated Lincoln Hall, one room of which, I'm delighted to say, is dedicated to the bass-baritone, "Sir Keith Falkner, 1950-1960."

I knew our father would have half an eye on the golf course, which, fortunately for him, was located directly behind the Music Building: one reason, he said, he had accepted Cornell's offer. Likely story, but it may have helped. Indeed, he headed to the greens at every opportunity, to swing and chase after those blasted little white balls, as Sir Adrian called them. Later, ever the sportsman, daddy would establish Cornell's first cricket team, which often played against the United Nations team.

Renwick Heights was a friendly and welcoming association, but our adjustment to it was not easy. The parents struggled to make ends meet. After the abundance of Italy, daddy's salary, though I didn't know it at the time, was a mere $2,500 a year; so there was much scrimping and saving. Mother took on piano students, and the car, bought from the Kirkpatrick in-laws, an old 1942 two-door Ford, remained in the garage, the cost of running it being prohibitive, even though gas cost about thirty-five cents a gallon. So, we walked everywhere, no matter the weather, drivers constantly slowing to offer rides which daddy refused, muttering after these kind people had gone on their way, "Why can't they realize we walk for pleasure!" Often drenched in rain, sleet, and snow, I did not often walk for pleasure. "If Americans," he continued, "keep riding around in cars, they'll all be fat and legless within a hundred years!" His first observation and prediction seem to have come true. I was given an allowance for doing chores, such as helping with cooking and cleaning. None of us had to do such chores in Italy, with help so cheap, but in Ithaca I leapt heartily to the job. With the exception of being able to replace a light bulb or rewire a plug, our father was hopeless at home maintenance. Mother, who had never had to do any serious cooking, was also pretty dismal, so I began to take over the evening meals, making something other than the seemingly endless and disastrous ham, creamed carrots, boiled potatoes, or stewed lamb. Mother's desserts were good; her specialties crepes, beignets, Duchess puddings, and fruit "fools."

Flip, not yet at school in Peekskill, and I received one slim dime per week, working up to a whopping $12.50 per month four years later. Just recently, I had to giggle when I discovered these allowances were listed under "Charity" in father's well-kept accounts. So, I babysat for the princely sum of thirty-five cents an hour, which allowed me to buy teenage "must-haves" or use toward Capezio shoes, decorated ballet slippers actually.

We never seemed prepared for the changing weather of the area during that first winter. It was probably the last balmy evening, leaves still a-rustle in early November, when daddy, ever the enthusiastic walker, had us striding uphill in summer-like clothing: up Wyckoff Road to Thurston Avenue, across the swing bridge over Judd Falls, and on to the campus, to Bailey Hall for a concert. Several hours later we emerged to find freezing conditions, a blizzard blowing in howling winds, inches of snow already sweeping across the campus. Eventually, sopped, frigid and snowmen-like, having slipped, slid and shivered our long and frigid way home, we made it back to Renwick Heights. Eventually we thawed out with hot baths, hot cocoa, hot toddies, and into beds heated with hot, hot water bottles. Thus did we learn how quickly weather can change in this region, winter storms enshrouding all in icy whiteness. I, bless my soul, would learn to drive in the stuff.

Another Italian now popped into my life, none other than the grandson of Luigi Einaudi, first president of the Republic of Italy following WWII, whose son had arrived on the Cornell campus about the time we did. Mario, the grandson, was a handsome lad blond of hair and blue of eye, being of northern extraction. Fluent as I was, a meeting was arranged, he to be my first date, both families approving: yet it was ill-fated for no sooner arranged than Mario broke a leg skiing. By the time he recovered, I was too involved with my peers to care much, soon forgetting him and only occasionally thinking of Ilario, though we were still writing.

ITHACA HIGH SCHOOL

Shortly after arrival, early October, mother marched us to different schools, Flip to junior High, and me to Ithaca High School, where she informed guidance counselors her daughters' studies must be in the arts; not realizing algebra, geometry, chemistry, physics, and so on, were necessary for higher education. Nonplussed by this British-accented rather opinionated woman, said counselors did not argue. So, here I was, a newly installed freshman dabbling in the arts, with, as a sophomore, lots to make up for graduation. My courses that first year were: English, French, singing, and, because I had juvenile dreams of becoming a big star with a capital "S," acting. Even though it was interesting to get another point of view, I held my tongue in social studies, having learned the British view of these same events.

Their grandparents recruited years before to help build the railroad system through the state, many of my new classmates were second-generation Italians. These fellow students were not Italian speaking, so naturally, I was a curiosity, having enrolled late, spoke with a funny accent, dressed oddly with long pigtails worn around my head, perhaps a peasant daughter from the old country? The British accent or phrasing often caused giggles: once saying to a new friend, "I'll give you a ring," only to have her say, "I don't want a ring, just call me!"

Having known each other since kindergarten, passing through the grades together, these kids made it difficult for a foreigner to be accepted. Those first weeks were an agony: as a novelty, I'd have to prove myself worthy. Until then, except for school, most of my time had been spent with adults or rigorous school situations that were never coed. It was difficult, for apart from some very unwelcoming girls, I was not sure what to make of these gangly, sometimes short and acne-covered boys, how to react to their childish behavior. After Ilario, it was "Yuck" time for boys. Well, not all; but most.

For the last few years, school uniforms had been the norm for me and everyone else, regardless of status. Here I found it an oddity, both trivial and expensive, that most girls dressed in fashions suggested, if not actually decreed, by the latest issue of *Seventeen* magazine: remember the poodle haircut, poodle skirt, not to forget bobby-socks and saddle shoes? Of course, I had to have a pair of these. Mother finally bought me a pair, but in size eight; far too big for my size-seven, in case my foot-size increased. It never did, but that's how poor we were at the time.

The while, mother was growing increasingly concerned. "Are you aware," asked other Cornell wives with girls enrolled in the Ithaca school system, "that your daughters, at least Julia, will be subject to rampant promiscuity? Half her class will be, if it isn't already pregnant, will be so by the senior year!" Naturally, mother was shocked, horrified enough to warn both, of us, but particularly me: "If either of you should ever find yourself in this condition, meaning "pregnant," never, I do mean NEVER, bother to darken my doorstep again!" Her remarks were unwarranted, uncalled for and highly insensitive, causing my sister to go one way, I another. In any case, mother's information had been incorrect, for in our class of 1954, I only heard of one, guessing others had perhaps been lucky.

Many of the freshmen girls decided to try out for the position of baton-twirling cheerleaders, a status thing, each vying to be chosen to cheer on the crowds at school football and basketball games. I too learned to twirl, chant slogans of "rah, rah rah," but my heart was not in it, so, in a detached sort of way, was not disappointed as either too shy or perhaps lacking self-confidence, I was not chosen. The positions going to those overly vivacious, adorably pretty, perky, empty-headed girls who swooned over jocks. There were other clubs, though I never felt totally comfortable joining them either. Mother was constantly urging individuality, her constant admonition, "Be yourself!" Wise words, but difficult for a teenager who wanted to fit in.

In Ithaca High in the 1950s we either bought our lunch in shifts for twenty-five cents, brown-bagged it, or walked the few blocks uptown to eat at a drugstore soda-fountain or five-and-dime, ordering an egg or tuna fish salad sandwich, a drink, and pie a la mode for almost nothing by today's standards. There was also the tasty *Home Dairy Bakery,* a bakery and cafeteria, all of us particularly fond of their orange frosted angel food cake. One spring afternoon, a bunch of us girls skipped school after lunch at the drugstore to run up to Marilyn's nearby house for an afternoon of sunning, hose spraying, toe nail painting, and gossip. At 4:00, I just managed to catch my school bus driven by that delightful ever-flirting middle-aged Frank, back to Renwick Heights, there, luckily, finding the parents out so that I could fabricate my excuse for that afternoon's absence. And so, hastily typing one, I illegally traced mother's signature, thinking as I did so, how very clever I had been. Not so, for, having turned in my excuse, I was summoned to the principal's office, chastised for unexcused absenteeism, forgery, and lying. My punishment, for there would have been one in Italian schools, was nothing more than not to do it again, or there would be consequences. Lesson learned. I should have told my parents, for, when I confessed, Mother surprised me: "Why didn't you tell me? I would have covered for you. Everyone plays truant once in awhile! But, don't let it happen again." I never quite knew what to expect from mother, she giving confusing messages so that I never quite knew which way she would jump.

Absorbed in the school system and its activities, my grades remained dismal, for, unchallenged, I was set on a more playful path. Courses were too easy to worry about after Italy's hard challenges. But I was involved, my interests as listed in *The Annual* for 1954:

> Julia Christabel Falkner: "Julie," (also known as Ju-Ju-Babe): Choral Club 4; Chorus 2; Dramatic Club 3,4; Itheteria (Latin Club) 1; Le cercle Francais 1,2,3; Madisquem (musicians, acting, dancing, instrumentalists, singers, quartets, ukelele, entertainers and magic); Tatler

Staff 3,4; Sectional All State Chorus: Junior Committees; Senior Committees.

Not bad, I thought, for one who had belatedly arrived on the scene, despite poor grades.

A BIRTHDAY PARTY

For my fifteenth birthday on January 10th, 1951, it was the parents who suggested I invite eleven friends to come to the party. It was set for a Friday afternoon, and, with no help, mother had cooked; she so new to cooking but, in this case excelled, working her butt off, (excuse me, Mum) to provide a special occasion for my new friends and me. The menu included a large Smithfield ham, bought at no small expense, and orange Duchess Pudding, but, no birthday cake: that was for family later on. Classmates arrived an hour or so after school; luckily, no one had turned down the invitation. I dread to think how I might have felt if they had, but they all came, seeming to enjoy the British party games organized by daddy.

Dinner was served, my friends and I gathering in the dining room around a highly polished table, elaborately set with silver, crystal, china, and linens, all crated from England, via Italy, to America. It was then, to my horror, it occurred to me my guests were probably all Catholic; unable to eat meat on Fridays. Predictably, all politely declined the delicious ham, but gobbled everything else in sight. Still, I thought my parents had made the biggest gaffe of my young life. The party obviously made an impression on the girls that long ago evening; for, at a recent reunion a few years ago, they remembered it all, and they laughed to say that had this occurred today, all of them would have partaken of the ham. Eating meat on Fridays is no longer a sin.

But to my surprise, the evening was not yet over, for, after another round of party games, Charades among them, just before our curfew at 10:00 p.m., daddy, amid dimmed lights to oohs and aahs, marched in with the traditional flaming English New Year's, belated in this case, large silver bowl laden with brandy-soaked raisins, bluish flames guttering and spluttering, as daddy urged everyone to dip in, grab a handful of pixilated grapes for the new year, and to wish me a happy birthday. I had had no idea this was planned, and I loved it. It was a great ending, the success of the evening, despite the ham fiasco, everyone seeming pleased to have shared my strange birthday party; so very unlike their own.

First summer back: Mary Kirkpatrick and me

SUMMER JOBS—1951
AND
POLIO SCARE

Suddenly, my freshman year was over, and, just as suddenly, it was summer. Daddy, still financially pinched, put an ad in *Time*, not too proud to offer his and mother's services as cook and butler, his daughters as maids. There was only one reply, one from a fruit grower in South Carolina: "Come pick my apricots, share proceeds. Daughters can sell ice cream on the highway." Not accepting this, Daddy departed for England for part of the summer while Mother received an offer from new friend Wilma Perkins, niece of the original owner and author Fannie Farmer. Farmer wrote the first definitive American cookbook, which created the standardized North American measurement system. Accepting the challenging position and a small salary, mother went off to Kennebunkport, Maine, to learn "cookery," greatly improving her techniques and gaining enough knowledge to write her own, unpublished cookbook.

For my sister and me, it would be a divided summer, she off to girl scout camp while I, for a small stipend, joined John and Hope Kirkpatrick's family as babysitter for their children, Daisy, David, and Mary, at their summer home in Danbury, Connecticut. The grounds, owned by Hope's parents, consisted of two main houses, a barn-like conservatory for John's practicing or entertaining; a guest cottage, my abode for the summer, along with a further studio-type cottage, residence of the family friend Erica Von Kaga, painter in the 1950s of charming greeting cards for Hallmark. In my off time, I studied with her.

It had been an enjoyable summer so far in this musical environment, Mr. Kirkpatrick often at the piano, Mrs. K easy to work for, their children easy to care for, with pleasant excursions to the shore and elsewhere. Danbury was nearby and one evening the K's took me to see *The Merry Widow*. How I loved that show! Having a place of my own on their beautiful grounds was fine, too, in off hours, to read in a quiet grove, be off by myself, or have a painting lesson with Erika. In fact, all was quite blissful until halfway through the summer.

We had enjoyed a fine day at the beach, returning exhausted, damp, salty, and somewhat chilled. Nonetheless, the children and I, all rather cranky still in our bathing suits, sat on the lawn playing games, before supper. For some reason, I felt cranky too, the late afternoon seemingly endless. At table, I, who loved Campbell's cream of spinach soup, could barely swallow it, or the rest of the meal. Later, and not soon enough for me, I managed to bathe and get the children into bed, then join Hope and her mother for our usual game of Parcheesi. It was a desultory game, during which the usual chocolate chip cookie and Dubonnet, did not go down well, causing me to ask to be excused, as feeling very odd, it was all I could do to toddle, in semi darkness, across the lawn to my cottage, and fall into bed.

It was about midnight when I awoke, and for one who has never suffered headaches, this was a killer, one of such throbbing proportions I felt my skull about to blast open, feeling at the same time, totally nauseated. Raising myself slowly, I found I could barely stand but somehow managed to reel into the bathroom, managing then, somehow, to return and crawl back into bed, unable to do more. I must have dozed until the clock registered seven, the very hour I was supposed to be up at the main house getting the children up for the day. Fortunately, all buildings on the property were connected by phone and so, just able to lift the receiver, I called the main house, to whisper to Hope that I was unable to move, would have to take at least the morning off, and hung up. What was happening to me? Why did I feel so awful, why couldn't I shake this awful bug? More importantly, why could I barely move?

From then on, others took over, and my days were a blur of time and faces. A doctor arrived at some point, as did mummy, in time to hear his diagnosis: the dreaded polio, he scheduling me for a spinal tap the following week. Everyone was shocked, not least the Kirkpatricks, worrying about their children. Then, the day before the spinal tap, my fifteen-year-old body began to fight back. The headaches eased, I began to eat, to stand unsteadily at first, was gradually able to take the few steps to the bathroom, to grow stronger every day, so much so that the doctor cancelled the tap. Mother told me later, that all she could think about was Roosevelt, who had suffered from the same disease, caused, so it was thought at the time, by sitting around in wet bathing suits. Well, that is exactly what I had done! Mother dreaded a life for me in an iron lung, the treatment of the day, perhaps paralysis, her daughter in a wheelchair for life. Today, of course, it is known polio is a highly infectious disease caused by a virus which invades the nervous system, often causing paralysis within hours. I was lucky. Polio has almost entirely been eradicated, except in Pakistan, Afghanistan, India, and parts of Africa by the Salk and Sabin serum.

Obviously, I had caused an agony for the Kirkpatricks, worried about their own children, and the parents, all wondering how and what to do next with this burden on their shoulders. Of course the sooner I could be removed from the Kirkpatrick enclave, the better; less likely for the children to be affected. Fortunately, they did not catch the virus. It was now the ever-caring and generous Aunt Dodie who came to the fore yet again, offering the loan of her newly built house in the woods near Cornwall, providing that daddy and I cleared underbrush and trimmed trees during my recuperation. I did so on these late summer days, helping daddy in woodland surrounding the house, and seeding a new lawn. It must have been the right remedy, for in no time at all, I had regained my strength, to wonder what all the fuss had been about. But how fortunate I had been, how lucky to have overcome the virus with no aftereffects.

SOPHOMORE YEAR

It was time to get back to Ithaca, where we immediately moved into the home of the Morris Bishops. Professor Bishop was the eminent chairman of the Romance and Literature Department, compiler of the history of Cornell, biographer and composer of limericks, and instrumental in getting Vladimir Nabokov to come to Cornell in 1948. The Bishops, Morris, his painter wife Alison, and daughter, were off to Greece on Sabbatical, their home just a stone's throw from Renwick Heights, to Cayuga Heights, the wealthy, wooded suburb northwest of the Cornell campus. We came to call the professor's home affectionately as "the Bishop's Palace," a large white-painted brick edifice overlooking the lake and western hills of Tompkins County.

Before we left Renwick Heights daddy took me aside. "I need to talk with you," he said. What, I wondered had I done or not done now, so often feeling I never quite lived up to parental expectations. "We have a problem," he continued. "We're unable to send both you and Philippa to boarding school next year and have chosen to—I was all ears at this point—send your sister to St. Mary's in Peekskill, paying her fees by giving recitals. You, and we hope you don't mind too much, will continue at Ithaca High, all we can do for the moment." Mind too much? I was ecstatic! Why would I want to go to yet another boring nun run boarding school, then under the Episcopal Diocese of New York? After all, by now I had been accepted. Furthermore, I had discovered some boys were not so ghastly after all, some too eager for manhood status, in a terrible hurry, to run off to fight. I doubt they knew what they were in for, for it, the Korean war, was a proxy between two countries separated by the 38th parallel, the south supported by the United Nations and United States,

231

the north by the Republic of China. The fighting was brutal, American deaths mounting to over thirty-three thousand dead; some eight thousand missing between 1951 and 1953. Before leaving, these benighted fellows made a round of high school girls, asking them to write with news from home. I did, too, for one fellow but never heard back, he probably one of the casualties listed above. Those of us still in school, though, had little interest in the mayhem; though I do remember General MacArthur's farewell speech when dismissed by Harry Truman, broadcast throughout the school: "Old soldiers never die, they just fade away . . ."

Meanwhile, the Ithaca Public School Board had hired an exchange teacher from England for a year, a Miss Stone who managed to ingratiate herself into her classes, teaching world geography. It was a course considered by many of the guys, who needed a passing grade for graduation, to be a breeze, and so, Miss Stone's classes were full, with guys like Harold (Harry) James, full of fun, our own aspiring trumpeter of the same name. Mary Ketchem, a new friend, and I took the course out of genuine interest, pleasure. It was a fun class but probably trying for Miss Stone, for we were not kind. Mary and I sat one behind the other, front row center, and when attendance was called, or one of us was asked a question, the other one would stand up in her place, thinking, as other students giggled, we were so clever: how about, so juvenile?

Our masquerade was soon discovered for when the parents heard an English woman was in their midst, they invited Miss Stone for a proper Sunday lunch. At the appointed hour, as I opened the front door to Miss Stone's knock, she exclaimed: "Oh! Ho! So, you who are the real Julia Falkner, and not, Mary Ketchem. Just as I thought! Your accent gave you away, you know." Oops! Foiled again. With G & T, in hand and wine with lunch, Miss Stone was a charming guest, rosy cheeks much in evidence from the imbibing while enjoying the traditional lunch of roast chicken, bread sauce, new potatoes with minted peas, followed by a Summer Pudding.

But, all this was superfluous stuff, for I was now into, Boys! Generally, my preference has been for older men; here were all these boys turning into handsome young things; well some were, aging from embarrassing pip-squeak tenors and acne, to baritonal tones, downy faces showing stubby bristles. It was this year that a junior named Bill Z. took a fancy to sophomoric me, inviting me to the first prom of the year. But, what was I to wear? I didn't own a prom dress. As always, Mother urged me to be individualistic, not to worry what others were wearing, so the result was a full black but short skirt with crinoline, black peasant blouse (hey, you can do wonders with elasticized off-the-shoulder sleeves), a wide black belt and black Capezio slippers. Heels were out for I would have been taller than my date—horrors! And, yes, the outfit was certainly different! So totally different that Bill must have been nonplussed having gone to the wild expense of buying a black orchid which he presented to me, carefully wrapped in clear cellophane box with black bow. Wow! I wore it on my wrist to be envied by others, for elsewhere it would have been unnoticeable. But, poor Bill, our relationship was not to be. He, thinking himself to be intellectually brilliant, and a virtuoso pianist, was neither. All he ever played in my presence were snatches of Khatchaturian's *Saber Dance*. Nor, did I find him attractive, he with pear-shaped body, belted trousers worn mid-chest. However, he seemed enamored of me for, at the dance, as we swept around the floor, he kissed his way from my knuckles, up an arm, across a bare shoulder, thankfully skirting my mouth, on to the other shoulder. It was embarrassing, revolting even, and I could hardly wait for the evening to end. I didn't date him again; my attention soon absorbed elsewhere.

Meanwhile, the school year had passed in a haze as did most of the musical events on campus which the parents expected me to attend, fortunately not all forty-one of them. I did attend a number with important artists including the brilliant soprano Eileen Farrell, frequent soloist with the New York Philharmonic under Leonard Bernstein. There were also Rudolf Firkusny, the Czech pianist who managed to escape the Nazis in 1929 to become one of the great pianists of the century; the Cleveland Orchestra under George Szell; the Hungarian and Walden String Quartets; and the highlight of the year, presented on May 16, the performance of Handel's

Alexander's Feast with Leona Scheuneman, soprano; the Hungarian tenor, Leslie Chabay and, Keith Falkner, bass-baritone: it was a great success.

While still in the Bishop's Palace, it was also that year, if memory serves, that my parents gave a dinner party for one of twentieth century's finest violinists, David Fydorovich Oistrakh, then on campus. Mother pulled out all the stops, serving a rather eclectic dinner starting with borscht, ending with Russian blini. Espresso and brandies, expensive cigarettes and cigars, their odors suggesting a coffee cum chocolate aroma, ended a splendid, but smoke-fugged, evening.

TOM, WITH VIRGINITY LOST

While all this was occurring, I was more interested in Tom C. What did we call "hunks" in those days: "Super Dude," "Swell Guy?" Unlike some others who preferred the flamboyant "Zoot Suit," first popularized in Harlem Jazz culture of the late 1930s, Tom usually wore fatigues. Zoot suits consisted of high-waisted, wide-legged, tight-cuffed peg-legged trousers with long jacket, with wide lapels and padded shoulders, often with chains dangling from belt to knee. Shirts had outrageous collars, with hair styled in a "duck tail." The best representative of this style was classmate Tom Flynn, (not the Tom of what follows), he so fun and sports-minded.

Tom C. was tall, fairly good-looking, had the curliest red hair I'd ever seen, with a certain charm, and an eye for the girls. He was certainly deeply involved with DeMoley, the Masonic-sponsored youth fraternity for young men founded in Kansas City in 1919, its objective to teach young men to be better persons, and leaders. Tom was into varsity sports until he developed water on the knee. Rest was prescribed, with ice and elevation of limb. Before his injury, Tom and I had occasionally dated; then began spending hours after school at my house listening to the hot tunes of the day: *Fly Me to the Moon;" "Purple Shades at Eventide"* as Tom hummed and strummed his ukulele. Years later he would tell me I had been the inspiration for his composition, *"Julia."* Though touched, I never heard it. On these long afternoons, Tom taught me to "Jitterbug," perfecting the intricate steps; the flips, turns, swish overs, around and through, eventually to become very good at it. "Jitterbug" is attributed to Cab Calloway, wearer of "Zoot Suits," while the term Jitterbug derives from an early 20th century term to describe alcoholics suffering from the DTs. Lyrics to "Call of the Jitter Bug" are:"

If you like to be a jitter bug,
First thing you must do is get a jug.
Put whiskey, wine and gin within,
And shake it all up and then begin.
Grab a cup and start to toss,
You are drinking jitter sauce!
Don't you worry, you just mug,
And then you'll be a jitter bug!"

So when Tom was side-lined and confined to bed rest for some months, after school, as encouraged by his parents, I'd walk to his house. It was always Tom's father who escorted me, teasingly, upstairs to his son's room who had watched my approach, with pony tail swinging. I was surprised to find his parents so relaxed about our being together for long periods of time. In fact, they seemed to encourage it. It was a mistake.

One afternoon, visiting as usual but with no one else at home, I made my way upstairs to Tom's room, finding him relaxed in an arm chair, foot on hassock, curls damp from a recent shower, tension in the air. Until then, the extent of our love-making, if you can call it that, had been kissing, and fumbling in the back seat of cars. But now we were alone. As I leant over to give Tom a kiss, his arms went around me, pulling me onto his lap, where I sat on a bulge impossible to ignore. What power I had, I thought, able to arouse a man; well, in this case, a young man full of testosterone.

Pushing me inches away, Tom gazed into my eyes: "Let me see you, I want to see your body, to make love to you." I noticed the absence of "with," but that was me, always wanting to totally share monumental moments; this, to my mind, such an occasion. Compliant, and too young to play vamp, temptress, seductress, or whore, I modestly turned my back and disrobed. I know not what I wore that day except for a pearl choker which I didn't bother to remove. Turning again towards my seducer; terribly vulnerable, I attempted to cover my nakedness, as Tom, who had not risen from his chair, gazed. "No!" he ordered. "Lie down on the bed." I did as told, noticing his newly made bed, thinking all this had been planned. He arose then to look upon my body, from my point of view breasts which looked like eggs in a frying pan; flat stomach, curly fringe. What was so erotic about that? It was both an embarrassment and an arousal, certainly it seemed the ultimate turn on for my lover to be. He stood gazing the length of my body, my only clothes, pearls. "You're beautiful," he barely whispered before his body loomed over me. We kissed. His hand caressed me, but I reached out, pulling him to me. Ah youth, testosterone, his insensate need taking over, though I sensed his body clenching for self-control, my deflowering a sudden rush, which, after a small hurt, his need being far greater than mine was just a thrust or two before he spasmed. I did not follow, but then, he had little knowledge of how to please a woman. For that matter, I knew nothing of pleasing a man, or to know what was missing from this juvenile "bedding." I did wonder why all the fuss about sex, if this was all there was to it.

It would be years before, with the right partner, I found ecstasy could be had. From our conjoining of course, Tom and I were often "at it," at the lake, woods, my house or his, his appetite unquenchable, instant gratification for him, while I was just pleased to be the girlfriend of a senior hunk in school. Yet, we were "playing with fire," sex always unprotected, neither of us thinking much about it, astonishing I didn't get pregnant, but somehow, foolishly, felt I was getting back at mother, testing her "Never bother to darken my doorstep again" attitude. As mentioned earlier, this remark to both her daughters caused us to react differently: Philippa, whom I sometimes found "saintlier than thou," and myself, who had to find out what all this hush-hush sex was about: devil take the hind-most, suggestive in itself! Too, I was too smitten to care, though it was quite a different "smitten" from what I had sensed would have been Ilario's treatment of me, had I ever been so lucky to have got that far.

Before parting for the summer, Tom to a swank resort in Bar Harbor, Maine, I not yet sure where, we spent hours at Beebe Lake, located on the northwestern edge of the Cornell Campus. Here, according to lore, couples, who walked the mile path around the lake holding hands, were destined to marry. I didn't know that then; certainly we spent many hours swimming, walking, and smooching under the waterfalls cascading from above, I in a Jantzen bathing suit bought for me by mother, the only one I owned, which left nothing to the imagination, nipples to the fore: so embarrassing. Needless to say, summer over, we would resume our juvenilia "pairings."

KENT & MARTHA'S VINEYARD
SUMMER 1952

Spring had edged toward summer. School let out in early June, not to reconvene until after Labor Day. But, where was I to spend the next few months, and with Tom away? Aunt Dodie, as so often, came up with the answer, knowing of an older couple in Kent, Connecticut, who needed a minder for their six-year-old son, Lanny. It paid well, and the summer would prove interesting and fun. The McDowells, an older couple, had only one child, a darling and charming red-headed six-year old. My duties, other than caring for him, were to cook evening meals, and after Lanny had been put to bed, to serve the meal and eat with his parents. They had a lovely garden full of flower beds and green lawns, where bees hummed, dragon and butterflies flittered and fluttered. There was an orchard, and further, acres of blueberry bushes which I had to harvest, while day-dreaming about Tom, who was far away in Maine.

Summer in Kent alternated with trips to Martha's Vineyard via Woods Hole, site of the oceanographic institution. My first weeks in Kent were spent gearing up for such a trip, as Mrs. McD, Lanny, and I whizzed around the countryside in her classic green MG. As the three of us tore down country lanes, with everything bought on these expeditions piled up beside Lanny on the almost non-existent back seat. By the time we reached home, it was not unusual to find that some goods were missing; having been swooshed out by the rush of air.

Kent Military Academy, all male then, co-ed today, was nearby. How those fellows learned a new girl was in town, I do not know, but soon there were calls from cadets asking me out. These young men were supposedly on campus for tutorial assistance; though I doubt they achieved much, for they seemed to party most of the time; often drinking themselves senseless. I did occasionally accept an invitation from Rich, and was immediately envious of his red convertible as he drove us to Kent's country club, there where I had to vie with rich, attractive, well-heeled, and spoiled young gals. But Rich, too, was over privileged. From the club's bar, drinks flowed, no questions asked. Rich introduced me to Tom Collins, too heady for me at the time, so sometimes found myself lolling on lawns, kissing this rather inebriated fool. In our condition, driving back to the McD's, could be hair-raising.

I had more fun with Lanny, though I did not care for his entomological interests. The garden attracted myriad butterflies, colorful specimens which he collected in his little net, speared them with pins, and placed them into glass-covered boxes. Fortunately, beetles and spiders were out. One evening before bedtime, Lanny and I walked to the orchard where, choosing an apple tree, at his request, I plastered a ring of molasses around the trunk. Early next morning, Lanny rushed out to see if he had captured anything, and indeed he had: the thrilling prize of a large pale-green lunar moth, stuck to the black gunk, dead. So sad.

A few weeks later, we piled into Mr. McD's large car and headed for Wood's Hole. From there we took the ferry to Martha's Vineyard, the island originally inhabited by the Wampanoag, thereafter named "Martha" by British explorers, yet no one seems to know why. Before sailing, we ate supper in a seafood restaurant near the wharf where a black male and his white companion entered and sat nearby. Whereupon, the atmosphere suddenly changed, fraught now with tension as some diners scowled and whispered, even moving to tables further away from the couple.

"Discrimination," had never been a word in our family, a musician, after all, was a musician whatever his skin's color. In school, though they were few, I felt at home with blacks. The Brown v. Board of Education ruling had not taken effect until May that year, declaring "separate educational facilities are inherently unequal." In Ithaca High School there had been no such discrimination, for, in New York State then, there were no racially segregated schools except when whole neighborhoods were involved. So, I was amazed by the fuss elsewhere, admiring the courage of the racially mixed couple sitting nearby, challenging the status quo, the bigotry.

Our disturbed yummy seafood supper over, we were aboard the ferry and soon arrived in Edgartown to drive to the McDowell's modern summer home near the nor'-eastern shore. Their house stood amid older, well-spaced houses whose weather-beaten gray shingles had been buffeted by wind-blown sand and salty spray for years. Lanny's bedroom was in a small crow's nest a-top all; the main floor with multiple floor-to-ceiling windows, surrounding verandas overlooking the Atlantic with its endless roar, echoing throughout the house. Life was relaxed. Informality was everywhere, as we cycled the island, swam, surfed, sailed or fished. Lanny loved the latter but hated to bait, so I did it for him, trying not to think as I impaled each poor worm. One day, fishing off a nearby breakwater, Lanny caught a twenty-inch baby sand shark, which somehow, I managed to unhook and throw back into the sea. It appeared grateful, as, waggling its tail, it swam off into deeper waters.

Wearing only halters, shorts, or swim suits, we were all soon nut-brown. My duties with Lanny were light, but the evening meal was, as usual, my responsibility. So, many a late afternoon, I strode down to the shore, through razor-sharp sea grass, over dunes, and through tangles of beach plums, carrying a large pot to fill with sea water. I'd lug the thing back up to the house, heave it onto the stove, turn on the heat, and bring it to a boil. Then there was the awful task of throwing live lobsters, legs and pincers flaying, into the cauldron, and slam down the lid. At least I did not have to deal with the gigantic ones in Honduras, where a friend of mine had found them ferocious, fighting and jumping their way out of pots, to scramble up walls or to drop to the floor with large pincers waving as they tried to escape. No, thank you! What I was doing was cruel enough, though in some ways, beautiful too, for in their death, carapaces turn a ravishing pink; flesh, dripping with lemon-butter, quite sublime.

With one day a week off, I had a chance to meet and make friends, but, unlike them, had a summer job. All of us were bronzed, lithe, nubile, energetic and equally giddy, as we bicycled around the Vineyard, bowled, or played endless games of tennis, hung out at soda shops, or went to the movies. There were moonlit evenings on an anchored raft in deep water, where, over and over again, we proved our supposed invincibility by diving into the darkened depths, swimming under the platform, and up, and over again. We flirted outrageously, lying top-side, basking in sunshine or brilliant moon-star shine: all pure fun, a wonderful way to spend a summer.

In many ways, I was sad to see the summer wane, though I was eager to get back to my "Joker." Well, that's the way I felt about Tom, he who had spent his summer as an "attendant" at a swank resort in Maine. Tom had written often, enjoying a racy summer, so he was proud to tell me, and I knew he did not mean "racing." I was sad to say goodbye to Lanny and his parents who, on parting, gave me a beautiful leather bag which, they said, had had my name on it. So I was on my way back to Ithaca, eager to meet up with Tom, he for his senior and my junior year. We were definitely, a "pair."

At that first prom in November, having re-rehearsed our jitterbug steps, we decided to show off. And we did. Before leaving Kent on a day off, I had taken the train into Hartford to buy a long strapless tulle dress in order to fit in with everyone else. Compared to what I had worn at previous dances, this was "in." Many were on the floor that evening before realizing Tom and I were "cutting a rug." The floor soon cleared, and as the only couple on the floor, we exhibited in an intricate blur of energy, the fast-paced steps of the Jitterbug. I loved it; yet was embarrassed to be on exhibition, for that is what this was. I was doubly embarrassed when, ending the performance, I looked down to find my strapless dress had slipped, fortunately with bra still where it should be. Everyone clapped and slapped Tom on his back.

About this time Daddy wisely began to introduce me to liquor; hoping, he said, to inure me from disastrous binges so many young people fall prey to. Then, I started to smoke, it being the "in-thing" to do at the time. I tried to keep this secret from my parents, who would not have approved. After I conquered the cough, cough, splutter, splutter, choking, tears rolling down cheeks, I thought I had arrived; the total sophisticate for sure!

SCHOOL YEAR 1952/53

Back home from the summer, I found the parents had moved again, the third house in three years. This one was located at the southern end of State Street leading up from downtown, in turn to become Danby Road, southward out of town. Not too far away on State, lived Mary Ketchem, already mentioned, who, over the years, became a good friend. Her parents were wonderful, always making me feel welcome whenever I stayed. Meanwhile, our new abode, though less impressive than the Bishop's Palace, was comfortable enough, with large airy study/music room, grand piano, and a modern monaural LP record player and speakers.

That year, the music department, in its element again, presented thirty-six concerts and recitals. There was the Danish National Orchestra; William Warfield, Baritone; Isaac Stern, violinist; the Cleveland Orchestra; the Robert Shaw Chorale; the Juilliard and Griller Quartets. My father appeared in recital with the British pianist John Hunt, a visiting professor that year. Some other literati and illuminati on campus that year were, aside from Nabokov, Freeman Dyson, son of Sir George, a predecessor of father's as director of the Royal College of Music. Freeman, a physicist, author of *Disturbing the Universe* (1979)—a must read—was a lover of music, as are many physicists. Also on campus were the Clinton Rossiters, he historian and political scientist, author of "*The American Presidency*" and "*Seedtime of the Republic.*" I often sat for the children, saddened to hear of the Professor's suicide in 1970, caused, it was said, by acute depression.

Early in September, mother flew to England to visit family; not to return until Christmas. She was in London on December 5th, during the Great Smog of 1952, which lasted until the 9th. She wrote to say it had been almost impossible to find her way through yellowish murk that was so thick at night she couldn't see her feet or the pavement on which she stood. The fog resulted in many deaths and inconvenienced millions. This, and other "Pea-Soupers," over the years, had been caused by belching factories and innumerable coal fires, all spewing toxic fumes into the air. Such obliterating smog no longer occurs thanks to pollution legislation, slum clearance, and urban renewal. However, in other parts of the country you are likely to run into a different kind of fog, caused by atmospheric depressions. They are both treacherous, and quite wonderful in the density of the blankets of dewy wetness settling on everything, as tendrils of fog waft wraith-like and ghostly over Scotland and Yorkshire dales. In later years, I drove through some both day and night, and always they were eerie; sometimes, frightening.

Back in school besides course work, there were voice and piano lessons and life-saving classes in the YMCA pool. Daddy and I often went to sporting events, especially on Saturdays in the fall, for the Big Red football games at Schoellkopf Field. Mother took no interest in these "rough and tumbles," as she called them, she who had once attended a prize fight in 1934, between heavyweights Max Baer and Primo Carnera at Madison Square Garden. As she and daddy arrived a bit late, taking her seat, she glanced up at the boxers, to jump back up, stunned: "He hit him!" she shouted over the roar of the crowd. "But, of course!" Keith shouted, "What did you expect?" From then on mother preferred to occupy her time elsewhere. So, it was left to daddy and me, to enjoy the varied sports on campus together. Flip, you may recall, was still at school at St. Mary's. I didn't mind, though much preferred swimming meets and basketball to wrestling matches.

That year passed as fast and as hazily as had the previous one, though on mother's return, she had seemed increasingly concerned about me and my supposed, wayward ways. We often upset each other, she mostly sarcastic when it came to dealing with me, while I grew ever more angry and resentful. Aunt Dodie suddenly appeared for a week's visit, and she made it her business to spend time with me. Aside from her continued interest in my welfare, she seemed keen to know my views on any given subject, and what I might like to do in the future. At the time, I thought I might like to be an archeologist, and Dodie encouraged this. It was not until she left, and having said goodbye to the parents, that, as I helped her into her car, she turned to me, theoretically her adopted niece, who, as a strict New Englander, had been horrified by my painted nails and lips with a product called "Hot Tomato." She said, "Keep going the way you are, my dear, and you'll end up a slut!" I felt this judgment totally unjustified, knowing only too well who had suggested this castigation; none other than my mother! Small wonder, I suppose, for I had pronounced on my 16th birthday, that I would be moving to New York City to become a model. I had it all planned. I would live in the Barbizon Hotel, then a hotel for young ladies, and hunt for such a job. With that announcement mother had flown into a tizzy, and had taken to her bed for a week. I'm not kidding! Daddy, bless him, though busy elsewhere, trusted me, which kept me, well, more or less, on an even keel.

The class of 1953 graduated that June. Tom had been accepted at Bowling Green, Ohio, for the next year, would be leaving in the fall; we, necessarily, to part. I had met his great pal Dick S., a tall, rangy rather attractive red-head who, at his unlikely age, affected a pipe. Tom entrusted me to Dick's care, which I did not particularly mind, for I liked this senior who, because of poor grades, would return as a post-graduate student next year when I would be a senior. But for now, another summer loomed, I hired by the New York jeweler Baumgold; he and family summering in Cos Cob, Connecticut, an arrangement which would last for two years.

SUMMER 1953—COS COB

So, instead of what mother had called "my ridiculous plans," I was off to Cos Cob, near Greenwich, Connecticut, to care for the Goldbaum children: eight year-old Julie, Buzz, six, and three year old Adam. Familiar now with the Lackawanna's reliable "Phoebe Snow," I boarded in Owego, a one-horse stop with no station or platform, located between Elmira and Binghamton, which ran to Hoboken, the route vying with the New York Central's line to Buffalo. Daddy, dear daddy, was always in Owego on my return. The history of the train spans the seventeen years between 1949 and 1966. The the name Phoebe was meant to evoke snow-white services, as the trains engines burned anthracite, a clean-burning fuel. Traveling several summers on this spectacular route through the Poconos, I got to know the friendly staff of the dining who served delicious meals on tables draped with crisp white napery and polished silverware. Black waiters served impeccably, and were immaculately dressed in highly polished black shoes and socks, black trousers, white jackets and gloves. But, sadly, with the onset of faster travel, the "Phoebe" and other trains lost passengers and went out of business, though not forgotten as a classic mode of travel.

The estate in Cos Cob was entered through tall wrought-iron gates with, to the right, stables and a groom's cottage. A long uphill drive lead to three mansion-like houses, each hidden from the other by woodlands near a large over-grown lake, with terraces where Romanesque statuary eroded. Behind the Baumgold's ivy covered stone house, was a large swimming pool with changing rooms, along with tennis courts and acres of woodlands. The Pomerances lived nearby, he the architect Ralph Pomerance, whose house, which I loved to visit, had an open floor plan with floor to ceiling windows, a see-through staircase, all of which created a sense of airiness in a bucolic setting. Their daughter, Pamela, became a summer friend, while her brother, several years younger, is, I believe, the Steve Pomerance involved in politics; their father, the architect of course, while their mother Jo (Josephine), an early advocate of nuclear arms control, was the granddaughter of Henry Morgenthal, Sr.

Summers in Cos Cob were for the most part fun. I was earning a decent wage, had separate quarters, most evenings free, and one day off a week. Fortunately, most of our days were sunny. On rainy ones, which weren't much fun for the kids, I managed to keep them entertained. They particularly loved the wonderful children's recordings by Danny Kaye: "Clocks and watches and watches and clocks, make terrible ticks and horrible tocks . . ." On better days, there were tennis lessons, matches; and swimming and diving lessons taught by a hunk of a pro. Endless afternoons were spent poolside, or hiking, or horseback riding. At supper time, the children and I munched on trays in the TV room watching "Howdy Doody," which, because of its popularity, became the very first show to be extended to five evenings a week. Bob Smith, host, played Buffalo Bob. There was also Clarabelle the clown, with marionettes Phineas T. Bluster, Dilly Dally and Flub-a-Dub all so human-like, they gave the impression they could cut their strings and walk off the set at any given moment.

The previous year I had passed my driver's test, thanks to mother's instruction. She was an excellent driver herself, having been taught in the 1930's by Philip, that road-racing brother of hers. On one weekend with the Baumgolds away, their 1950's green Cadillac remained in the driveway, keys in the ignition. This was just too tempting, and so, after I put my charges to bed, I left them temporarily in the care of the cook. It was dark as I gathered Pam and a few other kids, and drove the big car down the long drive and out through the estate gates into to Cos Cob. From there, I joined the Boston Post Road, where, several miles north, I stopped at Howard Johnson's for coffee milkshakes. After our adventure, we returned safely. I must have been crazy and totally irresponsible: damned lucky to get away with this joy-ride without incident. I was not proud of this escapade.

I usually spent days off in Greenwich, for a haircut, light shopping, a movie, but, occasionally took a train into the city. There was the long morning I spent in Bergdorf Goodmans, the store located since1897 on the west side of Fifth Avenue, between 57th and 58th streets. After an hour or two, I found the right dress: a short princess-styled moiré dress with shoulder straps and a full, though short, skirt in "Hot Tomato," no less! It was a perfect cocktail dress. Then, it was on to buy high-heeled silver sandals, before taking the train back to Greenwich.

Just as suddenly as summer had arrived, it was over, time to say goodbye to the Baumgold's who presented me with a gold watch for my services and invited me back for the following summer. It was an offer I could not refuse, though stipulated my salary would have to be raised from $55.00 to $75.00 per week. Mr. Baumgold didn't blink, and so it was arranged.

On return to Ithaca, I found the parents had moved yet again, this time to a house located just off East Buffalo Street, several blocks up from down town. It was at 3 Fountain Place, at the end of a small cul-de-sac overlooking one of Ithaca's many gorges disgorging into Cayuga Lake. The house belonged to Henry Guerlac, Cornell professor of History of Science with a PhD in European History, and author of the official history of the U.S. Radar Program. He, Rita, and three daughters, were off on sabbatical.

Three Fountain Place, built in the 1800s, is an odd mix of gingerbread and monstrosity; yet with some charm. Built of gabled grey wood where one expects gargoyles to leer from nooks and crannies, there are none. Instead, icing-shaped doodads and spirals decorate various roof lines of the three storied edifice. Below, a large veranda runs across the front and part of the far side, embrasures allowing for private conversations, even trysts, in shaded privacy, the building able to grace any antebellum movie set. It was a tranquil place, except on late summer evenings when raucous raccoons rummaged, creating havoc among trash cans; and devouring the late summer harvest of a small vegetable plot.

Massive double front doors opened onto a hall with highly polished parquet floor. To the right and ponderously dark, but equally polished, a wooden balustrade led upward in three stages: on the second, one passed three tall stained-glass windows proclaiming Caesar's assertion to the Roman Senate of his victory (at Zela, now Turkey), in 45 B.C. "Veni! Vidi! Vici!" To the left of the front doors, in a room full of light overlooking the southern veranda, the same polished flooring ran the length of a large music room with grand piano, harp and other instruments. All five Guerlacs were musical.

In the entrance hall, directly across from the front door, double doors opened into an intimate sitting room complete with built-in hi-fi system, with two small sofas facing each other on either side of a small fireplace. Beyond, a large bay window with cushioned window seat looked out on to the eastern facing garden where a large bed of brilliant-colored zinnias nodded in late summer breezes. A door from this small anteroom led directly into the large dining room, a long polished table and comfortable chairs its centerpiece, the only light, except from another larger bay window with cushioned seat, was a dim chandelier. Beyond, was a "butler's pantry" which led into a large kitchen and scullery; then, on out to a grape arbor and herbal beds.

We ate dinner around this highly polished table discussing the news or personal events of the day, and, when those subjects were exhausted which wasn't often, we played word games such as "I have in my body ten Spanish noblemen, what and where are they?" There was the game of collective nouns such as: "a pride of lions; gaggle of geese; a volery of birds; an exultation of larks; a charm of hummingbirds; tidings of magpies; a parliament of owls; an ostentation of peacocks," to name a few. Our mealtimes always fun and educational. However, woe betide either Flip when she was home or myself, should we slouch; for seated either side of daddy, we were likely to get a thump across our backs with little warning, with the command to sit up straight; posture to him, all important for body and lungs; otherwise, how could one project or sing?

The rest of the ground floor contained a guest suite with a magnificent library with fireplace, and a nook of an office where daddy wrote and paid bills. We all enjoyed the library; I in particular, just discovering the wonderful writers of past and present. Each book, tome and volume in this library was worth reading; all encased in wall-to-wall, floor-to-ceiling glass cases, opened by keys. That year, I made it my goal to plow through the six volumes of *The Rise and Fall of the Roman Empire"* by Edward Gibbon, he known for the quality and the irony of this history which, some critics think, is a denigration of organized religion. Was it strange I should dwell in and on those books? Not at all, for I found the history described fascinating, perhaps because I had lived in Rome. All the above were of interest, that is, when my mind was not absorbed with boys, friends, acne, grades, and the never-ending lows and highs of high school life.

Upstairs, there was a master suite and three more large bedrooms. I never investigated the attic rooms. My bedroom faced east with bay window overlooking a pergola of grapes and in season, the riotous zinnias. There was a bathroom and then, before a sleeping porch, a back staircase led to the kitchen. Out back stood a time-worn barn which must, at some stage have housed carriages, but was now garage for our Plymouth station wagon. From there, a narrow lane led to East Buffalo Street, where, if you turned left, you would soon find yourself on the Cornell campus; turn right, and you were in downtown Ithaca.

Photo deemed by one teacher as, inappropriate!

SENIOR YEAR 1953-1954

For all three hundred and fifty of us, plus one postgraduate, our final year stretched before us. I was happy to return from that second year in Cos Cob to my redheaded boyfriend Dick Stewart, the cool young dandy with pipe, who sometimes ostentatiously wore an ascot. Much admired for his harmonica playing, Dick was also a wonderful dancer, having studied in an Arthur Murray Studio. Waltzing with him was like dancing with Fred Astaire, being swept graciously around the floor.

One afternoon, as I rode a city bus across campus, who should hop on but my father. As we rode, he asked, in serious tones, what I hoped to do with my life, or short of that, what I wanted to do next year. This was difficult to answer, for I didn't know. Everything, so far, had revolved around parental decisions. It seemed they now expected me make choices rather than wait for fate to deal out its next hand. Was I ready? No.

I found it odd that nothing was ever mentioned about musical studies, but when the parents offered further voice or piano lessons, I spuriously announced I could get all that at school. I regretted this especially when, some years later, both my father and some coaches said it had been a pity I had not pursued a vocal career. As it was, tryouts for me always brought roles in high school musicals; yet my parents never allowed me to accept, for, said they, I was in school to study; not to prance around a stage at all hours. Better for me, they said, as a very indifferent student, to concentrate on my studies. However, when I got a role in the senior play, a French Farce, they let me accept the role of a sexy school girl. Perhaps they thought allowing me this might compensate for the loss of musical roles. I resented their attitude and brought it up several times in later years, only to hear: "Enough, please! Let's not dwell on this again. We did what we thought best at the time." Not a word of apology. Perhaps too, daddy, having tried the stage in both film and opera, knew the ordeals of rehearsal and performance; though one can hardly compare his ventures to high school ones. Though disappointed at the time, I was soon more interested in fashion, archaeology, and the theatre.

So what was I to do next year? I could be an airline stewardess, I thought, until I discovered I was too tall. Perhaps I could join the air force; though, being a non-citizen, I did not know how that might come about. So, it had to be the theater, but first, I had to face the dreaded college boards, and knew after taking them, I had not done well except for history and English, math being quite beyond me. In the meantime, many of us were hoping to go on to college or university and so filled out endless applications, that is, except for me. Following antiquated British rules, the parents allowed me to submit only one application, this to Cornell's School of Dramatic Arts. If I failed to be accepted, I would only be good for a technical school: this, the old British way.

At our last Christmas prom, my old boyfriend Tom, back from Bowling Green, put in an appearance. As he surveyed the floor, he spotted Dick sweeping me about the dance floor and marched over to say hello. Then, before I had time to think, he maneuvered me proprietarily out of Dick's arms and into his. As we danced, Tom whispered: "Pretend you have a headache and let Dick to take you home. Then, I'll come pick you up, for," as he put it, "some old-time 'lovin.'" The bastard! No sooner were the words out of his mouth when the devil's advocate in me, flew across the dance floor to tell Dick of Tom's perfidy. Despite the row that followed, when needless to say I did not claim a headache, the two remained friends until Dick's death some thirty years later. And now, Tom, too, is gone; though we shared many telephone conversations reminiscing our time together; this before he died in 2009.

I had awaited the response from Cornell with trepidation, for I knew my grades probably were not good enough in spite of father's professorship at Cornell. And, in due course, rejection, followed by dejection, arrived. Of course, the news had to be shared with the parents; though they may have already heard, so I chose their "cocktail hour." Perhaps then, in more relaxed mood, more mellow, they might not be so disappointed in their errant daughter. Not so, for mother, un-delicately, set her glass on the table, and, though not exactly calling me stupid, exclaimed: "Well, there you are, you silly girl! The only thing you're good for is to become a secretary! Tomorrow you will apply for the business administration program at Ithaca College!" I left the veranda in tears, hurt, angry, and frustrated, and, too, for being such a disappointment to them. I knew I was not stupid, merely a late bloomer, deserving better understanding. Yet, it would be some years before my parents came to respect, admire, and praise my achievements. Dick had read me well for, in the Annual, our 1954 year book, he wrote: "You are very talented scholastically if you'd only apply yourself." The same could have been said of him, who had to repeat his senior year; yet was accepted at Cornell and the fraternity Delta Tau Delta. His major may have made a difference, that of agricultural landscaping?

The year wore on. Again the Cornell music department had outdone itself with performances of the Boston Symphony under Pierre Monteux. There was violinist Yehudi Menuhin, the pianist Rudolph Serkin, the mezzo Jennie Tourel; George Szell; then Erich Leinsdorf with the Rochester Philarmonic, the Walden and Hungarian Quartets; Morris Bishop and Keith Falkner in a program of "Words and Music;" Honeggar's *King David* with the Sage Chapel Choir conducted by John Kirkpatrick; and a concert performance of *Dido and Aeneas*, with student soloists.

Few weeks of the school year remained. My final courses were great: world literature, beautifully taught and full of discussion mostly regarding Russian writers; the other, advanced American history, wherein I still kept my mouth shut; not wishing to argue the British point of view of its onetime colonies. As we took final exams, graduation loomed, with the hustle and bustle of posing for photos, measurement for robes and mortar boards; announcements sent, guests invited; bouquets ordered. Few presents were expected. Those received were usually from parents, who, in the case of girls, often gave matched luggage. Was this an unsubtle invitation to be gone, to either marriage or college? Half my life, or so it seemed, I had lived out of other people's cases, so I was pleased to receive my own, a set of three in brown with green leather trim. But, would I be gone?

Just before graduation, at an assembly in the school's auditorium, the class of 1904, holding its fiftieth reunion, paraded across the stage. We clapped yet vowed the class of 1954 would never look that "ancient" at our fiftieth. In 2004, many did return for our fiftieth, and, lo and behold, some of us were indeed unrecognizably ancient; others changed but little.

Time now, for the class of 1954 to exit onto the stage of the big wide world. The ceremony, held in Bailey Hall on the Cornell campus, was accompanied by, what else, Sir Edward Elgar's" (March No. 1) *Pomp and Circumstance,* synonymous with school graduations countrywide, first played at such an event in 1905. Sir Edward's ability to convey emotions of both triumph and nostalgia, were perfectly suited for graduations, as one phase ends and another begins. Played endlessly, the music accompanied our slow progression to the stage, up, on, and across it; to receive diplomas. Posies distributed, speeches over, we flowed out to disperse to the four winds. Though I was only an average student, those past four years had been an eye-opener in so many ways after the cloistered existence of Italian schools. Would the parents wallow at our possible parting? No, for we had already parted any number of times; what was one more? There would be no empty-nest syndromes. Anyway, separation is, in whatever form, inevitable, as one travels through life.

Time, again, to say goodbye to Dick, as I was off to yet another summer in Cos Cob via the Phoebe Snow. And a fun summer it was. Oh, there was the usual routine with the children; sharing their evening suppers in the den watching Howdy Doody. My evenings and days off were more fun now, for I was dating the tennis/swimming coach, a fellow some years older, Dan C. His Italian background and looks attracted me to him. Similar to his Welsh cousins, he aspired to be the next Caruso or Pavarotti, and though Dan took innumerable lessons in the City, his was a lost effort. At the time he owned a red Chevy convertible. It seems the few convertibles in my life have always been red, just the sort of car to excite a young girl. Sometimes, as a special a treat, Dan would let me drive to the shore. Aside from coaching, Dan's life seemed fast-paced and was, I suspect connected with "I Mafiosi," for money never seemed an issue as he escorted me about. We often drove into the City or over to some rathskeller in New York State where the drinking age was lax. There he wooed me with wine, dine and dance, and succeeded. We'd go to State or local fairs where he was pleased to show off his prowess by removing his jacket, and flexing his muscles in fighter stance. Then, he'd lift a heavy mallet and smash it down onto a small platform, which, in turn, sent an object sky-rocketing up a chute, there to hit a gong at the top. He could do this a number of times without effort, then hand me his winnings, a stuffed teddy-bear or two which I passed on to the children. In the end I found him, despite his macho image a "wimp of a wop." "Wop," is an epithet for those of Italian descent, meaning for those "Without Papers." However, the word "Wop" may also derive from "Guappo," members of the Guapperia, a Naples criminal organization similar to the Sicilian Mafia. The term is certainly derogatory in America. Despite this possible background, I found Dan to be an old "softie" and, in the end, a loser. After that summer, I would not see him again for five or six years until my sister and I happened to stop at an out-of-the-way restaurant somewhere in New York State, and there was Dan, reduced to waiting tables. Awkwardly, we acknowledged each other and passed on.

Midsummer, Uncle Adrian (Boult) was conducting at the New York City Stadium Concerts during its thirty-seventh season. Each concert, whether classical or pop, was a sellout. One evening he and wife Ann, invited me to New York, to share a light supper in their hotel suite before being driven by limo to the Stadium. It was an appreciative audience under moon and starlight, crowds later gathering at the stage doors for autographs as artists emerged to go home. The limo dropped me in time for the last train back to Connecticut. I cannot say I knew him well, never feeling truly comfortable in his presence, as he appeared rigid in behavior and eating habits. He was, however, generous with gifts. At one point in his life, so daddy told me, Adrian had created quite a scandal when he "kicked up his heels," to dash off with another man's wife, whom he eventually married.

On another evening, I went into the City with a friend for supper and a performance of *Pajama Game,* newly opened on Broadway, starring the much admired John Raitt, with Carol Haney, and Janis Paige, Raitt admired not only for his talent, but his physique. The show would give Shirley MacLaine, understudy for Carol Haney, her big break when the former broke an ankle. Later that fall, in speech class at Ithaca College, our professor, (possibly gay and definitely a frustrated actor who had also seen the show), proclaimed to no one in particular, yet to all, and admiring his own delivery, opined in his most eloquent stentorian theatrical tones: "If I haaaad a bowdy like John Raitt's, (long pause), I'd walk arrround aaall dayyy in the nuuuude!" Leer-like grins greeted this disquisition.

Before the summer was over, there was the exciting experience of two major hurricanes, both of which hit the New England area twelve days apart: Hurricane Carol on the first of July, and Hurricane Edna on the thirteenth, both causing wide devastation. The parents were vacationing on Nantucket Island at the time and so saw the worst of both. Of course, daddy was in his element, loving every moment of the thunderous, roiling skies, the roaring gale-force winds and the furious spray of tumultuous seas, I wishing I had been there to share it with him. For us in Connecticut, it was bad enough. We had experienced the ominous pre-storm calm, and had the overwhelming sense that something big, something powerful was imminent. It was. It is Edna I remember best. She struck in the dark of night, blasting torrents of lashing rain in gale-force winds, strong enough to make the stone house groan: its lights to fail. In contrast, the next day, the morning sky shone, newly cleansed from the night's tumult, a day almost too brilliant, as we pitched in to clear the gardens of broken limbs, branches and debris. We had no way of knowing then, but brewing off the western coast of Africa, was a far more vicious storm. Her name was Hazel.

Dick's photo of me before Senior Prom

FALL 1954—ITHACA COLLEGE
AND
RVW

As summer waned three events took place, the first was Hazel, the storm being spawned off Africa's coast before I left Cos Cob in late summer. She became a category 4 hurricane, with winds of one hundred and fifty mph, blasting her way, between the 5th and 18th, from Grenada to Toronto. Heavy rains and wildly violent winds caused over one thousand deaths, damage estimated at $420 million. Ithaca was fairly lucky, just catching the western edge of the storm while sustaining considerable damage. It was a fearsome night, the darkness seeming to make everything more wildly alarming. At the time, we were still living in that lovely monstrosity at 3 Fountain Place when, just as I was going to bed on the evening the storm struck, daddy asked if I would like to go outside to watch "the elements," as he called them. Well, of course! Outside, it was exciting with flashes of lightening, thunderous claps, the roar of wind, as the storm raged around us. Teeming rain drenched hair, face, and clothing even though we wore raincoats, as the storm grew stronger. So magnificent it was, we decided to roam further into the garden. The old house had well-worn shutters on most windows, and we happened to be standing below my bedroom window with shutters, when we heard a rending, tearing, wrenching noise, and looked up to see one being torn off its hinges. What happened next, would have been unavoidable, that is, if we had been standing a foot or so further from the house, had started to walk further in the garden, for both of us would have been decapitated, the shutter sailing over our heads, missing us by inches. I believe "Gambu" had been at work again saving both his son and me, his granddaughter. It was at that moment we decided it might be prudent to disappear indoors.

Other events that fall, my enrollment in Ithaca College, meeting my husband to be, and most important of all, the much anticipated arrival of Dr. Ralph Vaughn Williams (1872-1958), prolific composer of symphonies, chamber music, opera, choral music, film scores, and arranger of hymn tunes. From the age of six, RVW's focus had been music and he began composing at that age. He had no interest in his relation, Charles Darwin or his theory of evolution, nor in china and pottery, the interests of the Wedgwood side of the family. RVW continued to compose until his death some eighty years later, a prodigious outlay. His visit to Cornell came about as follows.

In December 1953, the Sage Chapel Choir had performed *The Three Kings*—an epiphany "carol" by German composer Peter Cornelius—with father as soloist, before sailing on the Queen Mary for engagements in England: the Royal Albert Hall for Mozart's *Requiem*, then Bailliol College, Oxford, and elsewhere. In superb voice and accompanied by his pianist friend John Hunt, Keith received rave reviews. The British music world was excited by his return to the concert platform, RVW (or Uncle Rafe as we knew him) among them.

At a luncheon given for Keith by British composer Gerald Finzi who had invited among others, RVW and his poetess wife, Ursula. During lunch somehow father persuaded Uncle Rafe to at least consider visiting Cornell for a semester of lectures. Surprisingly, RVW immediately agreed. Wheels turned and soon, with the aid of pianist Myra Hess and others, arrangements were made, Cornell University offering RVW a visiting professorship in the music department, for fall term 1954. It was a feather a in their cap! Also arranged, a lecture tour during which the good doctor and his wife could see the Pacific Ocean, and visit the Grand Canyon.

Daddy, gone over the holidays, had missed my eighteenth birthday in January, but returned home energized from his successes and heady acclaim; ready to get back to teaching, to go on singing: "So much work to do, so little time," he wrote mother. Both of them looked forward to

RVW's visit as did I, but with some trepidation, for with mother ailing, I was asked to step in as hostess. Who? Me? I would do so while feeling totally inadequate to the task. That is, until I put on that red "Hot Tomato" cocktail dress bought the previous summer. That was when I seemed to come into my own, shyness evaporating, sense of assurance gained, as perforce, I played the role. The trick, I quickly learned, not an easy task at my age, was to forget about self, and make others welcome.

The Vaughn Williams' arrived and housed in an elegant suite in Cornell's University Club. On that late September evening, I was full of nerves as my father drove to meet this great man. As I entered the foyer of the University Club, I wondered what to say to such a personality. Then, suddenly, there he was, a bear of a man with bushy eyebrows, his large imposing eighty-two year old figure, striding toward us. "Hello, Keith!" he bellowed at daddy, before heading straight for me. "And this must be the delightful Julia! How are you, my dear?" as his arms wrapped around me. My reply was lost as I disappeared into his enormous embrace, into the folds of his scratchy tweed jacket hoping not to suffocate. What had I been worried about? From then on, I was his acolyte. Then, releasing me, he greeted father, ushering us into his suite of rooms, where we met his wife, the redheaded Ursula. Their suite, large and comfortable, had a grand piano installed in one end of a long room and it was at this piano that RVW, with beetling eyebrows, white hair in disarray, began composition of his Eighth Symphony, given its first performance two years later. As he worked, the piano, floor, every conceivable surface was strewn with manuscripts covered with black-inked scrawls.

Uncle Rafe was an immediate success, enormously popular with students, and conquering all hearts, so fond of young people was he, particularly the girls. All his lectures, illustrated by my parents, were jam packed, many mobbed, crowds spilling out into hallways with amplifiers. At Q&A, the hard-of-hearing RVW would, to everyone's bemusement, lift an old-fashioned ear trumpet to his right ear: "Eeh! What did you say?" he'd ask. Some questions seemed deliberately asked sotto voce, just to hear the great man say: "Eeh?" again and again. RVW loved parties and held court seated comfortably in a large armchair. There female students flocked, perched on the arms of the chair, while others sat spellbound at his feet. I remember two stories, the first concerning a young lady who, perched on the arm of RVW's chair, innocently asked if he knew the tune *Greensleeves*. Uncle Rafe, well known for this composition based on a theme by Thomas Tallis, was kind. "No, my dear, do sing it for me." Not so on another occasion as he listened to a male student's dissonant composition. The good doctor interrupted: "If a tune should ever occur to you, my boy, don't hesitate to write it down." Ouch!

On November 9th, a concert of the great man's music was presented with the Buffalo Philarmonic, the Cornell Acappella Chorus, and the Sage Chapel Choir of an orchestral version of his *Songs of Travel*, with Keith as soloist. This was followed by *The London Symphony* conducted by the composer. Another concert on November 21rst presented more music by the maestro.

On Thanksgiving eve the RVWs' gave a party to thank the music department and friends. It was a gala affair catered by the Statler School of Hotel Administration, otherwise known as the Hotel School its grads called Hotelies. It was a fun evening, again in my red cocktail dress and silver heeled sandals, professors flocked around, I fairly comfortable now with socializing. Was I chic, or was I chic! I had a great time. Next day, we escorted the RVW's to the home of famed musicologist Donald Grout and his wife Martha for the traditional Thanksgiving spread, which went on and on. Afterwards, and stuffed to the gills, all sat sipping coffee and brandy while at Uncle Rafe's request, Dr. Grout played Bach.

Too soon, the whirl-wind visit was over, for the day after Thanksgiving, the RVWs' flew to New York with the parents, to attend an opera at the "Met," their loge provided by good friend, the Manager Rudolph Bing. A visit to Yale followed, where Uncle Rafe was presented with the prestigious medal, the Howland Award, and one thousand dollars with which he indulged himself on those last few nights in the City, before sailing back to England. The campus missed RVW's great presence, I know I did, after one all embracing goodbye hug from him, a real charmer. Unfortunately,

I would be the one to tell my parents of the dear Doctor's death in August 1958, all of us too saddened to say much. Ursula survived him for another fifty years, dying in 2007 aged ninety-six, known in her own right as poetess and for her biography of RVW.*

Ralph Vaughn Williams' music is highly evocative: what about his wonderful "Songs of Travel" try listening to "The Lark Ascending," but in particular, his "Seventh Symphony" based on his music score for the 1948 film "Scott of the Antarctic." Some years ago, teaching a class, I tested this by playing a movement of the 7th and asked students to picture verbally, some with drawings, what they had heard. Afterwards, all twenty were right on target, agreeing the music had something to do with cold, of ice and windswept places: that's how evocative Uncle Rafe's music can be.

Keith Falkner with students at Cornell University.

Meanwhile, I returned to college life, but as Christmas came and went, discovered the New Year to be full of surprises. At that age when most of us think we know everything, I had decided my parents were

* *RVW, a Biography of Ralph Vaughn Williams*, by Ursula Vaughn Williams. Oxford University Press, 1964. Printed by Riochard Clay and Company, Ltd., Bungay, Suffolk.

insensible, too judgmental and old-fashioned fogies, this when my parents were but fifty-four and fifty-two, young in retrospect! Such arrogance! Still, I wanted to be thought bright and independent enough to make my own decisions, to pursue my own way. But, what did I know? Nothing, as it turned out.

Taking the College's entrance exam, the first person to finish and passing with top scores, I began my studies in Business Administration. Then suddenly, I found myself being swept off my feet with my first serious pursuer. I had dated and been "deflowered" by Tom, and was presently dating Dick, when I met on campus no, not a Harry, but a Bill, one William Hawley Wheeler; the name alone sounded impressive. Bill, eight years older, had recently been discharged from the Air Force, as sergeant in communications in Darmstadt, Germany. At college on the GI Bill, he was majoring in TV/Radio & Film, secondary interest: theater. Tall and fairly good looking though beginning to bald, he was "big man on campus," and, one of few with a car. One afternoon he happened to seat himself across from me in the cozy coffee bar on campus. Though we had not met, never spoken before, he told me, having seen me about the campus, I was to become his wife. Really? I thought I might have a thing or two say about this but was floored by this declaration, in fact, bowled over, and being impressionable, was snowed and deeply impressed. Some afternoons later, again in the coffee shop, he embarrassed me as he proclaimed in stentorian tones to everyone's amusement and my embarrassment, oh dear God!

Julia! My jewel, my Ruby, my Pearl!
My heart is joyous you are a Girl!
For, if you were a He,
It would certainly be,
With a body like Yours,
A Catastrophe!

Bill shared a small rented house on one of Ithaca cheaper side streets with his Italian friend, another on the GI bill, a Bill George. With limited resources, Bill entertained me one night a month with T-Bone steaks, salad served with an inexpensive bottle of wine; more often, it was Cheese-Whiz sandwiches, pickles and cold beer. When George was around, it was a heaping bowl of pasta topped with homemade tomato sauce which included his secret ingredients, those of sugar, a pork chop and fennel seeds. It was nothing but superb.

With Bill in my life, I was not paying attention to my studies: it seeming to be a year of romance for that spring, Prince Rainier the III of the tiny Principality of Monaco, wooed and wed the actress Grace Kelly. On Valentine's Day, Bill handing me red roses at a dance, proposed, though not on his knees. Swept away by the moment, I accepted. And so, in due course and with trepidation Bill presented himself to my father in the Guerlac library, asking for my hand in the old-fashioned manner.

My father had recently asked what I wanted to do next year, and I had replied: "Marry Bill!" Mother, reading by the fire, leapt to her feet: "Never! I will not allow it! You will go back to England to marry a nice Englishman!" "No! I will not!" I retorted and told later, though I do not remember saying this: "If you won't let me marry Bill, we'll elope!" Mother sat down. Daddy was silent. It seemed to be a stand-off, both parents hoping I would outgrow this infatuation for a man they felt totally unsuitable. In hindsight, I realize they were right, I more in love with love than of being so. At any rate, Bill emerged from his interview with a grin on his face and hugged me: we would become engaged in October, 1955, not before, the parents I suppose, giving me the chance to change my mind.

1954 Family photo at 3 Fountain Place

THE CRESTMONT INN
SUMMER 1955

Our fifth home, in as many years, was on Highland Avenue, built of stone and somewhat less impressive than previous ones, but comfortable, belonging to the Meisners; he professor of plant pathology, currently on sabbatical. I often wondered how the parents put up with the constant moves, but by house-sitting, they paid no rent, a big help to daddy's budgetary worries. It would not be until the following year, when they made a last move into the home of the well-known political scientist, Robert E. Cushman and his wife, that they had any sense of permanency, before returning permanently to England in 1960.

Ithaca College is private, founded in 1892 as a conservatory of music in downtown Ithaca, relocating to South Hill overlooking Cayuga Lake in 1960, with satellite campuses in London, Washington, D.C., Los Angeles and Antiqua, world-renowned for its Communications program. Needing to be closer to the downtown campus, Cornell professor William Moulton and wife Jenni offered me a room in their home on Llenroc Court (Cornell spelled backwards) where, in lieu of rent, I cooked the evening meals and served at their innumerable cocktail parties. The Moultons were an interesting couple. He was a linguistics professor, fluent in German, who, as an army captain in World War II, wrote the language series *Spoken German*. His Americanized, German-born wife, Jenni, ostracized on the east coast during the war for her Teutonic background, faced the ordeal despite being a United States citizen. She was very lucky not to have been forced into a camp similar to those for the Japanese on the west coast. Civil rights violations occurred. On the east coast five hundred persons had been arrested without warrant. Others, some United States citizens, had been held without charge for months, or had been interrogated without benefit of legal counsel. Yet President Franklin D. Roosevelt did not hesitate to award top war jobs to many of German extraction, General Dwight D. Eisenhower for one. Eventually the Moultons with their girls, Betsy and Suzie, moved into the new house they had built on Highland, which wasn't far from my parents to whom I returned. Each evening, though, I continued to prepare the Moultons' dinner; this time for a small salary. The challenge was to get the meal on the table within the hour, training that I found invaluable.

I was dating Dick when I met Bill. While it was nice to have Dick as a steady beau, our relationship was not the greatest. It was after a fiasco of a weekend spent at Dick's fraternity, Delta Tau Delta for Cornell's home-coming I realized we should part, and was left with the awful task of telling him so. The separation was upsetting as we said goodbye. He claimed he loved me; I was miserable for hurting him. Both of us were in tears at one point. Somehow, I knew it for the best in the long run: and, how right I was. Mother's remedy: "Come! My dear! Have a nice cup of tea and you'll feel better." I did.

Bill graduating with a communications degree from Ithaca College in June, was immediately hired by radio station WEEU in Reading, Pennsylvania. Meanwhile, Flip and I headed for Eagles Mere, Pennsylvania, a charming village blending Victorian country charm with contemporary comfort. Eagles Mere's population, according to the 2000 census, was one hundred and fifty three during the winter. Summer was a very different matter, as the area offers miles of hiking and mountain bike trails, country inns, and, in the winter, a toboggan run. There's a fine golf course, scenic vistas plus Eagles Mere's private lake, with summer festivals staged on the tree-shaded green, excellent dining at several inns and at The Barn Restaurant & Bar. The Crestmont Inn, built in 1900, was, and is, famous for its cuisine, its golf links, tennis courts, and natural lake. Flip and I were lucky to be hired for that summer to wait tables at this prestigious Inn. Its owners, the Dickersons, at the time, hired high school and college students to work in summer as groundskeepers, valets, and waitresses. The guardian par excellence of morals, dining room regulations and etiquette, was the hawk-eyed Mrs. Worthington, who oversaw her charges not only at their stations, but also in the segregated dorms, where curfew was at eleven p.m., no excuses accepted. Did she ever sleep? Perhaps not, for I learned later she was always in dreadful pain from cancer.

My roommate, Dinah, was the most gorgeous girl on the premises. A recent displaced person from Latvia, she had arrived in the United States in 1950, as we had, so we had much in common regarding travel, though with differing aspects of the war. Daddy called her Dido, after the opera *Dido and Aeneas*: she, the queen of Carthage, who fell in love with Trojan hero Aeneas; who, abandoning her, caused such despair, that she committed suicide in a funeral pyre. Why daddy called Dinah thus, except for her great beauty, I have no idea, but so indeed she remains.

Waiting tables three times per day, seven days a week, was hard work as we were constantly rushing back and forth to the kitchens from our stations to serve all in record time. The kitchens were chaotic, waitresses rushing in and out, shouting orders, bellowing chefs, banging of pots, clatter of dishes, occasional clashes and crashes. The mumbling of sous chefs, combined with the prima donna egos of the masters,' often escalated from muttered swearing to venomous bitching, insults flying, often a pot or two added to the mix. Once I witnessed, with some alarm, the head chef go after a subordinate with meat cleaver in hand with, thankfully, no blood spilt. I heard it was quietest at 4 a.m., when the baker showed up, though seldom sober after a night of bingeing, so it was said, to bake the daily breads, rolls, pastries and desserts. His raspberry and butterscotch Bavarian cream pies, his chocolate rum torte, were exceptional. Having miraculously created these, he would disappear until the following morning, repeating the process day after day.

After initial training, I was assigned a station, waiting upon a number of vacationing families, all tipping generously. My first $100 for a week's service was not bad for the mid 1950s; the sight of that first C-note quite a thrill. Our routine was to be up early and head for the dining room before it opened at 7 a.m., making sure stations were in order, tables shipshape before battle-ax Worthington inspected. We boiled eggs always, it seemed, a rotten one in the mix; made toast, collected bowls of fruit, cereal, and oatmeal. There were hotplates where bacon, ham, sausages, omelets, and pancakes were made to order, as we ten waitresses tried not to bump into each other as we bustled about. Gathering our orders for each one of the four or five tables we serviced, along with juices, jams, syrups, butters, coffee, or tea, we carried them into the dining room on three foot heavy metal trays. The most difficult part occurred when moving from kitchen to the dining room and back again, for two sets of double swinging doors had to be negotiated, one In, the other Out, this while carrying trays loaded with food or dirty dishes. If caught between a set of doors, as a few were, the results were disastrous, for the tray, slammed from behind by the swinging first door and then the front, crashed to the floor. Fortunately, this never happened to me. Once breakfast had been cleared, we polished silverware, coffee pots, and urns; inspected plates from the giant dishwasher, and reset tables for lunch. We poured leftover coffee into large glass pitchers, added sugar with generous amounts of heavy cream and a stick or two of cinnamon. By lunch time, this refrigerated concoction was ready to serve as iced coffee, or as a rich dessert when poured over vanilla or coffee ice cream served in large soda glasses with long handled spoons and straws: lusciously fattening!

After morning chores, we were free until noon. We were in pale gray uniforms, white aprons, stockings and sensible shoes, for, in spite of the heat in kitchens and non air-conditioned dining room, Mrs. Worthington insisted her waitresses wear nylons despite tanned legs. Several times Dido and I refused because of the heat and clammy conditions, though Mrs. W's beady-hooded hawk-like eyes, soon confronted us: "Appear without stockings again and you're gone!" she'd mutter. But, she needed us and so we remained, conforming to her wishes except on the hottest days.

After lunch, with tables reset for dinner, we had a few hours to frolic in the sun by the lake before reappearing to start serving dinner at 7:00. This, from the kitchen's point of view, was the important meal of the day, serving anything from rare roast beef, to lamb, pork, veal and sweetbreads; even hamburgers, if so ordered.

Our schedules were exhausting, maybe why younger folk were hired, yet it was a fun time. When not tied up with duties, we sunned, swam, canoed, and flirted. There were dates too. On several occasions, another waitress and I were invited by two business men to the Barn Restaurant & Bar after dinner, treating us well for a few hours of innocuous fun. There was summer-stock to enjoy, the occasional square dance, movie, or just hanging out at the local teenage spot in Eagles Mere, where the juke box played the hits of the day: *Cherry Pink and Apple Blossom White, Mambo Italiano, Three Coins in the Fountain, Stranger in Paradise, and Teach Me Tonight* among others.

There were other things happening in the world, though we paid scant attention, with few exceptions. For instance in June, President Eisenhower became the first chief executive to appear on color TV; while, on the same date, the "$64,000 Question" premiered. By 1959, of course, contestant Charles van Doren, an English professor at Columbia University, became reviled across the nation for having cheated on the answers. Too, the very first seat belt legislation was enacted in Illinois, and, early in August, hurricane Connie struck the North Carolina coast, followed by Diane five days later. These two, following each other, caused devastating floods from there, all the way up to Massachusetts, leaving 184 dead, $832 million in damages. On the twenty-seventh, the first issue of *Guinness Book of World Records* was published, while on the twenty-eighth we heard of the horrible fate meted out to a black teenager in Money, Mississippi, who, it was said, had whistled at a white woman. He was killed, assassinated is more like it, by a posse of white men. This did shock us.

When Bill could get away, he drove up from Reading for weekends, where, when I was not at work, we meandered about the beautiful countryside, going to summer fairs, and spent an unseemly amount of time in his motel. I had realized on arrival that it had been unfortunate I had mentioned my upcoming engagement. I lost out on a lot of fun, and was avoided by some really neat guys. I did pal up with Tim for evening dances on the Inn's veranda, where, one evening, Lionel Hampton played for the crowd. Too, there was my sister's recent reject, a lad named John Paul Jones, if you can believe it. On many an eve, he and I would canoe around the lake under dazzling moon and stars, commiserating with each other. There was also the musical duo hired to entertain in the Inn's lounge following dinner, for which everyone "dressed"; a tenor and his Russian-born pianist wife, performed, he, later inviting me out for the evening after our duties. It was soon obvious this gentleman adored young women and was always pleased to have them fawning over him, me included. So, I played my part, though was put off by this man's cavalier attitude toward his wife.

Again, I found the summer over too quickly, for despite the hard work, it had been enjoyable with some freedom, in spite of rules and curfews. Too, there were the generous tips. However, I had yet to realize I was about to lose most of the above.

A portrait by Bill

FALL/WINTER 1955

As my parents had insisted, my engagement to Bill occurred late in October, and the wedding set for the twenty-seventh of December. William Hawley Wheeler, born in Plattsburg, New York, was eight years my senior, brought up with an older brother David, in Warsaw, Wyoming County, New York. Their recently deceased father, Edgar Edson, had been county commissioner for some years, Edgar's great great grandfather, Edson Wheeler, was related to the Renssalaers of New York fame. Jane Wheeler, soon to be my mother-in-law, was a Post, considered a character in a family of two witty older brothers: Howard, who farmed in Allegany County near Alfred, New York, and farmer, David Post, of Perry in the same state. Then, there was Jane's younger sister, Vida, a rather prudish old maid, longtime missionary to Japan who did not marry until well and safely into her eighties.

I first met Mother Wheeler, as I would be expected to call her, around Christmas 1954, finding her Dutch heritage evident in her once blonde but now gray hair, faded blue eyes, broadness of thigh, and narrowness of mind. She was an avid Baptist in the small community of Warsaw, who took pleasure in denouncing smoking and the devilment of alcohol at every opportunity, especially when presiding at meetings of the local Monday Club, whatever that was. Some years later, she could be found enjoying a sherry or two, for medicinal purposes only you understand, while continuing to denounce the evils of smoking. However, there was no mistaking the odor of tobacco hanging about her as she chewed a "chiclet," trying to hide her addiction.

The parents always encouraged attendance at any number of performances on campus. There was Handel's *Messiah* performed on campus in November with the Sage Chapel Choir, soloists, John Kirkpatrick conducting; also, the Budapest String Quartet performed in the Chamber Music Series. On December 1, Donizetti's opera *Don Pasquale* was presented by the great popularizer of opera in America, Boris Goldovsky. There was Gian Carlo Menotti's opera *Amahl and the Night Visitors* also presented in December, first performed four years earlier, to become classic television Christmas fare for some years; sadly, seldom performed today. For the Cornell performance, African-American law student Ellie Applethwaite, a fine mezzo taught by father, was chosen by him to sing the role of the mother. This caused much muttering, but Keith was not concerned with the color of her skin; rather, the quality of her voice. He would choose Ellie again, the lone black soloist, to sing with him in a 1956 performance of Bach's Cantata 140: *Wachet auf* (Sleepers Awake!) in St. Paul's Chapel at Columbia University; Tom Sokol conducting the orchestra and Sage Chapel Choir. It was Professor Falkner who gradually eased the boycott of African-Americans from taking center stage at Cornell.

Our engagement party was a small affair. Just before it, I received a phone call from that crazy young man, Rich, whom I'd known in Kent three summers before, and who was presently visiting a fraternity on the Cornell campus. Somehow he had found our number and rang to ask me out for the evening. The timing couldn't have been worse, and I had to tell him I was about to celebrate my engagement. Just how ready was I to marry and settle down? In hanging up, I found myself regretting I couldn't have said "yes." As it was, following my engagement, and with my betrothed miles away, I giddily continued to date.

As the date for the wedding drew near, I was in a dither of excitement. Anxious too, to escape from a mother I thought insensitive, uncaring, and tyrannical; nothing could, nor would stop me now! At the ripe age of eighteen this empty-headed creature knew exactly where she was going; or thought she did. Bill, whom I thought of as my savior to be, professed to love me, and I supposed I loved him. The possibility of being delusional never entered my airy head. Such burdens do we often lay upon another!

For the Thanksgiving break, we drove to the "Mountain House" sitting atop East Hill, with views of the highest Adirondack peaks. The Inn, originally built in 1890, had been run by the Beseimeyer family since 1945, and is a georama in all seasons. We had been here before on walking holidays in springtime; in winter, it was even more spectacular, glittering on cold crystal-clear days, Whiteface Mountain loomed over all. In 1980, the winter Olympics would be held here; now, the area a mecca for skiers.

The main building of Mountain House had a large living room with fireplace; the outside, surrounded by open decks with outdoor fireplace, overlooked unspoiled natural beauty. Our lodging was in Gulf Brook Cottage, long house-like, similar to the Iroquois Indian's bark-covered structures. Ours was pine, redolent with the scent of resin. Rooms opened off a long corridor, with a bathroom at the far end, for which use, guests juggled for first dibs. Meals in the main house were served home-style at a long communal dining table, the abundance of food delicious and more than satisfying.

A fellow guest, a small man named Doctor Herr Von "Something-or-Other," cockily strutted about proclaiming his prowess at having been the pre-eminent instructor of Nazi Ski troopers during WWII. Daddy somehow inveigled him to give us girls a skiing lesson, And so, we and the "Herr," set out one beautifully crisply frigid morning in snow sparkling in pristine whiteness, shadows appearing dark blue amid the green of pine, the white glare of sunlit snow. Slowly at first, then faster, we began to get the feel of the skis; learning the necessary side-way steps up slopes, falling less and less as we began to find our ski-legs, stance, and balance. By mid-afternoon we were no longer falling; instead, we skied, enjoying the thrill of it! Doctor Herr Von "Something or Other" had certainly done his job, which turned out to be a day-long session, as we made our way down from the peak of Whiteface Mountain's 4867 feet, to ground level. While utterly exhausted at the end of our long session, I was exhilarated. Alas, despite the good Herr Doctor's remark that I was a "natural" it would be my one and only lesson. It was too bad, but by now I was pining to get back to Bill's arms, such being the blindness of young love!

While in Keene, we visited a maple sugar factory driving in a sleigh through a large snow-covered grove of mature maples where sap dripped, drop by drop, into pails suspended from "spigots" hammered into the trunks. Full pails were collected by horse-drawn dray, and were transported to a low slung barn-like place to be emptied into a huge vat simmering over a huge pit of hotly burning logs to bring the sap to a boil; then, gently, as the fire lessened, to bubble down into various qualities of syrup, from light to dark; this last being the most flavorful. Some syrup was further reduced to become maple-sugar candy, fondly remembered from my stay with the Stantons in the 1940s.

Nearby was a sawmill where the scent of shaved pine, plus sawdust permeated everything; the wood being cut into planks and planed for local building needs or for the making of paper products. Inevitably, the main activity, were father's enforced five to ten mile hikes "Good for the soul, good for the body!" he declared. "Quit, you're grousing! You'll get your legs and second wind. Just keep moving!" And so we did, this time having the proper boots for such ventures; and we always returned tired, yet refreshed, and very, very, hungry. In some respects, this holiday was over far too soon. It was the last one in which we'd all be together for some years to come. So, after a fabulous Thanksgiving feast, a day or so later we returned to Ithaca to face the rest of the year; indeed the future. I was full of anticipation, yet so unprepared for it.

So it was back to university or college we went: Cornell, Flip to Keuka College near Keuka Lake, I to Ithaca College. Mother continued to give piano lessons, yet she seemed increasingly difficult to deal with, prone to debilitating headaches, and short of temper, wanting to be left alone. She was hard to cope with, or to love, when in the throes of what I can only assume to have been menopause. I, years later, hardly noticed the event. However, bless her, she managed to pull herself together for the wedding, going through the motions calmly and gracefully, though I sensed her deep disappointment and disapproval. Perhaps she still clung to the hope

I'd come to my senses, if I had any, and change my mind to return to Britain to marry a "fine young Englishman."

Instead, the invitations were sent out, the traditional British wedding ordered: a three-layered fruit cake, lined with marmalade and marzipan then covered with a hard lemon-flavored white icing. My wedding dress, bought in Syracuse, was simplicity itself: an elegant off-white poie-de-soir dress, with scooped neckline, long tapered sleeves, and a three foot train. It cost, if you can believe it, $90, a fair price for the 1950's. My "something borrowed," was Auntie John's off-white veil of Alencon lace, worn at her wedding sixteen years earlier when she married Uncle Phil; I, aged three, their flower girl. Philippa would be maid of honor; friends Mary and Hilda, bridesmaids, for whom I chose green velvet dresses; their flowers, bouquets of variegated ivy intermingled with Stephanotis; mine the same but longer.

The house was awash that Christmas with guests and wedding presents. Dido came, much to daddy's delight, while ever dear Aunt Dodie arrived full of bon ami, all enjoying our time together despite things left to be done, meals to cook. As usual, I had decorated the tree, and there was music when, to my surprise, daddy danced, for more than once he said he didn't know how and when wooing mother, so he said, had worn crepe-soled shoes to avoid doing so. Now, though still professing his inability, he swept me around the floor, and what's more, he was good. Happiness, good food, and wine flowed, and we opened gifts, just as "niggles" began to worry my soul. I was beginning to realize all I would lose and miss.

On the eve of the wedding, Mother and I were hobnobbing in the kitchen when my, oh so innocent sister, caused me to raise my eyes in the Italian mode, that of mock agony, as she asked: "Don't you want to talk with Mother about what happens on the wedding night?" Gulp! Was she kidding? By now I had had a fair share of "bedding," and could have joyfully shot her! Yet Flip knew it was traditional, at least in England in my mother's generation, that the mother explain just what might occur on the wedding night. Didn't I want to know, asked Philippa? Historically,

Edwardian women had no idea what to expect upon marriage, with the very mention of sex, being taboo. It is assumed Queen Victoria was initially naïve, having no mother to advise her, though she may have come to enjoy sex with her Prince Albert, who, no doubt, enlightened her on a number of subjects, including the intimacies of the bedroom. At that time, most female newlyweds, if given any instruction at all, or just a book to read, were left in the dark, and so went blindly to the marriage bed. When "it," whatever "it" was, for they had no idea, happened, they had been told to "lie back and think of England," to remain either shocked, disgusted, most certainly un-pleasured, as little response was expected from them. Rare was the young woman who enjoyed the pleasure, so it was no wonder an underground sex trade flourished for men. My own mother seems to have been unaware of sexual needs until told of her likely duties by her mother, and no doubt learning more with father, though how knowledgeable he may have been, I have no idea. Thankfully, I had no such inhibitions, though I had a lot to learn.

Engagement photo by Bill

THE WEDDING
December 27, 1955

While I had been happy to be engaged in late October, it had been a difficult and tragic time for Princess Margaret, a situation I recall the parents talking about; they, feeling the right choice had been made. Well, they would, wouldn't they! Princess Margaret at twenty-five was free from her sister's bidding and had been seen everywhere with Group Captain Peter Townsand. It was therefore presumed by the public that an announcement of their engagement was forthcoming as Margaret had proclaimed Peter to be the love of her life. However, old English Church Law, initially, forbade divorce, further declaring that persons whose divorced spouses were still living, could not remarry until their former partners were diseased. Really! Therefore, the Captain though distinguished, was anathema to the royals who had not forgotten the effects of Edward VIII's abdication in 1936 to marry the twice divorced American, Wallis Simpson. The queen, first and foremost, had to consider what was best for country and family; so the big guns were brought out. Princess Margaret was informed that if she persisted, she would have to give up all royal rights, income and leave England for five years. As she knew her love could not give her all the perks that go with being a royal, the Princess issued a statement said to have been written by both, to announce their relationship over:

> "Mindful of the Church's teaching that Christian marriage is indissoluble, and conscious of my duty to the Commonwealth, I have resolved to put these considerations before any others."

I suspect if Princess Margaret had been allowed to marry her love, she might have been a far happier person. Fortunately, I had no such problems for, albeit begrudgingly, I had received parental blessing.

St. John's Episcopal Church, located at the corner of North Cayuga and West Buffalo streets, was bedecked for the Christmas season. Red, white and pink poinsettias and greenery were everywhere, interlaced with gold and white ribbons, intermingling with the red and green of holly and the white of mistletoe berries. Tall tapers, affixed at the end of pews, flickered in gentle currents of air as the long red-carpeted central aisle led from the narthex to the chancel, to the altar within the apse; there to match the same abundance of color as in the nave. There was the entry door to the vestry, the organ to the forefront, choir stalls on either side of the apse. All were decorated in the same riot of color amid the altar's various-sized white tapers in their golden candlesticks: perfect decorations for a wedding.

The rehearsal was held in the early evening, but, as we had no tradition of dinner afterwards it was just a small party where a few drinks were served. Most guests on the Wheeler side, professed to be teetotalers. Guests were on their own, most staying in the charming old Ithaca Hotel, one of many older structures of the city which no longer exist, for the incentives of urban renewal in 1963, were too attractive to save many of them. There is now an Historic Ithaca organization to preserve the past and oversee the building of a new Ithaca Hotel on the original site. The hotel will house the original infamous Zinck's Bar, an Ithaca institution for both Cornell faculty and students who often sang:

> Give my regards to Davy
> Remember me to Tee Fee Crane.
> Tell all the pikers on the Hill
> That I'll be back again
> Tell them just how busted
> Lapping up the highball
> We'll all have drinks at Theodore Zinck's

When I get back next fall!

Ours was a simple wedding with no lavish reception or professional photographer to record every detail. All was very cost efficient and, I hope within the parents' limited income, though I never knew for sure. A wedding portrait was taken several months later, this in comparison with the outrageous costs of today's weddings which seem totally out of all proportion and, to my mind, not only extravagant, but unrealistic. What a business, what a rip-off; especially when many marriages soon end in divorce.

The 27th arrived, and while others bustled about, I spent a leisurely morning; the service not to begin until 11:00 am. Slowly, I got ready for the ceremony, the center of attention, feeling happy, finally to live my own life, or so I thought, and more importantly, without parental jurisdiction. Finally dressed and buttoned up within the hundreds of tiny covered buttons down my back, I was ready to embark on this adventure, ready to leave for the church with daddy in chauffeur-driven car. We did not speak on the way, it seemed unnecessary, he as taciturn as I. It was enough to hold each other's hands as we slid and swerved down Ithaca's hilly ice coated streets to St. John's. At the church, we walked up the steps, as I did my best to hold the hem of my gown out of the slush, and on into the vestibule where my pretty sister, even prettier in her green velvet dress and matching shoes, was waiting along with the bridesmaids. Mother had already been seated in the front left pew, and at fifty-three, looked stunningly beautiful, having made a great effort to celebrate the occasion.

Daddy left me as Frank Eldridge, organ professor at Cornell, began to play the Symphony from Bach's *Christmas Oratorio*; then a "pastorale and passacaglia," (the former evoking the peaceful, simple rural life; the latter, a musical form invented in 17th century Spain in which variations are repeated over a bass line,) composed by Cornell friend Gilbert Weeks. Bach's *"Toccata and Fugue in D minor,"* followed. Then, before daddy and I were to enter, he sang *Where'er You Walk* by Handel and *I Love My*

God Merrily by Ernest Bullock, English organist, composer, Master of the Choristers at Westminster Abbey, and participant in the coronation of King George the VI. Normally I would have had tears in my eyes as daddy sang, but I did not this day, for numbness had washed over me.

As we waited in the vestibule for daddy's return to escort me down the aisle, my sister, with no malice aforethought, I'm sure, dropped my train into a puddle of melting slush left by the feet of those who had preceded me into the church. It was not a particularly auspicious beginning. Daddy was beside me then, holding out his left arm for my right hand in its pointed poie de soir sleeve, holding my hand tightly in his own right as he escorted me down the aisle. I could feel how he cared in his very touch, just as when he had held my hand on the way to the church.

From then on I walked through the ceremony zombie-like, unable to feel much of anything. It was rather like being out of self, watching someone else going through the motions and emotion of a marriage. When had I begun to doubt, to ask myself what I was doing? Had there been a moment when I could have stopped the engagement; all the arrangements? Probably, but by then I was too in love with love, to escape. Now, it was far too late, too embarrassing to cancel, or so I believed, as I now found myself, arm in arm, dear father by my side, walking down the aisle to another favorite: Bach's _Jesu, Joy of Man's Desiring._

Bill stood grinning at the steps of the altar, little knowing what he had let himself in for, standing there with his good friend and best friend Lloyd Meeker, and Professor Moulton. Daddy released my hand and placed it in Bill's, and so the rite began. When it was time for my three year old nephew to be, ring bearer Charlie Wheeler to present the rings, he was gently pushed forward by his mother, Pat. Before performing his duty, standing in the center aisle, he turned to the congregation and proudly announced, "Hi! I'm the ring master!" There were amused giggles; even a brief smile from me. With vows exchanged in the rather short ceremony, arm in arm with my beaming husband, who looked as though he had captured some sort of prize, I remained remote as we walked down the aisle to the traditional wedding march. Then, as though awaking from a trance, I asked myself: What have you done? What, and why?

At the reception, I did enjoy the attention, the congratulations, and the congratulatory telegrams from family and friends around the world. At that time, a telegram message always ended with the word "stop," instead of punctuation. These wires therefore, after "stop," invariably said "love," from the sender, which daddy, reading the telegrams to guests, read as: "Stop Loving." Was this a subtle message, an omen, or his way of amusing our guests? Until the actual marriage, amid the excitement of getting engaged, of "showers," presents and all the attention, marriage seemed exciting, but now at this small reception held in the parish hall, I could not but wonder again what I had committed myself to. But the choice had been made and stick to it I would; that is until years later, in a need to find myself, I exploded.

The Ante-Communion
The Book of Common Prayer, page 67

The Collect for Purity, *all kneeling*

The Summary of the Law

Kyrie

The Collect at a Marriage, *page 267*

The Epistle, I Corinthians 13 R.S.V. *all seated*
see page 122
Glory be to Thee, O Lord. *all standing*
The Gospel, Saint Matthew 19:4, *page 268*
Praise be to Thee, O Christ.

The Marriage Service, Part 2
Prayer Book, page 301

The Wedding March   *Mendelssohn*

The Organ played by Mr. Frank Eldridge
The Solos sung by the Bride's Father

Saint John's Church
Ithaca, New York

on the

Feast of Saint John
Evangelist

Tuesday, December 27th, 1955
at 11 A.M.

J.C.F.   W.H.W.

Marriage Service

Honeymoon? What honeymoon? There would be none. There never was, never, come to think of it, any gift besides the old-fashioned platinum and diamond engagement ring, the simple silver wedding band, and an occasional rose, for Bill was poor, and together we would be poorer. Sometimes I wondered how Bill had convinced father to let him marry his eldest daughter, what he had said to convince him he could support a wife; possibly, a family. Had it been my threat, said in juvenile anguish, that if they did not let me marry Bill, we would elope? Perhaps. So, our so-called honeymoon was a one night stand in a motel, a fairly new commodity, somewhere in Pennsylvania, set in a grove of magnificent tall pines whose branches, weighed down from a recent heavy snow fall, would in the occasional strong gust of wind, dump pounds of the wet stuff heavily upon the roof and ground. Though there was no restaurant, the owners learning we were newlyweds, served a celebratory meal in our room, with a large bottle of champagne. So, in my lacy, sexy negligee and peignoir, I sipped plenty, nibbled less, and remember little, having bedded many times: always pretending, pretending, pretending, and pretending.

All this had occurred during Christmas break spent in the winter-grimy railroad city of Reading, Pennsylvania; in Bill's tiny apartment where dishes had to be washed in the bathtub and a hot plate serving as stove. It wasn't exactly a romantic beginning, though the landlady had tied sleigh bells to the bedsprings and Bill attempted to woo me by passionately playing Rachmaninoff concerti over and over again. I found I was more than happy to return from that depressing apartment, that grey, grey city, to my family and the clean snow-covered hills of Ithaca.

I resumed my studies, trying to finish my last semester at Ithaca College while living again with the parents. Bill drove up from Reading every other weekend. Still very much a cavorting teen, on going to bed one evening, I took a playful run across the bedroom and leapt upon Bill as he lay on my four-poster bed. There was a loud crack, as with a thud, the bed frame and slats tore free from the posts, to land us, momentarily stunned, on the floor amid a jumble of sheets and blankets. Seeing Bill's chagrined discomfort, I could only laugh: who was this person who saw little humor in anything except his oft told off-color jokes. So, as far as Bill was concerned, we had an uncomfortable night, I in disgrace, for we would somehow have to find the money to pay for repairs. I may have been immature, but I found he was far too staid.

Soon, with Bill's every other weekend visit to my newly repaired bed, it was not long before I was pregnant; quite extraordinary that it hadn't happened before. It was April, and I was quite happy to have a baby to love and cherish; something of my own; again showing my immaturity. When I told mother the news, she who had always advised: "Enjoy your lives for awhile, don't rush to have children," now said: "It's good to get your 'nursery' over with while you're young!" How two-faced could she be, I wondered? But, perhaps, she was just making the best of things?

I came to realize I had exchanged a rich and interesting musical life for a very ordinary existence: it was a rude awakening. To top it off, the parents announced they would be off on sabbatical to far-flung places, New Zealand in fact, and I, even if they had asked me to join them, was no longer free to travel with them. What I had wanted so badly was liberation from family restrictions and while I had them, had not found freedom, could not do as I pleased. Instead, I was under another's rather puritanical thumb, one who had nothing to offer anything in any way similar to my previous life. Too, the bleak railroad town of Reading, as it was at the time, offered few artistic events, and, what few there were, were unaffordable. Our entertainment became the occasional movie and things associated with WEEU. It was a lonely time that first year; so lonely, so boring, frustrating and miserable, and I realized I would soon be responsible for a baby. Women's Rights were just beginning to stir. As they did; well, for now, let us just say I had made my bed and would lie in it, but deep down, stirrings were afoot.

The parents and I parted on the twentieth of May after final BLTs and beer in the old Ithaca Hotel's bar before they were off for a flight to the Panama Canal to board ship, to sail forty-eight miles through the locks from the Atlantic to the Pacific. Bound for New Zealand, rising and lowering via locks, named one of the seven modern wonders of the world, the parents went and came back through this canal, fascinated to watch the maneuvering of large vessels raised from sea level up eighty five feet to the main elevation from the Pacific to the Atlantic. There is a plan afoot now to widen the locks for passage of even larger ships but, the Rankitiki, on which the parents sailed, fit comfortably within the Panama Canal's dimensions.

I was surprised to find how much I missed them, I who had done my best to escape their rule. Now I wondered why I had been so hasty; why, after our years of enforced separation, I had not appreciated them more. Obviously, I did not know my own mind, no doubt thinking at that age I knew all there was to know, what I needed to do. It was an eye-opener when I finally realized I had learned little, understood less, and behaved extremely foolishly in being so obdurate, so opinionated, and, so stupid.

RE-REFLECTIONS

As I returned it to the dealership, the images and memories which had so suddenly flashed in the rearview mirror of that shiny red convertible brought back both happy and sorrowful times. Some were agonizing, some less so, but certainly those of separation during World War II our worst. Fortunately, our suffering was less than that of many millions of others during the war. Despite the wrenching separation from parents, my sister and I had been very lucky in our placements in America.

Many thoughts, even arguments, have been waged regarding the uprooting of young British children during WWII. At the time, it seemed there was no question that Hitler, with all his might, would invade Britain. Too, our family's alarmist Uncle Phil, who had seen what the German Armageddon could inflict, urged his sister to send us, his nieces, to safety. And, of course, many other parents had done so, thinking it their duty to preserve the young for the future. A number of historians have suggested, even argued, that if Hitler planned to invade, he would have been unable to do so. For the majority however, there was no question that Britain was under threat of imminent invasion, and I cannot blame our parents for thinking so, and to wish us to be safe, overseas with good friends. They stood behind Churchill, not to mention King George VI, one hundred percent!

While we were safely away, our parents gave up brilliant musical careers to work for the war effort. Father rejoined the RAF at age 40, while Mother, at 38, went into some kind of undercover work. Sworn to secrecy, she took all the information about that work to her grave. They could not have done this if they'd constantly worried over our safety. Our stay in America that early in life, had been a horrible wrench, a time of loss when children our age need comfort and security. Yet we survived. I am proud to have been one of the many evacuees, individuals numbering 14,000 plus some 2,600 children evacuated through CORB, the Children's Overseas Reception Board. Our parents gave up so much when their country called, and yes, though torn from our lives, and because of their great love, did their best to save us.

Writing these vignettes has brought back a flood of memories, both sad and gay: what if we'd been torpedoed, what if there had been a train crash; what if we'd not survived childhood illnesses, the roof had caved in or we'd been swept away in a violent storm? Too, there was especial nostalgia for "La Bella Italia," along with any number of other "what if's." What if we had remained in Italy? What if, as mother had once insisted, I had gone home to England to, as she put it: "marry a nice young Englishman?" What if I had not been such a rebellious teen? What if I had not jumped into the marriage bed at such a young age, hardly realizing the responsibilities that come with being a wife and mother?

There had been so many breaks, so many separations which, as the title indicates, led to *A Not So Dolce Vita* during the Second World War. Yet we survived and remained optimistic that all would end well, holding on firmly to this attitude, despite portcullises raised or lowered over the years. But that is for another telling. By the way, has anyone seen my next red convertible?

Made in the USA
Lexington, KY
19 June 2012